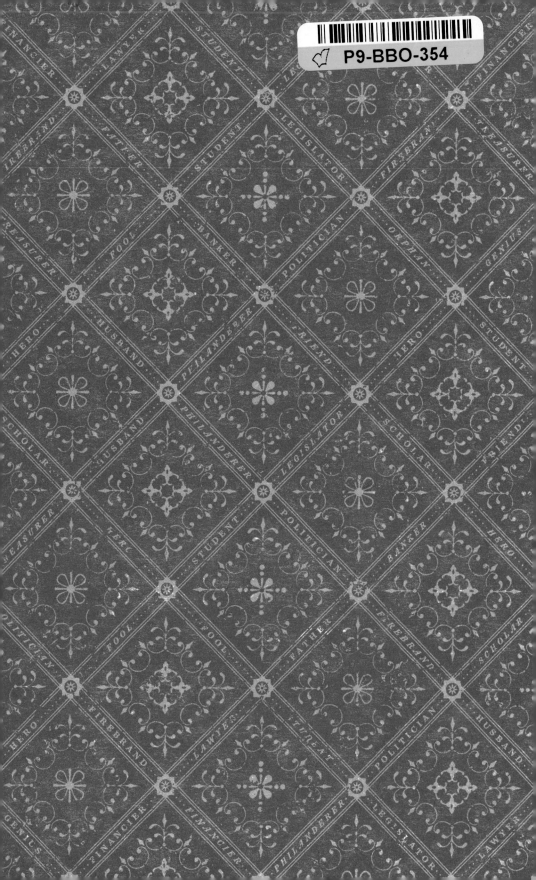

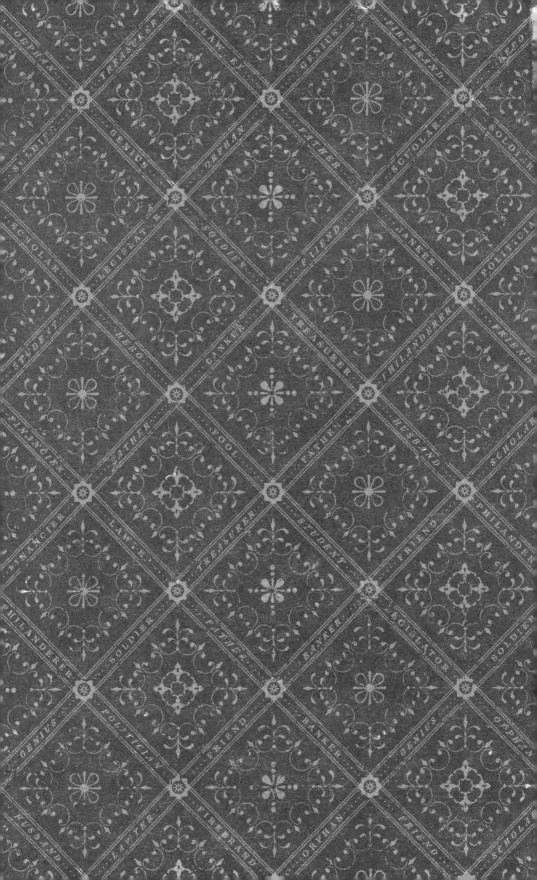

— ALEXANDER —
HAMILTON
REVOLUTIONARY

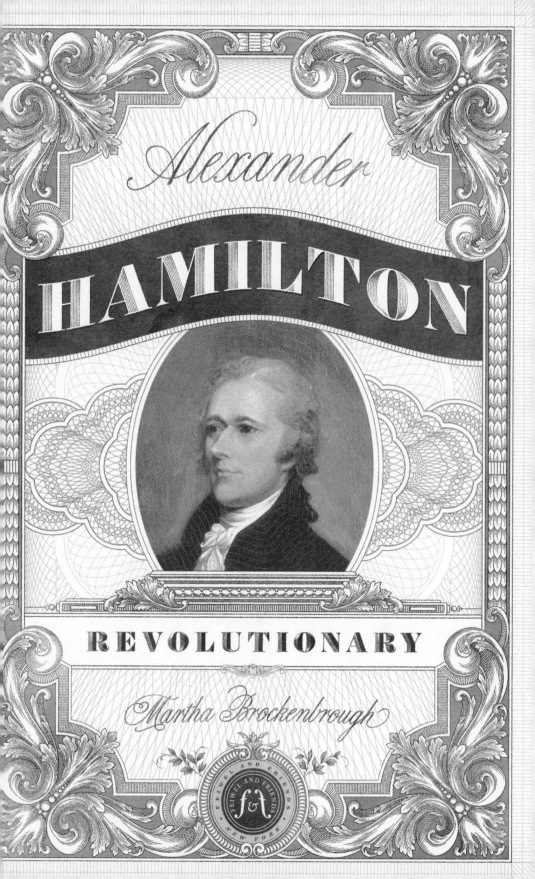

Alexander

HAMILTON

REVOLUTIONARY

Martha Brockenbrough

FEIWEL AND FRIENDS · NEW YORK

A FEIWEL AND FRIENDS BOOK
An imprint of Macmillan Publishing Group, LLC
175 Fifth Avenue, New York, NY 10010

ALEXANDER HAMILTON, REVOLUTIONARY.
Copyright © 2017 by Martha Brockenbrough.
All rights reserved.

Printed in the United States of America

All images appear courtesy of the New York Public Library Digital Collection except for
the following: pp. iii, ix, xi, 2, 9, 16–17, 19, 30, 40, 291, 318, 319, 328, 342—Wikimedia
Commons; pp. 4, 5, 6–7, 10, 13, 20, 25, 29, 47, 64, 315—Library of Congress; p. 23—
National Historic Site, St. Croix; pp. 60, 201, 205—National Archives; p. 123—Rare Book
& Manuscript Library, Columbia University.

Our books may be purchased in bulk for promotional, educational, or business use. Please
contact your local bookseller or the Macmillan Corporate and Premium Sales Department
at (800) 221-7945 ext. 5442 or by e-mail at MacmillanSpecialMarkets@macmillan.com.

LIBRARY OF CONGRESS CATALOGING-IN-PUBLICATION DATA
Names: Brockenbrough, Martha, author.
Title: Alexander Hamilton, revolutionary / Martha Brockenbrough.
Description: First edition. | New York : Feiwel and Friends, 2017. |
Includes bibliographical references.
Identifiers: LCCN 2016056559 (print) | LCCN 2016057839 (ebook) |
ISBN 978-1-250-12319-0 (hardcover) | ISBN 978-1-250-12320-6 (ebook)
Subjects: LCSH: Hamilton, Alexander, 1757–1804—Juvenile literature. |
Statesmen—United States—Biography—Juvenile literature. |
United States—Politics and government—1783–1809—Juvenile literature.
Classification: LCC E302.6.H2 B74 2017 (print) | LCC E302.6.H2 (ebook) |
DDC 973.4092 [B] —dc23
LC record available at https://lccn.loc.gov/2016056559

Book design by RAPHAEL GERONI
Feiwel and Friends logo designed by FILOMENA TUOSTO
First edition, 2017

1 3 5 7 9 10 8 6 4 2

FIERCEREADS.COM

CONTENTS

FOREWORD

EVEN IF YOU'VE HAD THE good luck to hold a crisp $10 bill, you've probably never studied the portrait on it or thought much about the man it depicts.

HAMILTON, the bill says.

He's famous now, thanks to a Broadway musical. Before that unlikely thing happened, Alexander Hamilton had become a historical footnote. He even nearly lost his place on the $10 bill. This isn't all that surprising. During his life and afterward, people misrepresented much of what he did and believed. But his work—often criticized and misunderstood—was genius. The United States simply would not be what it is without his visionary thinking and writing. Indeed, without his courage and wits, the Revolutionary War might not have been won.

Alexander was a warrior: fierce, brave, and more than willing to die for the cause. He was a strategist who, despite his youth, became George Washington's right-hand man. He was a philosopher who helped the rest of the Founding Fathers figure out what they'd meant with their declaration, and how the Articles of Confederation could be turned into a constitution that would endure. He laid the groundwork for the nation's economy—which was more controversial and complex than you could imagine. He founded the Coast Guard. The Customs Department. The Bank of the United States.

From the start, his life was complicated—a study in contrasts.

He was born in a place both beautiful and terrible.

He was an orphan and, worse at the time, a bastard, which meant he could not go to school with the rest of the boys.

But he was brilliant. Studious, hardworking, and brave, and people rallied to his side again and again.

He was a loyal friend. He was a forgiving enemy.

He was a fearless soldier. He was an indispensable military bureaucrat.

He doted on his wife and children. He cheated on them.

He wrote sensitive love poetry. He wrote blistering political pamphlets.

He saved a man accused of murder. The man who helped him do it shot him to death.

He was a scapegoat. A scholar.

Respected. Reviled.

A genius. A fool.

A penniless nobody who became one of the world's most powerful men.

He believed in the rule of law. He lost his life in totally illegal fashion.

ALEXANDER HAMILTON.

HE WAS COMPLICATED.

THIS IS HIS STORY.

CHAPTER ONE

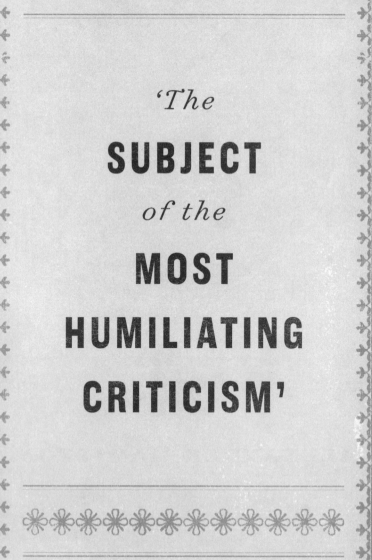

'The

SUBJECT

of the

MOST

HUMILIATING

CRITICISM'

ON THE LAST NIGHT OF August in 1772, as twilight descended on the island of Saint Croix, Alexander Hamilton thought he was going to die. He was still a boy, and he wanted to become so much more. He wanted to matter to the world. He wanted to be a man of courage and honor. He wanted to love and be loved. Instead, bracing himself against the winds of a hurricane, he waited for the blow that would end it all.

The storm tore homes and buildings off their foundations and sent wooden beams flying. It tossed huge stones a hundred yards and leveled a three-foot-thick wall around the storehouse of the king. And it wasn't just the wind. There were waves, too, huge ones more than seventy feet above their normal size. They flung ships a hundred yards ashore. Thunder boomed, and lightning lashed the sky, which spattered Alexander with torrents of salty rain. The air itself reeked of gunpowder and sulfur.

When the storm's eye opened over the island, the wind let up, but in an hour it returned with a vengeance from the southwest. The storm felt otherworldly in its power, as if Death himself had wrapped a cloak around the sun and pounded the planet off its axis with his scythe. All around Alexander, entire families ran screaming through the streets. Earthquakes and tidal waves punished the surrounding islands. No one had seen anything like it.

Alexander expected that he and everything around him would be obliterated at any moment.

Even after the storm ended, the suffering did not. Mangled bodies lay all around. Many survivors had grievous injuries. Homes and businesses had gone to wreck, and hungry children clung to the knees of their weeping mothers. There was no food. No shelter. There wasn't even good water to drink; the storm had made it too salty. Alexander's heart bled for these women he could not help. But what did he have to offer? He was poor himself. Fixing this was beyond his abilities.

He sought comfort in church a week after the storm, and a man named Hugh Knox stood to give a sermon. Alexander

ABOVE: ON AUGUST, 31, 1772, A HURRICANE PUMMELED THE WEST INDIES AND CHANGED ALEXANDER'S LIFE.

knew Knox well. He'd helped Alexander publish his first poems and had given him access to his library. Now, inside the church, Knox's words about God soothed and inspired Alexander. On the wings of this divine energy, Alexander picked up his pen and wrote his heart out to his father, describing the destruction and the aftermath, and what these things signified for humanity.

> *IT BECAME A TURNING POINT IN A LIFE THAT HAD BEEN UNLUCKY FROM THE START.*

Even if it wasn't enough to bring back his father, the letter was the best thing he'd ever written. It became a turning point in a life that had been unlucky from the start.

SEVENTEEN YEARS EARLIER, ALEXANDER HAD been born on Nevis, a steeply canted volcanic island not far from Saint Croix. His birth was so unremarkable that no record survived. But it took place on January 11, 1755, in a house on the main street of Charlestown, the island's capital. The house gave his family a view of the blue-green Caribbean Sea pounding sandy beaches made of pulverized coral and volcanic rock, along with all the commotion of trade in the harbor.

NEVIS WAS A HARD PLACE FOR ALEXANDER TO GROW UP.

Nevis was one of the sugar islands of the West Indies, which during Alexander's time played a major role in the world's economy. Everybody wanted sugar. Fortunes were made trading it. A lot of people grew to depend on it, and the sugar from Nevis was the sweetest of all, even as it required the work and suffering of vast numbers of enslaved Africans.

Nevis was a hard place for Alexander to grow up. The slave trade was grotesque, brutal, and deadly. Alexander hated it. And while he didn't have the catastrophic misfortune of being born or forced into slavery, his parents weren't married to each other. So, his mother was the subject of gossip, he and

ABOVE: *NAMED "LAND OF BEAUTIFUL WATERS" BY INDIGENOUS INHABITANTS, NEVIS IS A SMALL, VOLCANIC ISLAND WITH SANDY BEACHES MADE OF CORAL AND PULVERIZED LAVA.*

his brother were called names, and Alexander couldn't go to the church school, as other children did.

The subject of his birth humiliated him. One man was largely to blame for Alexander's suffering on this front. Johann Michael Lavien was a merchant who'd come to Saint Croix dressed in silk clothing with gold buttons and dreaming of making a fortune as a sugar plantation owner. He took a liking to Alexander's mother, Rachel Fawcett, who was on Saint Croix visiting wealthy relatives who lived a mile and a half southwest of the island's capital, Christiansted.

Rachel's mother, fooled by the glitter, thought Lavien would make a good match for her daughter, Alexander later said. Rachel hadn't wanted to marry Lavien. She was a teenager: beautiful, brilliant, and in possession of a small fortune she'd inherited from her father.

ABOVE: *ENSLAVED PEOPLE IN THE WEST INDIES MADE FORTUNES FOR SOME PLANTATION OWNERS.*

FOLLOWING SPREAD: *ALEXANDER'S PARENTS MET ON SAINT KITTS, AND HE WAS BORN SEVERAL YEARS LATER ON NEVIS.*

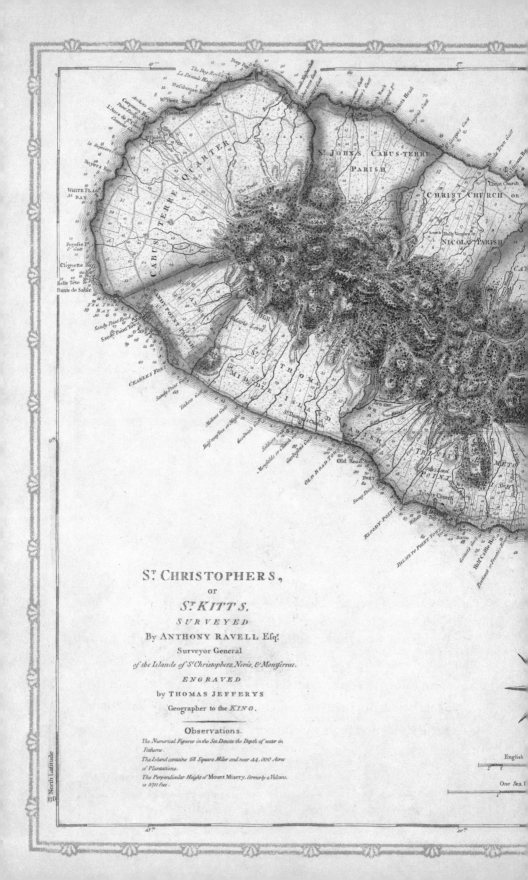

St. CHRISTOPHERS,
or
St. KITTS,
SURVEYED
By ANTHONY RAVELL Esqr.
Surveyor General
of the Islands of St Christophers, Nevis, & Montserrat.
ENGRAVED
by THOMAS JEFFERYS
Geographer to the KING.

Observations.
The Numerical Figures in the Sea Denote the Depth of water in Fathoms.

The Island contains 68 Square Miles and near 44,000 Acres of Plantations.

The Perpendicular Height of Mount Misery, formerly a Volcano, is 3711 Feet.

English

One Sea

17D. North Latitude

when it bears N.W. by N. 6 or 7 Leagues off.

NEVIS,
by
Thomas Jefferys.

Half a League

Statute Miles

Windward Pt.

St.

Grande Saline

Green Point

Mosquito Bay

Scotch Bonnet

Nag's Head

Hanana Bay

Pipers bay

The Cows

THE NARROWS

Horse Shoe Pt.

Newcastle

Hurricane Hill

Cades Point

St. THOMAS'S PARISH

GINGERLAND

Morton's Bay

Littleborough

The Mountain

PARISH

St. JOHN'S

New Bridge

PARISH

CHARLESTOWN

Great Fort

Bath

Makers Point

Little Bay

Hermit's Bay

Cayanna Bay

St.

Cayone

Pelham's Pt.

Barbers Pt.

Platform or

The QUARTER

SH

BASSE TERRE

Irish Town

St. George's Church

The Narrow Way

BASSE TERRE TOWN

Blue Water

Landnarhouse

BASSE TERRE ROAD

Moaring Point

Great Pasture Bay

Little Pasture Bay

The Fishery or

HALF MOON BAY

Parra Pt.

HORNBYHILL'S HILL

Saturday June 28. 1690.

NORTH FRIAR'S BAY

Well Cove

St. TIMOTHY'S

There he had his Foot

Hell Gate

Giants Cave

SOUTH FRIAR'S BAY

FRIGATE BAY

Robin's Bay

Water Hole

White House Bay

Guana Point and Hill

Pelican Rock

Grand Gulle

Grand Gulle

The Careening Places

Grande Saline

Green Point

ARSE-HOLE

SHITTEN BAY

Banana Bay

Banana Bay Head

Maggot's BAY

Bugg's Hole

The Nag's Head

Horse Shoe Pt.

THE NARROWS

Mosquito Bay

Jackson's Hill

Windward Pt.

Their marriage was miserable. Lavien was at least twelve years older, and he'd been nothing more than a fortune hunter. A poor businessman, he ran through Rachel's money. By 1750, Rachel had left Lavien and their son, Peter. Lavien was furious. She'd left him to the work and expense of raising their son, and she'd moved on with other men.

THEIR MARRIAGE WAS MISERABLE.

To punish her, he turned to the legal system. Danish law said a woman who'd twice committed adultery could be jailed. Rachel, found guilty, was thrown into a 130-square-foot cell with a floor made of brick. It wasn't the dungeon authorities forced enslaved people into, but it was a dismal spot nonetheless, mostly inhabited by drunks, thieves, and other lowlifes. For months, she lived in that tiny room, surviving on boiled cornmeal mush and fish, with nothing more than a glimpse of the wharf and the eastern end of cobblestoned King Street through the bars on her windows.

Lavien still held out hope that this punishment would force her back into submission. Instead, she fled to the nearby island of Saint Kitts. She supported herself by sewing and hiring out the labor of the enslaved people she'd inherited from her father. It was a drop down from the comfortable spot she'd had as the daughter of a doctor, but she was resourceful and smart, and she managed.

Before long, she paired off with a thirty-two-year-old Scotsman named James Hamilton. His upbringing was the stuff of fairy tales. He'd grown up in a Scottish castle called the Grange, southwest of Glasgow. His father was a laird whose estate was large and beautiful. As the fourth son, though, James wasn't in any position to inherit. Instead, he had to make his own way in the world.

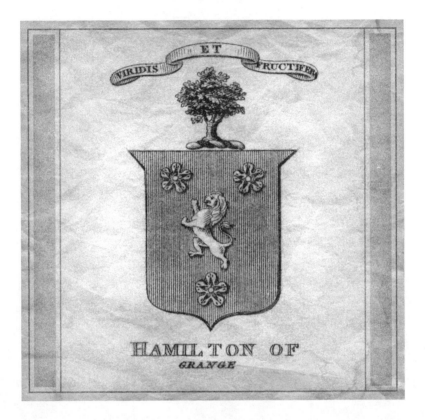

Unfortunately, he wasn't all that smart—nor was he a particularly diligent worker. After he failed to distinguish himself in a textile apprenticeship set up by an older brother, he went to Nevis, thinking he could make a fortune in sugar. Returning triumphant from abroad, some of Europe's upper crust had bought splendid estates of their own. Of course, many people who had hoped to turn sugar

ABOVE: *Alexander's Scottish relatives had a coat of arms that read "green and grow" in Latin.*

into gold were crushed by failure and debt. Some never made it home again.

JAMES AND RACHEL FELL IN LOVE IN THE EARLY 1750s, when he worked for a mercantile firm on Saint Kitts. They had two sons together, James Jr. and then Alexander, who was named for his paternal grandfather. Where they could, James and Rachel passed themselves off as a married couple, and for a while, the family lived on Nevis, surrounded by blue water rich with lobster and other delicacies. Alexander and his brother could climb through lush jungles that rose up the steep slopes of the volcano, surrounded by snowy egrets, monkeys, mongooses, and other tropical creatures.

ABOVE: *UNLIKE MOST OF THE FOUNDING FATHERS, ALEXANDER WAS BORN POOR TO PARENTS WHO WEREN'T MARRIED TO EACH OTHER. HE MOVED FROM THIS HOUSE ON NEVIS, PICTURED, TO SAINT CROIX.*

It wasn't quite paradise, though. In many ways, the landscape itself was a reminder that nothing was solid underfoot. The terrain was pimpled with sulfurous, undrinkable hot springs and steaming fumaroles. Earthquakes, tidal waves, and massive storms could strike at random. It could be rough in other ways, too. Pirates and privateers caroused at night in taverns and brothels. And sometimes there were bloody duels, fought by outlaws and would-be aristocrats alike.

THEY WERE FIGHTS FOR HONOR, AND HONOR WAS EVERYTHING.

The smallest insult could put a man in a mood for a deadly challenge. One famous duel happened after the victim called his shooter "an impertinent puppy." These duels fascinated Alexander. They were fights for honor, and honor was everything.

That was the sort of man Alexander decided to be—one with honor worth defending. He'd also be educated, even if he couldn't go to a regular school. It didn't matter if people made fun of him for being a good student, or for being skinny and small. He'd show everyone what he was really made of.

From his mother, he learned fluent French. He also took lessons from Jewish people from Spain and Portugal, starting young enough that he had to stand on the table next to his teacher when he recited the Ten Commandments in Hebrew. He had thirty-four books, a huge collection, which most likely included titles by Machiavelli, Plutarch, and Alexander Pope.

From these, he learned political philosophy, history, and the art of writing.

When he was still a teenager, he published his first poems, which were about girls and the glories of heaven, and were inspired by the work of Alexander Pope. Here are two stanzas of "The Soul ascending into Bliss, In humble imitation of Popes Dying Christian to his Soul," which ran in the *Royal Danish American Gazette* in 1772.

> HARK! HARK! A VOICE FROM YONDER SKY,
> METHINKS I HEAR MY SAVIOUR CRY,
> COME GENTLE SPIRIT COME AWAY,
> COME TO THY LORD WITHOUT DELAY;
> FOR THEE THE GATES OF BLISS UNBAR'D
> THY CONSTANT VIRTUE TO REWARD.
> I COME OH LORD! I MOUNT, I FLY,
> ON RAPID WINGS I CLEAVE THE SKY;
> STRETCH OUT THINE ARM AND AID MY FLIGHT;
> FOR OH! I LONG TO GAIN THAT HEIGHT,
> WHERE ALL CELESTIAL BEINGS SING
> ETERNAL PRAISES TO THEIR KING.

AS MUCH AS HE ENJOYED WRITING ABOUT heaven, he'd seen plenty of its opposite. If you weren't a rich plantation owner, life in the sugar islands could be brutal, especially for the enslaved people who'd been stolen from their homes, crammed into the bellies of overcrowded ships, and then displayed in marketplaces for buyers to examine as though they were animals or pieces of furniture.

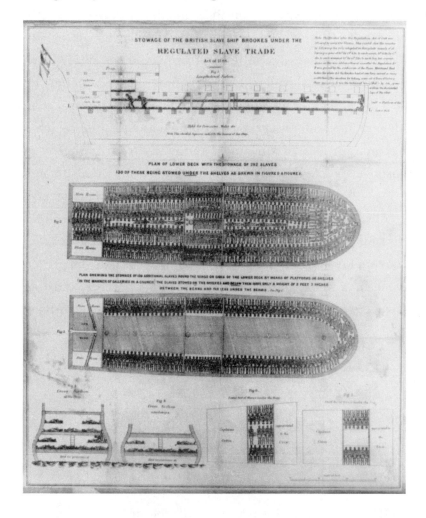

His own grandfather had been a physician inspecting the human wares at those auctions, and Alexander witnessed the brutality of these markets regularly. Even though he and his brother were masters themselves of a boy named Ajax,

ABOVE: *CONDITIONS FOR ENSLAVED PEOPLE ON SHIPS TRANSPORTING THEM FROM AFRICA WERE BRUTAL.*

Alexander grew up hating slavery. Enslaved Africans worked naked in the fields under a scorching sun, trying to coax cane out of the volcanic slopes. They also worked in boiling-hot sugar factories, where their lives and limbs were constantly at risk. To be enslaved in the sugar islands was essentially a death sentence, and millions of human beings suffered it.

On Nevis, enslaved people outnumbered white people by at least eight to one. On other islands, the ratio was even higher. Alexander and the rest of the white population lived in constant fear of uprisings, and many tried to terrorize enslaved people into submission through brutal punishments for small infractions—and worse for larger acts of resistance.

Alexander crossed paths with enslaved people throughout his childhood. As an older boy, he lived a half block from the Sunday market in Christiansted, where enslaved people came each week, spread their wares beneath trees, and sold a variety of food, candles, scarves, and cloth to each other.

HIS SPOT OF RELATIVE PRIVILEGE OFFERED ONLY SO MUCH PROTECTION.

His spot of relative privilege offered only so much protection. Life was difficult and could turn disastrous at any moment, as it did when Alexander was four. His mother's estranged husband, Johann Lavien, had continued to founder as a businessman. Moneylenders had seized his plantation, and he was reduced to being the overseer of someone else's.

He had to rent out his enslaved people to get by. But romance had found him, and he was living with a woman who wanted him to marry her. To do this, he'd need a formal divorce from Rachel. This was expensive and hard to get, which is why they'd never pursued one.

Lavien sent a court summons that went to an address on Saint Croix, where Rachel hadn't lived for nine years. She never received it and wasn't there to defend herself against the charges.

HE CALLED THEM "WHORE-CHILDREN."

The court papers were scorching. "She has shown herself to be shameless, rude, and ungodly, as she has completely forgotten her duty and let husband and child alone, and instead given herself up to whoring with everyone, which things the plaintiff says are so well known that her own family and friends must hate her for it."

Lavien didn't soften the language for Alexander and his brother James. He called them "whore-children."

Rachel was found at fault. As part of the divorce decree, Lavien could marry again. It didn't matter that he was living with another woman himself and was therefore guilty of the same things Rachel was. She was forbidden to remarry. This restriction wasn't from spite alone; it was also about money. It meant Alexander and James were officially branded as illegitimate, so that when Rachel died, all of the few things

FOLLOWING SPREAD: *ALEXANDER SPENT HIS LATER CHILDHOOD IN CHRISTIANSTED, THE CAPITAL OF SAINT CROIX.*

their mother had would go to their half brother, Peter—her one legitimate child under the law.

James, Rachel, and the boys moved back to Christiansted in May 1765. James had found work, but it was a terrible place for Rachel to live. She was known there as a bigamist and an adulterer. Under the weight of this shame, their long-term relationship collapsed. By July, James and Rachel had separated. In January 1766, Alexander's father went to Saint Kitts to collect a debt.

HE NEVER CAME BACK.

He never came back. Nor did he send money to support the boys. Alexander charitably figured his father could not afford to support them after his business dealings failed.

Family members helped where they could. Rachel's sister, Ann Lytton, had a wealthy husband, who pitched in on rent for Rachel and the boys. He even bought the family six walnut chairs with leather seats.

But there was only so much the Lyttons could do. Their son James Jr. had botched a business venture in 1764. Rather than face the consequences, he'd stolen twenty-two enslaved people and the family schooner and escaped to the Carolinas to start over. His devastated parents had sold their large stone house, which was called the Grange, just like James Hamilton's ancestral home. Gone were the sugar mill, the boiling house that produced molasses and brown sugar, and the quarters for the enslaved people who worked the land. The only thing they kept from the Grange was a small bit of earth that held the bones of their ancestors. The next year, Ann Lytton died.

Alexander, his mother, and his brother moved into a two-story wood-and-stone building on Company Street. The family occupied the top floor; on the lower one, Rachel ran a small grocery that provided supplies to plantations: pork, beef, salted fish, rice, flour, and apples. Alexander, always great at math, kept the books for his mother.

His work impressed her suppliers at a trading company called Beekman and Cruger. Thanks to Alexander, the family managed. They didn't have much: a half dozen silver spoons, seven silver teaspoons, fourteen porcelain plates, two porcelain bowls, a bed covered with a feather comforter, and the chairs from Uncle James. But, along with Alexander's treasured books, it was enough.

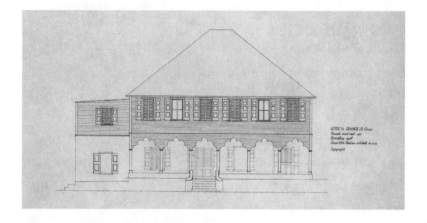

In February 1768, though, just after Alexander turned thirteen, Rachel grew violently ill, probably with yellow fever, an often-deadly virus that affects the liver and kidneys and makes the skin and eyes turn yellow from jaundice. After a week, they summoned a doctor, who bled her veins and applied an alcohol compress for her headache, medicine

ABOVE: *The Saint Croix home of Ann and James Lytton was called the Grange.*

that made her vomit, and provided an herb called valerian that caused terrible gas. Alexander got sick, too. The doctor drained some of Alexander's blood and forced fluid into his lower bowel through the rectum. For the rest of his life, he suffered kidney ailments.

ALEXANDER AND HIS MOTHER STRUGGLED SIDE BY SIDE IN THE FAMILY'S ONLY BED.

Alexander and his mother struggled side by side in the family's only bed. He was next to her when she died on the nineteenth of February. And even though it was nine in the evening when she passed away, the financial vultures arrived an hour later, locking away her assets to ensure they would go to her legal heir. They left only a few things unsealed so they could be used to prepare her for burial: the chairs, two tables, and two bowls for washing.

Alexander and his brother were effectively orphans, and so poor that a judge in town gave them money to buy shoes and black veils to wear to their mother's funeral. She was buried the next day in the family cemetery.

Then came the bills, including ones for the unhelpful medical care. The probate court—the officers of which had swooped in the night of her death—decided to consider three possible heirs to inherit her meager belongings. Two were Alexander and his brother. The third was their half brother, Peter. The process dragged on for a year. The court gave the entire estate—including Alexander's precious books—to Peter. The paperwork called Alexander and James "obscene children" born into "whoredom."

In November 1769, Peter Lavien returned to Saint Croix to pick up his things. Even though he was a grown man and a church warden in South Carolina, he left his young half brothers with nothing. He didn't even want the books. In one small mercy, Alexander's cousin Peter bought them back at an auction.

Alexander and his brother went to live with Peter Lytton, his girlfriend, and their son. Soon after the boys moved in, their cousin grew distraught about his finances and killed himself in his own bed. His death was bloody and traumatic, and in his will, he left everything to his girlfriend and their boy.

Alexander and his brother, left out again, went to live with their uncle James. And then their uncle James died. His will, which had been updated five days before his death, also left the boys nothing.

By then, James was sixteen and Alexander was fourteen. They'd lost their father. Their mother. Two guardians. They'd been branded as obscene whore-children. And now they were alone in the world, without a home, without money, and without any assurance of a future. It was a devastating series of blows, enough to fill anyone with doubt and despair. But Alexander and his brother persevered, even as their paths in life diverged.

James was apprenticed to a carpenter. For a while, he lived with Alexander in the home of a wealthy merchant named Thomas Stevens, his wife, Ann, and their five children. But he did not have Alexander's intellectual fire or ambition, and soon the brothers would part ways for good.

One of the Stevens boys—Edward—had meanwhile become Alexander's closest friend.

THEY WERE BOTH BRILLIANT.

Ned Stevens and Alexander had much in common. They were both brilliant. Both worked hard at their studies. Both spoke fluent French and had an interest in medicine and classical history, and an aversion to slavery. They had something else in common: they looked alike to an astonishing degree. Pale skin, bright blue eyes, reddish hair, slight builds. Many people noticed, and even when the men were grown, some people thought they were brothers by blood and not circumstance.

Alexander found a job as a clerk at Beekman and Cruger— the same trading company that had supplied his mother's store and admired his talent when he was keeping her books. Beekman and Cruger imported building materials, equipment for plantations, livestock, furniture, food, drink, and other necessities, as well as luxuries like crystal, porcelain, and silver for the island's upper crust. The company also exported

Nicholas Cruger

sugar and its derivatives, molasses and rum, as well as hard-woods and cotton.

Alexander was so good at his job that he temporarily ran the company for a few months in 1771 to cover for his sick boss, Nicholas Cruger, a pale-eyed man with unruly eyebrows and a swoop of short dark hair. Alexander was just sixteen at the time.

The job gave him a front-row seat onto the emerging economy of the day: international trade that pitted countries

ABOVE: *NICHOLAS CRUGER, PICTURED HERE IN 1780, SET UP A SCHOLARSHIP FUND FOR ALEXANDER.*

against one another in a race for power and wealth, and the territorial grabs that enhanced both. This thinking drove wars and revolutions and, over time, thrust Europe and later the American colonies into the beginnings of a modern age. Alexander soaked up vast amounts of knowledge about finance and commerce.

His math skills came in handy when he had to track freight and calculate sums in different currencies: Danish ducats, Dutch stivers, British pounds, Spanish pieces of eight, Portuguese reis. His French also proved useful.

THE WISH WOULD COME TRUE.

He learned the ins and outs of both legal trade and smuggling, what kind and how many guns a ship needed to keep it safe from pirates, and how supply chains kept businesses and communities alive exchanging everything from foodstuffs to building materials to livestock.

He also learned how to take charge of people and situations, even though most of the men he worked with were much older. He once scolded a ship's captain for not treating a shipment of forty-one mules with sufficient care in 1772. Then he let his boss know all about it. He'd never seen a worse parcel of mules:

"I sent all that were able to walk to pasture, in Number 33. The other 8 could hardly stand for 2 Minutes together & in spite of the greatest care 4 of them are now in Limbo. The Surviving 4 I think are out of Danger, and shall likewise be shortly sent to pasture."

He paid close attention to minute details. He knew what these signified, and he knew how to proceed in difficult conditions. The world could be a cruel place. He had little control over most things. But where he could influence situations with his sharp mind and tireless hands, he did.

As great as he was as a clerk, he hated the job. Tasks like checking flour for worms were demeaning. There was no future in such work, no way for him to truly change the world as he knew he could. When he was fourteen, he wrote Ned— who was studying in New York—a letter fretting about his lot. He wanted to be a great man like the ones he read about in Plutarch, and he was willing to trade his life—but not his character—for the chance.

"I wish there was a War," he told Ned.

The wish would come true. In the meantime, thanks to the hurricane, he'd impressed more than just his bosses. Hugh

ABOVE: *DATED JANUARY 11, 1773, THIS MINIATURE WATERCOLOR-AND-INK PORTRAIT SHOWS A YOUNG ALEXANDER AS HE FACED HIS FIRST WINTER IN NEW YORK CITY.*

Knox, the man who had delivered the inspirational sermon after the storm, thought Alexander's letter to his father was so stirring that he had it printed anonymously in the *Gazette*. Alexander's words read, in part,

> *It began about dusk, at North, and raged*
> *very violently till ten o'clock. Then ensued a*
> *sudden and unexpected interval, which*
> *lasted about an hour. . . . Good God! what*
> *horror and destruction—it's impossible for*
> *me to describe—or you to form any idea of it.*
> *It seemed as if a total dissolution of nature*
> *was taking place. The roaring of the sea and*
> *wind—fiery meteors flying about in the air—*
> *the prodigious glare of almost perpetual*
> *lightning—the crash of the falling houses—*
> *and the ear-piercing shrieks of the distressed,*
> *were sufficient to strike astonishment into*
> *Angels.*

Alexander's words struck astonishment into his readers. They couldn't believe the author was only seventeen. Everyone—even the governor—wanted to know who Alexander was. Once people learned who'd written the account of the storm, they wanted to help. Nicholas Cruger set up a scholarship fund that meant Alexander could become a student in New York City.

That fall, Alexander set out on a three-week journey by boat. Bad luck found him once more when the ship that carried him caught fire. Alexander and the rest of the passengers scrambled to scoop buckets of seawater to put out the blaze. It was a desperate situation. If they failed, the ship would sink, and they would die. But they managed to quench the flames. The damaged ship made it to Boston, and from there, Alexander traveled to New York.

ALEXANDER'S WORDS STRUCK ASTONISHMENT INTO HIS READERS.

When he stepped off the dock and into an entirely new world, he knew only one person in town: Ned Stevens. That was about to change. Even more, Alexander was about to change New York—and the world beyond.

CHAPTER TWO

A SON
of
LIBERTY

NEW YORK CITY IN 1772 was nothing like Alexander's childhood home. Even though Saint Croix was a busy port and a crossroads of international trade, it had less than half the population of New York, which was the second-largest city in the colonies, after Philadelphia. Twenty-five thousand people lived there, and they spoke at least fourteen languages among them.

ABOVE: *ARTIST THOMAS HOWDELL OF THE ROYAL ARTILLERY CAPTURED THIS SOUTHEAST VIEW OF NEW YORK CITY, LATER ENGRAVED BY P. CANOT.*

The city had tall buildings of painted brick, streets filled
with the clopping of horses pulling elegant carriages, and
churches with spires that reached for the heavens. Alexander
had never seen such grandness. A tree-lined Broadway was
the main thoroughfare through town, and most development
was concentrated on the south end of the island, where the
wharves were.

Cruger's Wharf was built in 1740, with thirty-foot tim-
bers sunk deep into the bed of the Hudson River. It jutted
southwest and ran parallel to Water Street. Ships moored
there unloaded imports and loaded exports, working at such
an intense clip that often leather shoes and glass bottles
and bits of pottery fell overboard and sank into the black fill
below. Here Alexander picked up his scholarship money, in
the waterfront offices of Kortright and Company. The money
came from profits made shipping molasses and rum from
Saint Croix.

At his old home, he hadn't always owned or needed shoes,
let alone a heavy coat. In New York, an epic winter was on its

ABOVE: *NEW YORK HARBOR CIRCA 1770.*

way. It was so cold that year that the East River froze. But Alexander found his place immediately, helped by letters of introduction written by Hugh Knox, whose endorsement opened all the right doors.

Alexander charmed everyone. It didn't matter in the colonies that his parents hadn't been married. He was worldly, his studies had paid off, and he impressed people with his intelligence. Even though he never liked to think of himself as handsome, other people couldn't help but notice his dashing looks. A friend said Alexander's eyes were "a deep azure, eminently beautiful, without the slightest trace of hardness or severity, and beamed with higher expressions of intelligence and discernment than any others that I ever saw." He did strike people as being diminutive because he was so slim—but at five foot seven, he was only an inch shorter than the average American man, and two inches taller than the average Englishman. Carrying himself with confidence, Alexander swiftly began to climb the social ladder.

IN NEW YORK, AN EPIC WINTER WAS ON ITS WAY.

Not long after he arrived in the city, he met an Irish tailor named Hercules Mulligan. Older than Alexander, Hercules was the younger brother of a Kortright and Company employee, and knew what it was like to be an immigrant. He was only a boy when he came over from Ireland, but he'd come with family, and Alexander was alone. Hercules took

Alexander under his wing and even housed him for part of the time he was in college.

Completing his education was Alexander's first order of business. He'd done well patching together his own schooling in the West Indies. But there were holes to fill before he was ready for college. He felt so behind. Other boys his age had already graduated from college, and he couldn't even get in until he'd brushed up on his Latin, Greek, and math.

COMPLETING HIS EDUCATION WAS ALEXANDER'S FIRST ORDER OF BUSINESS.

From the winter of 1772 through the spring of 1773, he plunged into these subjects at the Academy of Elizabethtown in New Jersey, learning enough that he could translate Greek Bible verses into Latin or English. He studied intensely at the school, which was run by the nearby First Presbyterian Church, and would slip out of bed at dawn and stroll through the churchyard cemetery as he ran through his lessons out loud. Then he would go to classes in a two-story brick building across the yard from the church. After school, he'd study past midnight.

He found the time to write poetry for fun and even penned the prologue and epilogue of a play performed to entertain British soldiers. His socializing turned out to be as important as his academic classes. Through Knox he met men like William Livingston and Elias Boudinot. They were

William Livingston

wealthy and worldly, and they ushered Alexander into the political and power hubs of the day. One person he may have met was a fellow orphan named Aaron Burr, who'd graduated from the College of New Jersey when he was only sixteen. (The College of New Jersey became Princeton University in 1896.)

The company Alexander kept tended to be ardent republicans, people who wanted independence from England. Some of them were mouthy. A poet and political firebrand

ABOVE: *WILLIAM LIVINGSTON, ONE OF ALEXANDER'S FIRST FRIENDS IN AMERICA, WAS A POET AND POLITICAL FIREBRAND.*

Elias Boudinot

nicknamed "the Whipping Post," Livingston loved ridiculing the king. He once wrote a letter telling his son that if a ghost of the ruling family ever visited, he should show him the door without so much as offering it a pipe of tobacco to smoke.

Boudinot was an attorney so well connected that he later became president of the Continental Congress. Alexander relished spending time at the Boudinot mansion, Boxwood Hall. It was full of books and lively debate—the sort of refined culture

ABOVE: *ELIAS BOUDINOT WAS A DEAR FRIEND OF ALEXANDER'S. THE BOUDINOTS LOST A BABY WHEN ALEXANDER WAS A COLLEGE STUDENT; HE WROTE A POEM ABOUT THE LOSS.*

Alexander craved. He became so close to the family that he kept a vigil by their sick baby in September 1774, when he was in college. He even wrote a poem after the child died, which began

FOR THE SWEET BABE, MY DOATING HEART

DID ALL A MOTHER'S FONDNESS FEEL;

CAREFULL TO ACT EACH TENDER PART

AND GUARD FROM EVERY THREATNING ILL.

BUT WHAT ALASS! AVAILD MY CARE?

THE UNRELENTING HAND OF DEATH,

REGARDLESS OF A PARENT'S PRAYR

HAS STOPED MY LOVELY INFANT'S BREATH.

ABOVE: *THE COLLEGE OF NEW JERSEY, LATER KNOWN AS PRINCETON, DENIED ALEXANDER ENROLLMENT.*

In six months Alexander finished prep school. His first choice for university was the College of New Jersey, a hotbed of revolutionary sentiment. Hugh Knox had gone there. Livingston and Boudinot were both on the board of trustees. What's more, the college was recruiting students from the West Indies. With these connections and his intellectual chops, Alexander felt confident enough to ask John Witherspoon, the Scottish-born theologian in charge, if he could speed his way toward a degree. The faster he could get through school, the faster he could build a life.

IT WAS A BLOW, BUT ALEXANDER HAD WEATHERED WORSE.

Witherspoon proposed the idea to the board—and Alexander was rejected by the trustees, who apparently said the plan was contrary to the usage of the college. Witherspoon hated saying no to Alexander, but his hands were tied. Another student who'd taken a fast track, James Madison, damaged his health by pushing himself too hard. He needed a year after graduation to recover.

It was a blow, but Alexander had weathered worse. Instead of packing his bags and traveling to the College of New Jersey in late 1773, Alexander began his studies at New York City's King's College, which was run by loyalists to the Crown. The urban campus overlooked a meadow and the Hudson River, which flowed alongside the western edge of Manhattan.

Built on land owned by Trinity Church, King's College offered classes in a three-story building topped with a cupola. Deciduous trees cast shade on the steps leading up to the classrooms. A fence wrapped around the campus, and students were required to be safely locked in after curfew, which was 10:00 p.m. during the summer and 9:00 p.m. during the winter.

The gate was meant to keep the young men out of trouble. Brothels surrounded the campus, and a high percentage of the city's population—about five hundred women—were prostitutes. Alexander's handbook offered a stern warning about consorting with them: "None of the Pupils shall frequent houses of ill Fame or keep Company with any persons of known scandalous behaviour."

Alexander managed to avoid landing in the dean's black book of students who'd broken the rules. Bent on making his way in the world, he threw himself into his academic work: philosophy, law, and medicine. Maybe, he thought, he'd become a doctor like his friend Ned Stevens.

ABOVE: *ALEXANDER STUDIED HARD AND STAYED OUT OF TROUBLE AT KING'S COLLEGE.*

As a private student working at his own swift pace, Alexander took some of his lessons from the college president, Myles Cooper, a published poet, an elegant scholar, and an ardent loyalist. His students took courses in natural law, physics, logic, ethics, metaphysics, math, philosophy, astronomy, geography, history, rhetoric, and ancient and modern languages.

ALEXANDER WASN'T EAGER FOR WAR—FAR FROM IT.

Alexander kept up his habit of rising early for a long ramble while he practiced his lessons aloud. Days were tightly scheduled. After his 6:00 a.m. walk, he'd attend chapel and eat breakfast. Dressed in his scholar's cap and gown, he'd work most of the day and after dinner follow the bells to evening prayer. Free time followed, and Alexander often spent his at the Mulligans' house with Hercules.

For fun, Alexander formed a weekly debate club with Ned Stevens and his new friends Robert Troup and Samuel and Henry Nicoll. He tested swiftly written political essays on them, and he sharpened his increasingly revolutionary arguments against Cooper. He also visited the Common, a park a block from school where radicals gathered. Alexander wasn't eager for war—far from it. But the idea of liberty and the natural human right to it entranced him.

The meaning of liberty hadn't always been such a flash point. In the middle of the 1700s, an English writer would expect his readers to view "liberty" as a birthright conferred to him as a subject of the Crown. This changed when the British started issuing certain taxes on the colonists. The taxes themselves weren't for unreasonable things, or for things that didn't benefit the colonies. The British empire needed to pay off the debt incurred fighting the French and Indian War, after all. Instead, the debates Alexander heard centered on *how* the English government chose to impose those taxes.

Colonists hated the Stamp Act, which Parliament passed in March 1765. It meant colonists would have to pay a small tax on every single printed page they produced, including legal documents, licenses, newspapers, ship's manifests—even playing cards. The revenue would fund the ten thousand troops stationed on the Appalachian frontier, a swath of land long cultivated, fished, and hunted by indigenous tribal nations but coveted by colonists and European empire-builders.

ABOVE: *THIS POLITICAL CARTOON MOCKS THE BRITISH BY DEPICTING A FUNERAL PARADE FOR THE STAMP ACT, REPEALED IN 1766.*

The colonists objected to the idea that England would be able to demand tax revenue without first getting approval from colonial legislatures. They feared the Crown would demand more money later. The act was repealed in 1766, but the outrage remained, especially when Parliament issued the Declaratory Act, which essentially said it could pass any colonial legislation it chose.

St—p!   ſt—p!   ſt—p!   No:

Tuesday-Morning, December 17, 1765.

THE True-born Sons of Liberty, are desired to meet under LIBERTY-TREE, at XII o'Clock, THIS DAY, to hear the the public Resignation, under Oath, of ANDREW OLIVER, Esq; Distributor of Stamps for the Province of the Massachusetts-Bay.

A Resignation ? YES.

Outraged by this act, many colonists, including Hercules Mulligan, formed a paramilitary political organization called the Sons of Liberty. Mostly members of the upper and middle classes—some of whom served as colonial legislators—they met secretly in Boston and New York to discuss their grievances. They adopted a flag with five vertical red and four white stripes, and the blunt motto "No taxation without

ABOVE: *THE SONS OF LIBERTY CALLED A MEETING IN LATE 1765 TO HEAR THE PUBLIC RESIGNATION OF A STAMP DISTRIBUTOR.*

representation." They also recruited "wharf rats" and other lowlifes to take part in their protests.

Their complaints extended beyond taxation. Increasingly, they saw King George and his predecessors as abusive manipulators. Some patriots thought the Crown had forced slavery on unwitting colonists, saddling them with the institution, and they thought the king not only failed to protect the frontier borders but sometimes worked with Indian tribes to threaten the colonists when it suited his aims.

IT WAS AN EXPENSIVE PUNISHMENT FOR THE TEA COMPANY.

The Sons of Liberty performed their most notorious act on December 16, 1773. Under the light of a watchful moon, more than a hundred colonists, some dressed as Mohawk Indians to underscore their allegiance to their adopted homeland over the Crown, boarded three ships in the Boston Harbor. They seized 342 chests of British tea worth 9,659 pounds, smashed them open, and dumped the goods into the water as some two thousand people watched from the docks. It was an expensive punishment for the tea company, which was already suffering financially after a colonial boycott of their wares.

The results were explosive.

Alexander was deep in his studies when a silversmith and engraver named Paul Revere galloped to New York four days later with the stunning news from Boston. Despite the love that many New Yorkers had for England, the news sparked a furor among Alexander and his friends. How should New York respond? Should they boycott English wares? Or would this eventually be self-defeating because they needed English-made cloth and other items? One of Alexander's first political pieces, which supported the tea protest, made the case for a boycott, as painful as it would be.

Until then, the thirteen colonies had acted like separate countries. Now they were asking many of the same questions. Their mutual concern about the English motherland led them to band together in 1774 and form the Continental Congress. Representatives from each colony—including Alexander's friend William Livingston—met to respond to the Coercive Acts, also known as the Intolerable Acts, a series of measures taken by the British government in retaliation for the Boston Tea Party.

The acts were harsh, but they weren't as bad as they could have been. One member of Parliament called Boston a "nest of

ABOVE: *PAUL REVERE WAS PART OF A WARNING SYSTEM OF RIDERS WHO ALERTED PATRIOTS TO THE ARRIVAL OF BRITISH REGULARS ON THE EVENING OF APRIL 18–19, 1775.*

locusts" that should be destroyed. Instead, Parliament closed Boston's port until reparations were paid for the ruined tea. It revoked the Massachusetts Bay charter of 1691, centralizing the authority with the Crown in the Massachusetts Bay Colony. It also permitted British troops to stay in unused buildings, prevented unauthorized town meetings, and tilted the scales of justice in favor of British officials by letting them be tried for capital offenses in England or other colonies.

Alexander and the Sons of Liberty gathered at the base of the liberty pole in the Common on July 6, 1774, to protest the acts. The British had long hated this pole and what it symbolized. Soldiers had burned and cut it down repeatedly until the colonists sunk a new one twelve feet into the ground and wrapped it in iron bands to keep it standing.

That day in the Common, standing in the shadow of the symbol of liberty, Alexander was just nineteen, and young looking at that. Dressed in a waistcoat, frock, breeches, and cravat, and with his hair pulled back and powdered in the style of the day, he gathered his courage and slipped through the crowd. Inspired by the moment, he decided there was something he needed desperately to say.

Nervous, he cleared his throat and began. What if he faltered? What if he failed to stir the crowd? It turned out he need not have worried.

Not even for a moment.

His words, once more, were about to change the course of his life.

CHAPTER THREE

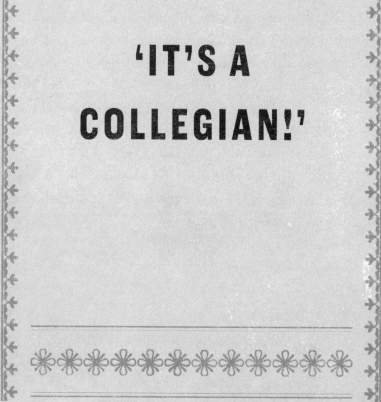

'IT'S A COLLEGIAN!'

AFTER A HESITANT START, Alexander found his voice. He condemned the British for closing Boston's port after the tea protest. He urged his fellow colonists to protest the unjust taxes. He called for a boycott of British goods, something that would make the colonists suffer, but would cause even more pain to the British.

His ideas and his energetic delivery lit up the crowd. No one could believe someone so young could be so persuasive, so passionate, so informed.

A murmur rose: "It is a collegian! It is a collegian!"

His time as a student was coming to an end, and his career as a revolutionary was beginning. He would bridge the transition from student to soldier with words, taking on the loyalists' own Westchester Farmer in a series of fiery essays.

The Farmer was the Reverend Samuel Seabury, a well-known loyalist who took vicious aim at the Continental Congress in anonymous pamphlets. The Farmer riled the patriots so much that they dunked copies in tar and feathers and tacked them to whipping posts. Perhaps because Seabury was a friend of Myles Cooper, the president of Alexander's college, and perhaps because he did not yet think of himself as a full-fledged American, Alexander wrote anonymously as "A Friend to America."

Samuel Seabury

A month after the first Farmer pamphlet appeared, he responded with a powerhouse thirty-five-page pamphlet. He wrote stirringly about freedom and slavery, and the God-given, natural right the colonists had to liberty. He'd seen firsthand how enslaved people suffered. He'd seen how courts could abuse the powerless. This would not stand.

"The only distinction between freedom and slavery consists in this: In the former state, a man is governed by the laws to which he has given his consent.... In the latter, he is

ABOVE: *THE RIGHT REVEREND SAMUEL SEABURY CALLED ALEXANDER AND OTHER PATRIOTS "SCORPIONS."*

governed by the will of another. . . . No man in his senses can hesitate in choosing to be free, rather than a slave."

The Farmer didn't intimidate Alexander. When Seabury called the patriots "scorpions" who would "sting us to death," Alexander fired back, intimating Seabury's critical abilities were so lousy that he preferred the man's disapproval to his applause.

Even so, Alexander wasn't yet arguing for revolution. He wanted Parliament to stop imposing taxes without the colonists' consent. One argument justifying this was that Parliament and the Crown were separate entities. The colonists could be subjects of the king but not subject to Parliament's laws. Impressed readers wondered who this Friend to America was. There were rumors that the author was Alexander, but people didn't believe someone so young could know so much about politics, language, and human nature.

Bloodshed could not be averted by words, though. Blood had already fallen in 1770 at a massacre in Boston, where British soldiers killed five men, including Crispus Attucks, the son of enslaved people—one African and one Wampanoag Indian. More was shed on April 19, 1775, when British

ABOVE: *ALEXANDER TOOK ON SEABURY IN THIS ANONYMOUS PAMPHLET, PUBLISHED IN 1774.*

FOLLOWING SPREAD: *NEWS OF THE 1775 BOSTON MASSACRE REACHED NEW YORK CITY FOUR DAYS LATER. ALEXANDER AND HIS CLASSMATES TOOK UP ARMS.*

soldiers quartered in Boston headed to Lexington to seize patriot leaders Samuel Adams and John Hancock, along with weapons and ammunition the colonists had stockpiled in Concord.

Colonial minutemen—volunteers willing to serve on short notice—had been tipped off. Someone opened fire in Lexington, and eight colonists died when the British blasted back. Two more were slain in Concord, but as the British retreated, the tables turned. Patriots fired from hiding spots along the way, killing or wounding 273, far more than the ninety-five casualties on the colonists' side.

FOUR DAYS LATER, NEWS OF THE VIOLENCE REACHED NEW YORK CITY.

Four days later, news of the violence reached New York City. The Sons of Liberty leapt into action. They seized supplies on British ships headed to Boston, as well as a cache of weapons held at City Hall—more than a thousand muskets, bayonets, and boxes of ammunition. These were used to arm outraged New Yorkers, including Alexander and his classmates.

Alexander immediately went to work practicing military drills. Every day, he and his classmates put on caps that read LIBERTY OR DEATH, along with short, close-fitting green military jackets. They marched through the churchyard of St. George's Chapel, practicing under the sharp eye of a former member of a British regiment.

Alexander drilled like a man possessed. Guns. Explosives. Maneuvers. Order. As relentlessly as he'd studied academics, he mastered the art of war, and not just the maneuvers, but the mindset.

And it was just in time. The patriots' rage in New York was percolating into violence.

On April 24, eight thousand furious men gathered outside City Hall. The next day, an anonymous handbill blamed five Tories, including Hamilton's professor Myles Cooper, for the deaths of the patriots in Massachusetts. On May 10, after a protest, a drunk and angry mob stormed King's College. The rabble knocked down the college gate and rushed the steps to Cooper's apartment. As the mob approached, Alexander stood his ground and launched into a speech, arguing that harming Cooper would sully the cause of liberty. In doing so, he bought his professor time to escape.

Even though he disagreed with Cooper politically, Alexander was more than willing to stand as a human shield when it was the right thing to do. He could have been beaten to death. He could have lost his stature as the young voice of the Revolution. But none of that mattered to him as much as human decency.

The two men never saw each other again. But Alexander, filled with courage and scenting war on the horizon, had set an important standard for himself. His life mattered less than his principles. He was above the witless rage of a mob. He was a man of honor.

THE SECOND CONTINENTAL CONGRESS APPOINTED
George Washington on June 15, 1775, to lead the Continental
Army. The challenge of this loomed large. The colonists were
in no way ready. Alexander's friend Elias Boudinot was with
Washington when the general learned they had enough gunpowder for only eight rounds a man, and they had fourteen
miles of line to guard. Washington, never much of a talker,
could not speak for thirty minutes.

Not long afterward, a 158-foot Royal British Navy man-of-
war called the *Asia* dropped anchor in New York Harbor. She
had three huge masts and sixty-four guns. The firepower she
represented was terrifying. Inch for inch, she had the most
guns of any ship the Royal Navy had yet built. The *Asia* could
burn down the city.

Washington had to take the Hoboken ferry into the city to
avoid her guns. On June 25, Alexander got his first glimpse of
the forty-three-year-old general as he traveled down Broadway

ABOVE: *AMERICAN TROOPS WERE INITIALLY OUTMATCHED BY
THE BRITISH, THOUGH THEY TOOK POSSESSION OF BREED'S HILL ON
JUNE 16, 1775.*

George Washington

in a carriage pulled by white horses. Washington was tall and fit, about six foot two, and he cut a deliberately impressive figure. When he'd served during the French and Indian War, he complained about the sad state of his regiment's uniforms, with their thin fabric and sorry waistcoats. Conscious that leadership required a certain look and bearing, Washington dressed himself in tall black boots, buff-colored wool breeches with a matching waistcoat, and a blue coat with shiny buttons and a purple sash, along with a curved sword of grooved steel.

ABOVE: *GENERAL GEORGE WASHINGTON TOOK COMMAND OF THE CONTINENTAL ARMY ON JUNE 15, 1775.*

King George

The next week, Alexander and the rest of the citizens of New York were on edge. The sultry heat of summer hung around the city like a blanket. The Second Continental Congress authorized an Olive Branch Petition on July 5 to send to King George. The king ignored it and, on August 23, fired back a royal proclamation of his own.

His American subjects were in open rebellion. His military would break it.

Hours later—even before word of the proclamation made

ABOVE: *HIS MAJESTY KING GEORGE III IGNORED AN OLIVE BRANCH FROM THE SECOND CONTINENTAL CONGRESS.*

its way across the Atlantic—the *Asia* opened fire from the East River.

The Americans had no warships to fire back, which meant Manhattan was vulnerable. An abandoned British military fortification—Fort George—was armed with two dozen cannons. The New York militia needed them. Alexander, along with Hercules Mulligan and fifteen other volunteers from his college, helped steal those weapons and bring them to the liberty pole. The men lashed ropes to the cannons, which weighed one ton each and were mounted on tiny wheels, and they dragged at least ten of them to safety before a barge from the *Asia* took aim at them. Under fire, the men pressed on, even as the rope blistered their hands.

UNDER FIRE, THE MEN PRESSED ON.

In a desperate moment, Alexander gave Hercules his musket to hold. He moved a cannon and asked Mulligan for his weapon back. Hercules, distracted by gunfire, had left the gun by the Battery. Undaunted by grapeshot and cannonballs screaming through the air, Alexander ran back and retrieved his weapon.

That night, a Sons of Liberty meeting place called the Fraunces Tavern was hit—a cannonball tore a huge hole in the ceiling. Fires blazed in the harbor, and their reflected flames lit up the windows. Alexander remained cool and focused even as terrified citizens panicked in the streets. He and the others managed to steal all but three of the Battery's twenty-four guns, which they stashed under guard at the liberty pole.

Not long afterward, he wrote a letter about the mission and sent it to Hugh Knox, who printed it in the *Royal Danish American Gazette*. "I was born to die and my reason and conscience tell me it is impossible to die in a better or more important cause."

His courage and drive made him a standout soldier, noticed by many. Elias Boudinot wanted Alexander to be an aide-de-camp to a brigadier general in the Continental Army, William Alexander, known as Lord Stirling. Other generals had noticed his talent, too.

Alexander hesitated. He didn't want a desk job. He wanted to fight for glory on the battlefield. When the New York Provincial Congress ordered the colony to put together an artillery company, Alexander decided running it was the post for him. He turned the generals down, persuaded key people to back him, studied everything he could about artillery, and in March 1776, at twenty-one years of age, became captain of the New York Provincial Company of Artillery.

ULTIMATELY, ALEXANDER HAD SIXTY-EIGHT men under his command, and he took scrupulous care of them, even using his Saint Croix scholarship money to buy some of their equipment, expecting to be paid back from their future wages. He dressed his men in buckskin breeches and deep blue, swallow-tailed coats with brass buttons and buff collars that had white shoulder belts running diagonally across their chests. They had three-cornered felt hats with cockades and hung their muskets from leather shoulder straps. Hercules made Alexander an even higher-quality uniform, with pants of white fabric (tough buckskin was for the men doing the physical labor).

HIS COURAGE AND DRIVE MADE HIM A STANDOUT SOLDIER.

Not all revolutionary soldiers had such smart uniforms—or any uniforms at all. But Alexander was a natural leader and organizer, and he knew such things were important. He kept track of food, clothing, pay, and disciplinary action in a small book. He faced his share of challenges with his men. Nine days after he officially took command, he had to give one soldier the boot for "being subject to fits." Two days later, another got kicked out for "misbehavior." The next month, he court-martialed four men for mutiny. Others were found guilty of desertion and punished with days of bread and water and even whipping. Many other leaders had trouble turning recruits into soldiers. Not Alexander. Through his drills and leadership, his men became known as a model of discipline and order.

He made sure his men earned equal pay for their efforts. The New York Provincial Congress was responsible for paying his troops. The Continental Congress—which funded the Continental Army—had raised pay for its troops, but New York's militia hadn't kept pace, threatening his men's

General William Howe

morale and willingness to fight. He wrote letters that secured equal pay and provisions. He also did his best to instill discipline and promotions alike. His name crossed Washington's desk when Alexander ordered one of his men to be lashed for desertion. Washington, a strict disciplinarian, approved.

There was periodic good news for the patriots. In March 1776, the Continental Army drove the British out of Boston. But on the whole, things looked grim. They'd even had to melt lead rooftops and windowsills to make more ammunition.

ABOVE: *GENERAL SIR WILLIAM HOWE WAS THE BRITISH ARMY COMMANDER IN CHIEF.*

Admiral Lord Richard Howe

They needed more than bullets. They needed warm bodies.
Here, the British had a huge advantage. Starting in June, the
massive British war fleet began to arrive in New York Harbor.
Led by two brothers, General William Howe and Admiral
Lord Richard Howe, the king's fighting force comprised thirty
battleships armed with twelve hundred cannons; thirty thousand soldiers; ten thousand sailors; and three hundred supply
ships. It was the largest and strongest military since the days
of the Roman Empire.

ABOVE: *ADMIRAL RICHARD LORD HOWE, WILLIAM HOWE'S BROTHER,
COMMANDED THE BRITISH NAVY. TOGETHER, THE BROTHERS LED THE
LARGEST MILITARY FORCE SINCE THE ROMAN EMPIRE.*

The colonies had fewer than twenty thousand rookie soldiers. Many were old men. Boys in their midteens. Raw, disorderly, and sometimes even drunk. Discipline was an ongoing problem, as was basic hygiene. Though ammunition was in short supply, soldiers sometimes shot their guns to make noise and even start fires.

ABOVE: *A COMMITTEE THAT INCLUDED THOMAS JEFFERSON AND JOHN ADAMS DRAFTED THE DECLARATION OF INDEPENDENCE. THE MEN BOTH DIED ON JULY 4, 1826, ON THE FIFTIETH ANNIVERSARY OF THE DOCUMENT.*

Nonetheless, the patriots forged ahead. On July 2, the Continental Congress voted to declare independence. (New York abstained.) It was a historic moment. No colony had yet broken away from its parent country and managed to set up a self-governing state. Even trying to do so was treason, which was punishable by death.

NONETHELESS, THE PATRIOTS FORGED AHEAD.

Hundreds of copies of the Declaration of Independence were printed and distributed. The document made its way to New York on July 9, and after it was read, a four-thousand-pound, gilded lead statue of George III astride his horse had its last stand in Bowling Green park. Patriots tore down the statue, cut it into pieces, melted the lead, and made 42,088 bullets intended for British bodies. (All but the head, which was rescued by loyalists and sent to England, where it disappeared.)

New York was difficult territory to defend, especially without a navy. But it was strategically important as a buffer protecting New England and as a corridor to Canada. Manhattan is long and thin, and the adjacent New York Harbor is deep enough to be filled with ships. Two rivers flanked the island, which was narrow enough for invaders to cross, trapping patriots between troops and ships.

The British made good use of this vulnerability.

On July 12, on a beautiful summer day, the British advanced. They sent the *Phoenix*, a forty-four-gun battleship, and the *Rose*, a twenty-eight-gun frigate, up the Hudson

River. The wind and tide moved in their favor. Soldiers and panicked residents ran pell-mell through the streets, accompanied by the clamor of alarm guns.

South West View of Fort George with the City of New York.

Alexander, in charge of artillery at Fort George, opened fire on the enemy. The ships sent back cannonballs that crashed into houses and bounced down streets thick with terrified women and children. The American shots caused hardly any damage, but they filled the air with smoke and the stink of gunpowder as British ships slipped past.

Alexander commanded four of the biggest cannons. In the midst of fire, one of them burst. As many as six men died, and four or five more were wounded. Some of his men were drunk and failed to wipe the powder and quench the sparks

ABOVE: *A SOUTHWEST VIEW OF FORT GEORGE AND THE CITY OF NEW YORK.*

from an earlier volley. Though he wasn't to blame and wasn't disciplined afterward, the ordeal devastated him.

At least his company had shown up. One soldier estimated half of the city's artillerists were either drunk at bars or consorting with prostitutes instead of fighting. General Washington wasn't pleased: "Unsoldierly Conduct must grieve every good officer, and give the enemy a *mean* opinion of the Army."

IN THE MIDST OF FIRE, ONE OF THE CANNONS BURST.

The development boded ill for the Americans. The two warships made it past all the guns with hardly a scratch. There was no reason to believe the entire British fleet couldn't do the same—trapping Washington and his men in New York.

Washington urged citizens to evacuate. Scouring the terrain from across the East River, Alexander didn't think the Continental Army stood a chance against the British. He wanted to retreat—but a letter delivered by Hercules Mulligan received no response. Washington sent out general orders on August 8, indicating that his men were to be alert around the clock. "The Movements of the enemy and intelligence by Deserters, give the utmost reason to believe, that the great struggle, in which we are contending for everything dear to us and our posterity, is near at hand."

A series of attacks began early on August 27. The British and their Hessian mercenaries crushed the American forces.

The debacle dispirited Washington, who could only watch from afar through a telescope borrowed from King's College. "Good God, what brave fellows I must lose," he said. Lord Stirling, surrounded, bought time for fleeing troops before he was captured—which would have been Alexander's fate had he chosen to work as the man's aide.

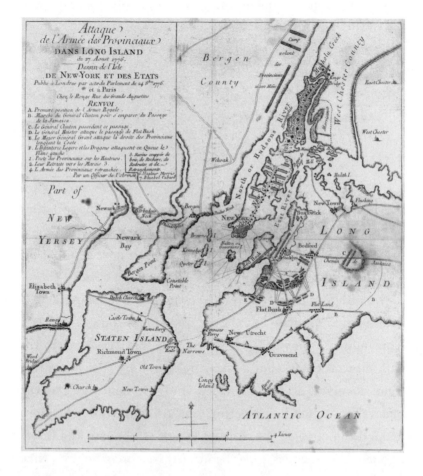

The next afternoon, England's General Howe ordered his men to dig trenches around the Americans, who were

ABOVE: *THE BRITISH ROUTED THE PATRIOTS ON LONG ISLAND IN AUGUST 1776.*

cornered in Brooklyn Heights up against the East River. After another day of attacks, Washington ordered an evacuation. Under cover of night, nine thousand Americans were rowed back to Manhattan. The sun rose before all the Americans had escaped, but a lucky fog rolled in, concealing the rest. George Washington was the last man to leave Brooklyn.

It was becoming increasingly clear to Washington that his army was a mess: soldiers who signed up for short-term engagements that they often abandoned; drunken men who took part in looting; Yankees who'd rather let their shirts rot on their backs than do the women's work of washing them. Washington wanted a well-trained standing army—which would become a huge point of contention with some, but an issue on which he and Alexander were in perfect alignment.

"GOOD GOD, WHAT BRAVE FELLOWS I MUST LOSE."

Weeks passed, and on September 15, five ships—including the *Phoenix* and the *Rose*—sailed up the East River and landed on the eastern shore of Manhattan at Kips Bay. They bombarded the colonists and unloaded barges full of British and Hessian troops, who aimed to keep the Americans trapped in the southern part of the island. Patriots—overwhelmed by the forces and their firepower—fled north.

Washington, enraged, ripped off his hat and threw it on the ground. "Are these the men with which I am to defend America?"

Alexander was one of the last to leave Fort Bunker Hill where troops had been stationed. He was flanked on the right by the enemy, blocking access to the rest of the army. Aaron Burr, an aide-de-camp to General Israel Putnam, arrived on horseback and urged the men to leave, else face capture or death. The men followed, and at one point Burr raced toward gunfire so that he could take on an enemy guard. Alexander arrived in Harlem Heights having lost a cannon and his baggage, but alive—thanks to Aaron Burr.

WEEKS PASSED WITHOUT FIGHTING AS THE troops made their way to White Plains. The battle there proved costly for both sides. The British lost more men, but the patriots were beginning to lose hope. On November 16, they lost Fort Washington, and thus the island of Manhattan. Four days later Fort Lee in New Jersey fell. A lesson was learned: no more open confrontations with the vastly superior British regulars.

By December, Alexander had become so sick he couldn't get out of bed. His company was down to about thirty men. Some had died; others had deserted. Thomas Paine, who had been with the soldiers during the dispiriting loss in New York, captured the mood on December 19, during the darkest part of winter and the darkest moments of the early war:

"These are the times that try men's souls. The summer soldier and the sunshine patriot will, in this crisis, shrink from the service of their country; but he that stands it now, deserves the love and thanks of man and woman."

Alexander was no sunshine patriot. Sick as he was, he forced himself down to the Delaware River on Christmas night. It was so cold that ice caked the boats, which men poled across the ice-clogged Delaware. Snow and sleet fell on Alexander and his troops, who then marched eight miles dragging a massive artillery train with the aid of horses.

ALEXANDER HAD BECOME SO SICK HE COULDN'T GET OUT OF BED.

When they reached Trenton, they spied a miracle: the glint of metal off the helmets and bayonets of Hessians. Alexander's men fired. The Hessians returned the favor. From behind, their footsteps muffled by falling snow, Washington and his men sneaked up on the Hessians as Alexander and his men blasted on, preventing the German mercenaries' escape. A thousand enemy forces were captured that night, thanks in part to Alexander's artillery company.

There was a second fight on January 2, and on January 3, Alexander led an attack on Nassau Hall at the College of New Jersey, the same school that had rejected his application. No one would reject Alexander now. A senior officer observed his arrival on campus: "I noticed a youth, a mere stripling, small, slender, almost delicate in frame, marching beside a piece of artillery, with a cocked hat pulled down over his eyes, apparently lost in thought, with his hand resting on the cannon, and every now and then patting it, as if it were a favorite horse or a pet plaything."

The victories at Trenton and Princeton boosted the hearts of Alexander and his men. And then, on January 20, 1777,

Hamilton received a note that should have thrilled him more than anything. It was from George Washington: an invitation to join his staff.

It wasn't the moment Alexander had been waiting for, though. Glory on the battlefield—that was his dream. He hated the idea of shuffling papers instead of shooting guns. But he was still getting over his sickness, so he took the job.

Before long, he'd made himself invaluable to the general, who was quartered at the Arnold Tavern in Morristown, New Jersey. The tavern was a solid three-story building with two chimneys and a wide front porch. Washington and his men, including Alexander, spent about five months encamped in the area.

As part of Washington's staff, Alexander was brought inside the heart of the Revolution. He saw the challenges of managing a Continental Army alongside state militias, as well as the difficulties in fighting a larger, better-trained, better-funded, and better-equipped enemy.

Alexander was the gifted wordsmith Washington was not, and a huge part of his role was managing the correspondence that flooded his desk: letters from Congress and from the colonial legislators; orders that needed to be sent, most of which Alexander wrote; disputes between subordinates that needed management. He was the best of Washington's writers.

ABOVE: *ALEXANDER HAMILTON LONGED FOR GLORY ON THE BATTLEFIELD, WHERE HE WAS A STANDOUT SOLDIER. HE IS DEPICTED HERE IN YORKTOWN, 1781.*

There also were supply chains to manage, including munitions, clothing, food. This he'd learned to handle in Saint Croix. And there were people who needed attention: prisoners, and soldiers in need of promotion—again, something that put his shipping-clerk experience to good use. Alexander

ABOVE: *PART OF A LETTER ALEXANDER SENT GEORGE WASHINGTON IN 1783. WASHINGTON'S FAITH IN ALEXANDER NEVER WAVERED.*

helped bring order to Washington's staff, and thanks to his study and drilling, he also knew a great deal about political and military principles. Before long, he wasn't just Washington's right hand. Alexander was thinking and writing on Washington's behalf, corresponding often with Congress and with leaders in New York. He also drilled troops and carried out vital missions.

After hours of writing and copying letters, sometimes as many as a hundred in a day, Alexander and the rest of Washington's military family would sit around the dinner table and share stories each night. Quarters at the tavern were close. Washington's aides often slept six to a room and two to a bed. (During the war, they even slept on the floor by the general's bed when necessary—and that's when they had shelter. Other times, they'd bed down under cover of trees and stars.)

ALEXANDER'S REGRETFUL REPLY WAS FLIRTY TO THE EXTREME.

Morristown did have one unexpected perk: Alexander had time to woo women, or at least try. Susanna Livingston, an old friend from Elizabethtown, inquired if she and a few friends might visit headquarters, and Alexander's regretful reply was flirty to the extreme. He even described himself as "a valorous knight, destined to be their champion and deliverer." He was so girl crazy, in fact, that Martha Washington named her randy tomcat after him.

John Laurens

He made friends with the other aides and didn't mind their calling him Ham or Hammie. One gave Alexander a nickname that stuck for life: the Little Lion.

Alexander was especially close with John Laurens, the strapping, intense-eyed son of a rich and powerful South Carolina politician. He and Laurens had much in common, an echo of Alexander's friendship with Ned Stevens. Like Alexander, Laurens was interested in medicine. He too was a bold and sometimes even reckless soldier. And, despite

ABOVE: *ALEXANDER'S BEST FRIEND, JOHN LAURENS, WAS A FIERCE OPPONENT OF SLAVERY.*

being from a slave state, he hated the practice of enslaving human beings.

Another friend was one Marie-Joseph-Paul-Yves-Roch-Gilbert du Motier, better known as the Marquis de Lafayette. Given all those names to protect him in battle, Lafayette was a French aristocrat about Alexander's age. He was so taken by the cause of liberty that he'd traveled to America with a ship and weapons he'd paid for himself. Like Alexander, Lafayette was an orphan. Together Lafayette, Laurens, and Alexander reminded people of the three musketeers from the Alexandre Dumas novel.

Older men in the military looked at Alexander as a source of hope. General Nathanael Greene, one of Washington's most respected leaders, called Alexander "a bright gleam of sunshine, ever growing brighter as the general darkness thickened."

ALEXANDER AND HIS MEN DOVE INTO THE CURRENT.

And the darkness did thicken. After a lull, the fighting returned. In July 1777, the British captured Fort Ticonderoga in upstate New York, and it felt as though victory had slipped forever out of reach. Alexander was at the front lines with Washington on September 11 for another brutal loss. The defeat at the Battle of Brandywine would lead to the British takeover of the new nation's capital, Philadelphia, on September 26.

A week after this disappointment, Washington sent Alexander, Captain Henry Lee, and eight cavalrymen to destroy flour mills along the Schuylkill River before the British could use them. To make sure Alexander had an escape route, he planted a flat-bottomed boat on the edge of the river.

As he and his comrades were destroying the mills, a sentry fired a warning shot. The British were on their way. Captain Lee and half the men took off on horseback. Alexander and three others scurried for the boat. The British took aim. One of Alexander's men was shot and killed. Another was wounded.

The river, swollen by recent rains, bashed furiously at the boat. The British fired away. Alexander and his men dove into the current. Lee watched the horror unfold. Alexander hadn't surfaced, and Lee feared the worst. As soon as he could, the captain dashed off a letter to General Washington announcing awful news: the death of Alexander Hamilton.

ABOVE: *ALEXANDER WAS SENT TO THE SCHUYLKILL RIVER, WHERE HE DESTROYED FLOUR MILLS.*

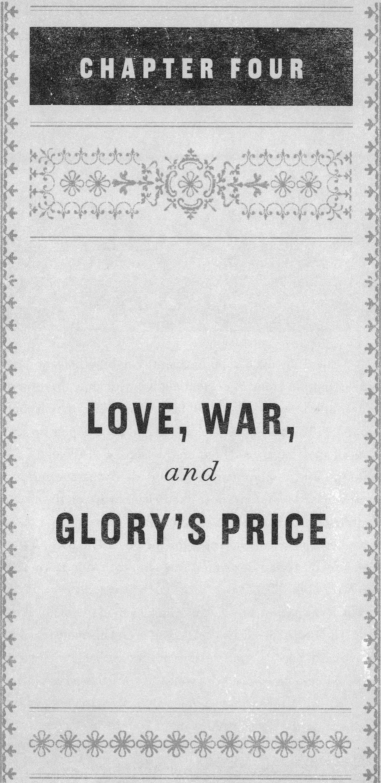

CHAPTER FOUR

LOVE, WAR,

and

GLORY'S PRICE

THE MOOD IN WASHING-ton's office was grim when the letter arrived. Then, when the soaking-wet lieutenant colonel walked through the door moments later, there was laughter, relief, and even joyful tears. He was alive. *Alive!*

Washington, who didn't have children of his own, called Alexander "son" and "my boy." Yet this didn't mean the general was warm. On the contrary, he cultivated distance from the troops he commanded to remind people who was in charge. Discipline and protocol were at the heart of military competence.

Alexander once challenged a friend of his to slap Washington on the back during a dinner party. The friend did just that. Washington sat, stone-faced, and moved the man's hand back where it belonged. No one said a word.

Later, the friend confessed to Alexander: "I have won the bet, but paid dearly for it, and nothing could induce me to repeat it."

That Washington wasn't warm didn't mean he didn't care deeply about Alexander. If there was any coldness between the two, it came as much from Alexander, who addressed Washington as "Your Excellency." What's more, the general also *needed* Alexander's brilliant mind and busy pen, now more than ever.

After Alexander had climbed out of the water on the far side of the river, he sent an urgent dispatch to Philadelphia recommending an immediate evacuation of the capital. Some congressmen fled because of Alexander's warning. Fear had also been sharpened by a British attack about twenty miles away. On September 20, under cover of darkness, soldiers crept through a forest toward the light of American camp-fires. Absolutely quiet, they had removed the flints from their rifles to prevent accidental discharges that could alert the patriots. Shortly after midnight, the British soldiers rushed into camp and stabbed relentlessly with their bayonets. At least fifty-three Americans died in the Paoli Massacre. One American corpse had been pierced forty-six times.

Equally urgent as the imminent arrival of the enemy in Philadelphia was the matter of supplies for the troops. They lacked blankets. Clothing. Horses. To ease that crisis, Washington gave Alexander a difficult charge:

> *I am compelled to desire you immediately to proceed to Philadelphia, and there procure from the inhabitants, contributions of blankets and Cloathing and materials. . . . This you will do with as much delicacy and discretion as the nature of the business demands.*

IN A WAR BEING FOUGHT FOR THE PRINCIPLES of liberty and property ownership, collecting supplies from civilians was delicate to the extreme. The army couldn't continue without food and horses and blankets, but it risked losing support of the citizenry in demanding them, even with the permission of Congress.

Alexander brought to the job all the diligence and diplomacy he'd displayed as a young clerk. He not only kept track of the items he'd received, but also prepared receipts for residents. He excused the poor and homeless from contributions, as well as people who needed their horses for their livelihood.

His thorough and effective work equipped the rebels to fight the Battle of Germantown only weeks after his miraculous return from the dead. The Continental Army was still reeling from the loss at Brandywine, but Washington was eager to strike back. The British had taken Philadelphia, and some of the redcoats—British soldiers named for their uniforms—were headed for American forts blocking access to the Delaware River. But a reduced force of nine thousand British troops remained camped at Germantown—and Washington decided to take them on.

He had eleven thousand troops and a complicated plan of attack in mind. It would require precise timing and the

ABOVE: *THE BATTLE OF GERMANTOWN ON OCTOBER 4, 1777, WAS A DISPIRITING LOSS FOR THE AMERICANS.*

cooperation of two Continental Army generals as well as a pair of detachments of state militias.

Alexander wrote Washington's long and detailed orders.

On the night of October 3, four columns of soldiers headed off on the sixteen-mile march to Germantown. The two columns in the center, led by General Greene and General John Sullivan, would strike at General Howe's center. They would be flanked on each side by a pair of militia detachments. They were to march all night and then attack before dawn: silent, quick, and lethal—bayonets only.

THEY WERE TO MARCH ALL NIGHT AND THEN ATTACK BEFORE DAWN.

There were problems from the start. Greene's troops were delayed, but at five thirty in the morning, Sullivan's troops attacked anyway, forcing Howe's advanced guard back. About a hundred British soldiers took refuge in a stone mansion. Sullivan kept up the onslaught. Cannonade and musket fire sounded like thunder and the crackling of thorns under a pot. He forced the British troops back a mile toward Germantown, all the while struggling to see in the darkness and through a thick blanket of fog.

An hour later, Greene's troops arrived. In heavy combat, they took part of the British camp. All felt promising despite the delay—and then it fell apart. Sullivan's men didn't have enough ammunition, and worse, Greene's men accidentally shot some of them through the fog. Although they'd put pieces of white paper in their hats, they still couldn't see each other in the darkness.

The British retreated into people's homes and shot from second-story windows. The two columns of militia men didn't perform as planned. The one on the right, a detachment from Pennsylvania, made no headway against a group of Hessians. On the far side, the men from New Jersey and Maryland arrived too late to help. Some soldiers were distracted by the redcoats in the stone mansion, which didn't help the main cause. Washington, Alexander, and the rest of the general's military family watched their hopes collapse in agonizing fashion.

After five grueling hours, Washington's many troops retreated, and for eight miles the British gave such swift chase that the patriots "were flying," one witness wrote in her journal. In the confusion, General Howe's fox terrier darted across to the American side. Distraught as Washington was, he couldn't resist a sad-eyed dog, and he had Alexander write a note and send the animal back to his enemy: "He does himself the pleasure to return him a dog, which accidentally fell into his hands, and by the inscription on the Collar appears to belong to General Howe."

The conflict left one thousand patriots dead, captured, or wounded; the broken corpses of American soldiers lay on the road. As crushing as the disorder of the American troops had been, there were some flickers of hope.

In the middle of October, British General John Burgoyne surrendered nearly six thousand men to General Horatio Gates in Saratoga, New York. The victory convinced France to ally herself with the Americans. And it also meant Washington could use some of Gates's troops for other battles.

Finding enough soldiers for the Continental Army remained an enormous problem and a constant source of worry for Alexander. It wasn't only that some of the soldiers were dead, ill, injured, or absent without leave. It was also that their enlistment terms had ended and that they were allowed to go home: an understandable choice, considering winter was on its way and the army was chronically short on food, clothing, and supplies.

ALEXANDER TOOK OFF ON HORSEBACK, GALLOPING SIXTY MILES A DAY FOR FIVE DAYS STRAIGHT.

Reassigning some of Gates's men was vital to Washington, and Alexander was the man to make this happen. Yes, he was young. Yes, his rank was lower. But Washington believed Alexander could make the politically difficult case better than anyone else. To complicate matters, Gates wasn't a fan of Washington's leadership skills and fighting style, which avoided major conflicts on open fields. And Gates himself was considered a hero because of the huge victory over Burgoyne (although much was due to the actions of Benedict Arnold and not the gloating Gates, whom Alexander had never liked).

Washington gave Alexander two options: let Gates continue to use his troops as he saw fit if it helped the army, or redeploy men if that seemed the shrewder move. Orders clear, Alexander took off on horseback, galloping sixty miles a day for five days straight. On the way, he delivered Washington's orders for General Putnam also to send brigades south to assist him. In return, Putnam would pick up seven hundred men from New Jersey.

Exhausted, Alexander arrived in Albany and made his case to Gates, who refused to comply. Instead, he offered the services of the weakest of the brigades he had. Alexander was incensed and thought the decision was "impudence . . . folly . . . rascality."

Gates wouldn't send as many troops as Washington wanted: two brigades of Continental Army troops had to stay. Both men walked away mad. Gates, offended he had to talk with such an upstart, began an angry letter to George Washington.

"I am astonished . . .

He thought better of that line and crossed it out. He tried another approach and crossed that out, too.

"I confess I want Wisdom to discover the Motives that Influenced the Giving such an Opinion."

He also crossed out a whole paragraph griping about having to obey the verbal orders of an aide-de-camp who was acting like a little dictator three hundred miles from headquarters. Eventually, Gates found his way to compromise on the number of troops. He wasn't happy about it in the least.

Meanwhile, Hamilton's college friend Robert Troup was in Albany. So Troup, Nathanael Greene, and Alexander met for dinner at the elegant three-story Georgian-style mansion of an important New York military leader, General Philip Schuyler. It was the sort of environment Alexander had thrived in before the war, one where power and privilege parted like

an ocean before his charm. Now, though, he was more than just handsome and charming. He was brave, brilliant, and instrumental to the war effort.

At that dinner party, Alexander met Schuyler's three attractive daughters. One of them was a dark-eyed, dark-haired, petite charmer named Elizabeth.

Alexander didn't know it at the time, but he'd just met his future wife.

HIS RETURN TRIP WAS ROUGH. GENERAL PUT-nam had failed to send the men he'd promised, and Alexander went berserk at the betrayal. On November 9, Alexander fired off an enraged letter.

ABOVE: *THE SCHUYLER MANSION IN ALBANY, NEW YORK, IS WHERE ALEXANDER FIRST LAID EYES ON HIS FUTURE WIFE.*

General Israel Putnam

Sir, I cannot forbear Confessing that I am astonishd. and Alarm'd beyond measure, to find that all his Excellency's Views have been hitherto flustrated, and that no single step of those I mention'd to you has been taken to afford him the aid he absolutely stands in Need of, and by Delaying which the Cause of America is put to the Utmost conceivable Hazard.

ABOVE: *GENERAL ISRAEL PUTNAM THOUGHT ALEXANDER WAS A HORRID UPSTART.*

In Putnam's defense, two brigades hadn't been paid—the funding problem was a cancer to the cause. But Alexander cut Putnam no slack and insisted he send all his Continental Army troops to Washington straightaway. In doing this, Alexander was operating under the principle that it's better to ask forgiveness than permission. Washington hadn't given him any such order. But Alexander had gambled shrewdly. Washington was pleased with his initiative. No forgiveness was required after all.

The ordeal ravaged Alexander's health. He had to stop his travels and recuperate. As he shivered with a fever and severe pain, he sent word to Washington explaining the delay. Despite his health, he tried to keep pressure on Putnam to send men. But by the end of November, Alexander was bedridden.

On November 23, Captain Caleb Gibbs sent word that Alexander was near death. His limbs were cold and remained so for two hours. Alexander rallied. But when the symptoms returned two days later, the doctor caring for him expected him to die.

Alexander was stronger, though, and he beat the illness. As soon as he could move, he set out again to join Washington and the rest of his military family—although he collapsed near Morristown just before Christmas. Washington's men had arrived at their camp in Valley Forge a few days earlier, and supplies were so low they had nothing for Christmas Eve dinner but rice and vinegar. Alexander joined them there in late January 1778.

The camp's location on the west bank of the Schuylkill River about twenty miles northwest of Philadelphia offered some protection in case of a British attack. But against all other enemies—hunger, cold, disease—it was vulnerable to the extreme. The darkest, most miserable days of the Revolutionary War had arrived.

Alexander and the rest of the aides stayed with the general and sometimes Mrs. Washington in a modest two-story stone house with windows and fireplaces. Soldiers slept on rickety bunks in tiny log cabins warmed by small fireplaces. The ground was covered in snow and the corpses of hundreds of decomposing horses, as well as blood from the feet of men who had to use rags for shoes. The lack of shoes was so dire that Washington had earlier offered a $10 reward to the person who came up with the best substitute using rawhide.

In the center of camp lay the artillery park, an open field where the men stored and repaired their cannons and where they would drill for hours on end if they weren't too ill.

Alexander was miserable. The war effort seemed like it could unravel at any second, and a group of rivals had been plotting behind Washington's back to have him removed as

ABOVE: *WASHINGTON AND HIS TROOPS SUFFERED MISERABLY AT VALLEY FORGE DURING THE WINTER OF 1777–78.*

the head of the army. Alexander also had to put up with accusations that he'd stolen correspondence from one of Washington's rivals, which he hadn't done. Alexander, hating the man who'd questioned his honor, came up with a suitable insult for his accuser: "vermin bred in the entrails of this chimera dire."

THE ARMY WAS BLEEDING MEN.

And Washington was so irritable all the time! Martha Washington confided to a friend that she had never seen her husband so anxious. Even as Alexander hated bearing the brunt of Washington's moods, he understood the stress the general was under. Congress was pressuring Washington to attack, but the troops had nothing to eat and not enough clothing. It was all well and good for members of Congress to criticize from their warm seats by the fire, but the lack of supplies was literally killing the army.

When Alexander and the rest of the men started their six-month stay in Valley Forge, the Continental Army had eleven thousand soldiers. By the end, two thousand had starved, frozen, or died of disease: smallpox, typhoid, pneumonia, dysentery, and typhus—known as putrid fever. The army was bleeding men in other ways. About two thousand men had deserted their posts; the situation was so urgent Washington threatened to shoot the men running away. Often, though, people left legitimately. Their terms of service were ending, and there was often not enough money to pay soldiers what they were owed. Even Washington's own state, Virginia, had lost nine regiments this way. It was increasingly hard to make the case for continued rebellion in the face of a better-organized, better-paid, better-equipped enemy.

Exhaustion was real. So was ambivalence. By some estimates, a third of the Americans were committed patriots. Another third were neutral and wanted stability. The final third were loyalists. A French-born brigadier general in the Continental Army thought the Americans lucky that the British had made errors and were sluggish. The Americans weren't used to the hardship of war:

> *It is easy to see that if their privations increase to a certain point, they will prefer the yoke of England to a liberty which costs them the comforts of life. . . . There is a hundred times more enthusiasm for this revolution in a single cafe in Paris than in all the united colonies.*

The patriots who stayed might not have expressed the enthusiasm of Parisians sipping wine in cafés. But they did endure great suffering. Starvation. Frigid weather. Sickness compounded the clothing problem because soldiers who got ill had to discard their clothing to prevent the spread of disease, which was rampant. It was no small thing to replace clothes. Not only were they scarce, but they were expensive —and getting more so by the day. The Continental Army was paid in paper Continental money, whose value was being eroded by inflation. A general was paid $332 per month. A pair of pants cost $1,000—if they could be had at all. This was the peril of global economics during wartime, which disrupted normal trade.

George Clinton

As Alexander filled spare moments in the stone staff house at Valley Forge, he threw himself into mastering the intricacies of finance during that long winter. He pored over two massive volumes he carried with him: Malachy Postlethwayt's *Universal Dictionary of Trade and Commerce*. Each book was the length of his forearm and several inches thick. This was information that he intended to master. There could be no nation without a stable economy that included manufacturing as one of its components.

ABOVE: *ALEXANDER AND GEORGE CLINTON, NEW YORK'S GOVERNOR, WOULD BECOME POLITICAL ENEMIES.*

But it wasn't just the cost of goods and the instability of the currency that dogged the patriots. Supplies of any sort— even food for men and their horses—were elusive because of management challenges. The person in charge of supplies and logistics for the army had resigned in August. His subordinates were angry about their pay; they'd wanted to get a percentage of everything they acquired for the army, but they'd been denied. They quit after he did, with disastrous results for the soldiers. Even if Congress had taken care of the situation, though, there weren't wagons to deliver the supplies, because the men who had teams of horses wanted more pay for the work.

Alexander, who'd been sending regular reports and insights back to his friends and colleagues in New York, drafted a lengthy letter to George Clinton, the state's governor. Washington signed it on February 16, 1778.

A part of the army has been a week, without any kind of flesh, & the rest for three or four days. Naked and starving as they are, we cannot enough admire the incomparable patience and fidelity of the soldiery, that they have not been, ere this, excited by their sufferings, to a general mutiny or dispersion. . . . If you can devise any means to procure a quantity of cattle, or other kind of flesh, for the use of this army, to be at camp in the course of a month, you will render a most essential service to the common cause.

FROM HIS SEAT AT THE CENTER OF WAR, Alexander saw clearly that defeat could ride up on many horses. And though he still craved the chance to fight with gunpowder and steel, he also threw himself into battle against his bloodless foes at Valley Forge. The situation was beyond critical.

Washington agreed, and worried that if help did not arrive soon, the army would disband.

Washington, Alexander, and a few other key staff members dug deep. Washington saw to it that medical conditions were improved. Nathanael Greene took over management of supplies. Alexander lobbied Congress, frustrated that state leaders were more powerful than congressional ones and were seeing to their own first. On January 29, Alexander sent a report to Congress outlining ways to improve the organization of the army and its recruitment, promotion, and compensation practices. He wanted Congress to ask France for help solving the problem of clothing. And he detailed plans to get food for horses. The poor creatures were starving, just like the men.

Soon afterward, a critical ally arrived at camp: one self-titled Baron Frederick William Ludolf Gerhard Augustin von Steuben, a Prussian military veteran who had been a staff officer during the Seven Years' War and an aide-de-camp to Frederick the Great, the king of Prussia. Von Steuben had been accused of improper same-sex relations, and as a result was unable to find a military position in Europe. That's where he met Benjamin Franklin, who was scouting European military talent. Franklin

Baron Frederick William Ludolf Gerhard Augustin von Steuben

recommended him to the Continental Army. On February 23, 1778, he reported to Washington for duty as a volunteer.

Von Steuben and Alexander became fast friends. Though he was no taller than Alexander, von Steuben cut a larger-than-life figure, reminding one soldier "of the ancient fabled god of war."

The baron didn't speak English, but he knew enough French to converse with Alexander and Laurens. Von Steuben's first task was to create a prototype model army.

ABOVE: *BARON VON STEUBEN SEEMED TO ONE OF HIS SOLDIERS LIKE "THE GOD OF WAR."*

With his Italian greyhound at his side, von Steuben ran the soldiers through drills twice a day. He taught them how to line up in columns, how to march, and how to load and operate weapons with efficiency and speed. He cursed at them in several languages and was willing to work with the men directly—a break from traditions of other leaders of the Continental Army, who considered that beneath them.

HE CURSED AT THEM IN SEVERAL LANGUAGES.

This and the swearing boosted his popularity among the troops. Still, there was some culture shock when it came to delivering orders. In Prussia, it had been different. "You say to your soldier, 'Do this, and he doeth it,'" he explained to a Prussian ambassador. But with the Americans, "I am obliged to say, 'This is the reason why you ought to do that,' and then he does it."

The men had a long way to go. They sometimes didn't even remember to bring their bayonets with them. "The American soldier, never having used this arm, had no faith in it and never used it but to roast his beefsteak, and indeed often left it at home," von Steuben said.

Two days after von Steuben started his program, Washington liked it well enough that he started using it on all the soldiers at Valley Forge. And he soon appointed von Steuben as the inspector general of the army. Laurens, Greene, and Alexander became unofficial advisers to von Steuben. He'd run his plans by them, and they'd suggest adjustments. The order and discipline was exactly what Alexander loved.

There were some difficult moments. Americans with more seniority and higher ranks bristled at von Steuben's presence. This jealousy was a threat, Alexander told a congressman from New York.

Also, the troops weren't sure about von Steuben's taste in food. "My good republicans wanted every thing in the English style," von Steuben wrote later, "and when I presented a plate of *saurkraut* dressed in the Prussian style, they all wanted to throw it out of the window. Nevertheless by the force of proving by 'God damns' that my cookery was the best, I overcame the prejudices."

Within a month, this force of nature—along with Alexander, Washington, Laurens, and Greene—had transformed the army. The men in their smart, matching uniforms could march together, work together in multiple battalions, and fire their guns faster. And it wasn't just their on-the-ground skills that were changing.

Before von Steuben, most military camps had been laid out haphazardly. (Alexander's and Greene's were exceptions; their men pitched tents in neat rows.) Von Steuben insisted on orderly camp layouts for all. Also, instead of relieving themselves anywhere, men would use latrines located downhill and far from the kitchen. They also took care to dispose of animal carcasses, instead of letting the bones rot wherever they'd flayed the meat off them.

The difference this made was huge in health, in appearance, and in morale. Reflecting on it years later, Alexander said, "'Tis unquestionably to his efforts we are indebted for the introduction of discipline in the army."

Meanwhile, on February 6, the French had recognized American independence. They signed commercial and military treaties with the states—a huge development.

Von Steuben and Alexander worked closely together. Von Steuben asked him strategic questions, which Alexander answered in French as though he were talking to a favorite uncle. He didn't just answer the baron's questions, though. He inferred von Steuben's strategy and explained why it wouldn't work. "I think I see the reason for these questions. You wish the army to gain ground in the Jerseys. This is a highly desirable thing, if only we had enough wagons to transport not only our army, but our invalids, munitions &c; but we haven't enough for all that."

ALEXANDER HAD BECOME A MILITARY LEADER IN HIS OWN RIGHT.

Alexander had become a military leader in his own right. He helped von Steuben write the nation's first military manual—*Regulations for the Order and Discipline of the Troops of the United States,* the army's Blue Book—which became an indispensable tool for organizing men into an effective fighting machine.

Although the winter at Valley Forge in many ways had been disastrous for the troops, the army hadn't fallen apart. It had grown stronger. And as winter became spring, the states had the beginnings of an allegiance with France—one that would inevitably send a fleet of ships to help America in its cause.

Fearing a French blockade, England's General Henry Clinton, who had recently taken over the British command from

General Howe, evacuated Philadelphia, moving nine thousand men with fifteen hundred wagons slowly across New Jersey. He made himself into such a plump target that Washington wanted to attack with the von Steuben–trained troops. If they won, the Americans could end the war.

Alexander wrote up Washington's orders to leave Valley Forge on June 17, 1778. In Hopewell, New Jersey, Washington called a council of war and explained his plan to harass the enemy. As Alexander took notes, he could barely conceal his disgust at the spectacle of second-guessing and fear. The men were acting unmanly.

General Charles Lee didn't like the plan. Lee didn't think the underfed, underarmed troops were ready. Better to wait for the French. Lee, who traveled everywhere with his dogs, was known for his temper; the Mohawks had called him Boiling Water during the French and Indian War. The general also didn't respect Washington's leadership, and he liked to poke fun at the baron and Alexander.

Irritated, Washington called for a vote. Other officers, including Henry Knox, who had been Alexander's superior when he was an artillery captain, sided with Lee. Lafayette, Nathanael Greene, and General "Mad Anthony" Wayne agreed with Washington, who decided to move ahead.

The plan was to harass the British Army from the rear with the first corps of soldiers. The rest of the army would cover as necessary. Alexander was to help Lafayette lead six thousand troops. For two days, Alexander rode day and night gathering intelligence so plans could be updated as necessary.

When Lee saw the ultimate size of the advance force, however, he insisted Washington give him the command, not wanting to lose the job to "the little French boy." Washington did.

General Charles Lee

Lee's initial orders were to attack the rear flank as soon as he got intelligence that they were on the move. In further orders delivered by horseback, Lee was to send several hundred men up to observe the enemy. If redcoats left, he was to send word. Otherwise, he was to skirmish, holding them there until the rest of the Americans caught up.

At 5:00 a.m. on June 28, the intelligence came. General Lee set out with the rest of the advance guard. The main body did the same. By seven, it was ominously hot already, and summer

ABOVE: *MAJOR GENERAL CHARLES LEE, NICKNAMED "BOILING WATER," LED A DISASTROUS ATTACK AT MONMOUTH.*

thunderstorms had pounded the roads into sticky mud. Confusion reigned on the battlefield, thanks to Lee's ambivalence. At one in the afternoon, Alexander heard the crack of small-arms fire, and Washington sent him ahead to investigate.

"I WILL STAY HERE WITH YOU, MY DEAR GENERAL, AND DIE WITH YOU!"

When Alexander arrived, he found chaos. There were fewer than a thousand enemy troops, which made the prospect for an attack good, but Lee's men were on the run. What's more, no one had sent word to Washington that this was happening. Alexander snapped into action when he found Lee: "I will stay here with you, my dear General, and die with you! Let us all die rather than retreat!"

Alexander ordered the fleeing brigade to attack with their bayonets. Fighting wildly, he lost his hat in the fray.

When Washington arrived astride a white horse, he cursed Lee so soundly the leaves on the trees in the surrounding forest trembled.

Lee sniveled. "The American troops would not stand the British bayonets."

Washington was unimpressed. "You damned poltroon, you never tried them!"

He stopped the runaway soldiers and rallied them once more to the cause. "Stand fast, my boys, and receive your enemy. The southern troops are advancing to support you."

Washington's beautiful horse died in the heat, so he switched to a chestnut mare and quickly reorganized the troops. As Lord Stirling's men covered the left, Greene's the right, and Lee's soldiers under Wayne the center, the British struck back. Stirling's men took the first blows. Then Greene's. And then Wayne's.

Henry Knox's artillery men volleyed cannonballs through the scorching air. The redcoats returned fire. At one point a British cannonball blew through the petticoats of a woman assisting her husband at his cannon. She glanced at her ruined skirt and carried on; a soldier noted in his journal: "It was lucky it did not pass a little higher, for in that case it might have carried away something else."

The heat was merciless. Many men fought without shirts. One army private described it as combat in "the mouth of a heated oven." Dozens of soldiers on both sides died of heatstroke. Women on the battlefield brought pitchers of water to the men.

Alexander's horse was shot out from under him by a musket ball. He was "much hurt" in the fall. Aaron Burr and John Laurens also lost horses this way, and Burr became so overheated he contracted sunstroke. Soon afterward he resigned from the military.

By early evening, both sides had exhausted themselves. The British Army escaped, having lost more men than the American side to injury or death, although the battle overall was considered a draw.

Alexander, who'd struggled with Washington's moods and with his own yearning to lead on the battlefield, saw his general in a new light. Unlike Gates, who had sat back and let Benedict Arnold win the Battle of Saratoga, Washington had been a hero. Alexander wrote to his friend Elias Boudinot, "America owes a great deal to General Washington for this day's work; a general route dismay and disgrace would have attended the whole army in any other hands but his."

What's more, the training Alexander and von Steuben implemented had transformed the army. The soldiers' performance impressed Alexander, who gained a certain amount of fame for his own battlefield exploits. On July 16, the *Pennsylvania Packet* carried an excerpt of a letter from Washington's aide James McHenry to Elias Boudinot: "He was incessant in his endeavours during the whole day, in reconnoitering the enemy and in rallying and charging; but whether he or Col. Laurens deserves most of our commendations is somewhat doubtful—both had their horses shot under them and both exhibited singular proofs of bravery. They seemed to course death under our doubtful circumstances and triumphed over it as the face of war changed in our favour."

After Lee requested a court-martial to clear his name, Alexander placed him under arrest for disobeying orders and making a shameful retreat. He worried a court-martial wouldn't be enough to bring Lee to heel. "A certain preconceived and preposterous opinion of his being a very great man will operate much in his favour," he wrote. "Some people are very industrious in making interest for him."

In many ways, Alexander's premonition was correct. A court-martial would *not* be enough to shut Lee up—and it would also be too much. The ensuing dispute touched off a series of events that would, by year's end, culminate in a bloody duel for the honor of George Washington.

Alexander would be in the thick of it.

CHAPTER FIVE

'ALL FOR LOVE'

LEE WASN'T SORRY. HE was fuming, especially because people were gossiping about the situation in camp. He sent Washington a letter on June 29—which he dated July 1 for reasons only he knew.

"I must conclude that nothing but the misinformation of some very stupid or . . . wicked person coud have occasioned your making use of such very singular expressions as you did on my coming up to the ground where you had taken post."

He wanted to know the reasons for the three charges against him. He made awkward attempts to flatter Washington, blaming the harsh words for his performance on Washington's underlings, chief among them Alexander. "I must repeat that I from my soul believe, that it was not a motion of your own breast, but instigaged by some of those dirty earwigs who will for ever insinuate themselves near persons of high office."

Washington fired back a letter saying he'd be happy to put Lee on trial. He reiterated that Lee's retreat was "unnecessary, disorderly, and shameful." He also let Lee know he'd misdated his letter.

If Lee had been heated before, he was boiling now. He dashed off another letter on June 30, misdating it yet again, expressing his great sorrow at having misdated the first letter. He also let Washington know that the dignity of his office was made of tinsel and that the bright rays of Lee's truth would burn away all Washington's mists.

Then he threatened to quit the army.

And then he sent a *third* letter demanding a swift trial.

He got his wish. On July 4, a day patriots celebrated by firing guns and skyrockets, Alexander was a witness in Lee's court-martial trial. Lord Stirling presided over the proceedings, which opened in a tavern at New Brunswick. In addition to being charged with failure to obey orders and making a shameful, disorderly retreat, Lee earned himself a third charge of disrespect to the commander-in-chief for two of the letters he'd sent.

THE MEN FACED OFF AND APPROACHED EACH OTHER.

Lee cross-examined Alexander himself at times, but Alexander, cool and thoughtful, was a devastating witness. Other witnesses backed Alexander up. Lee had defenders, including Aaron Burr, who'd been disappointed not to be chosen for Washington's staff, as Alexander had been. Nonetheless, after a trial that moved from place to place and involved the testimony of thirty-nine people, Lee was found guilty of disobeying orders, of misbehavior before the enemy, and of making an unnecessary and, in a few instances, disorderly retreat. He was also found guilty of disrespecting Washington.

Stirling took the word "shameful" out of two of the charges and suspended Lee from the army for a year. All things considered, it was a light sentence because the court thought he was incompetent rather than disobedient. This wasn't much consolation for a hot-tempered bonfire of vanity. On December 5, Congress voted to uphold the court's decision.

Lee did not learn any sort of lesson. He and his supporters kept up the calumny against Washington and Alexander. Eventually, Lee criticized Washington in print.

Laurens, another one of the "earwigs" Lee had disparaged, wanted Alexander to come to Washington's defense in writing. Alexander held back, most likely because he was being accused along with Washington and couldn't very well make an unbiased case. So Laurens challenged Lee to a duel, with Alexander as his second.

Duels were not uncommon in the Continental Army. They gave men a way to achieve a sense of justice when their honor had been insulted. A challenge to a duel didn't automatically mean one would happen. According to the rules of dueling, Lee could have apologized for his words until the day of the duel. But he didn't—no big surprise given the size of his temper and the wound to his pride. Lee had also insulted von Steuben's honor, but they resolved the matter before it came to bloodshed.

With Laurens, Lee remained obstinate. And so, at three thirty in the afternoon on that cold December day, Lee and his second, Major Evan Edwards, met Laurens and Alexander in the woods outside of Philadelphia, four miles down Point No Point Road. Each man received a brace of pistols. Lee, a spindly fellow who'd lost the use of two fingers in an Italian duel, proposed they advance upon each other and fire when they'd reached a certain distance. Laurens agreed.

The men faced off and approached each other. When they'd reached the agreed-upon distance, they fired. Laurens, uninjured, prepared to shoot again. Then Lee announced he'd been hit. Laurens and the seconds rushed toward him, offering help. Lee waved them off. It was nothing. A flesh wound.

He wanted a second go; he had killed the Italian and lost fingers in that earlier duel.

Alexander and Lee's second both objected. Unless Lee was motivated by personal hostility, Alexander said, he ought to drop it. Lee wouldn't agree unless his second did, too, so Alexander and Edwards stepped aside for a chat. They both agreed the fight should end. As Lee dripped blood, the foursome headed back to town, hashing out the points of honor that would close the books on the conflict. Lee insisted it was right to gripe about Washington's military performance with his friends. He also denied saying the worst things he'd been accused of saying. What's more, he said, he'd always "esteemed General Washington as a man." That concession was enough for Laurens, and thus concluded Alexander's first duel.

Afterward, Lee took his dogs with him and moved first to Virginia and then to Philadelphia. Seven other men who'd been insulted by Lee challenged him to duels, but he apologized sufficiently to head those off. Congress voted on a resolution to dismiss him permanently after his suspension ended. It didn't pass, but it made Lee so mad that he dashed off another round of insults. Provoked, Congress booted him out of the army on January 10, 1780. Within four years, he was dead of tuberculosis.

MEANWHILE, ALEXANDER'S ROLE IN MANAGING the Revolution broadened again, though still not in the way he wished. Both France and Spain—longtime rivals of England— had entered the war on the side of the states. Encouraged by

Alexander, Lafayette convinced Washington to deploy French troops on the ground. Alexander continued to use his French with aplomb, both in diplomatic documents and Washington's communications.

Alexander struck the French officers as smart, well read, witty, and charming. The French impressed Alexander somewhat less. He disliked how they insulted the competence of his countrymen. And then there was the ridiculousness of certain administrative tasks he had to perform on their behalf while he was busy managing soldiers, spies, correspondence, and the movements of the enemy.

Mr. Chouin the French Gentleman who lives at Head Quarters informs he has heard you had a bear-skin, which you would part with; and requests me to inquire if it is so. I told him I thought it very improbable you should have any but what you wanted for your own use; but for his satisfaction would inquire how the matter stands.

Still, Alexander knew how vital the French alliance was. In the early days of the war, they'd smuggled weapons and powder; outright support now was just as vital. Granted, the French did it for their own interests, not for any nobler purpose. But this was the compromise of war, so he grudgingly wrote stupid letters on behalf of petty men who felt entitled to the bearskin rugs of others, all the while growing increasingly frustrated with his role as Washington's chief aide.

He wanted to command troops, not pen and paper. Death by glory, not by paper cut. Still, he kept at it. By spring, the army remained understaffed. Alexander had a solution—one he'd mentioned in his earlier list of suggestions to Congress, and one he'd talked about with John Laurens. With Laurens at his side, he wanted to bring it up again, no matter how controversial it might seem.

Alexander believed it was time to recruit enslaved men to fight on behalf of the Continental Army. He proposed forming a few battalions of black soldiers to serve in the Revolutionary War—paving the way for their emancipation. Some were already doing so on behalf of the enemy, after all.

ENSLAVING PEOPLE WAS INHUMANE AND INHERENTLY UNJUST.

Laurens had been particularly bold on this front. His father was a major owner of enslaved people and a powerful man in government. And yet, even before the Declaration of Independence was signed, Laurens had taken a different stand: "I think that we Americans, at least in the Southern [colonies], cannot contend with *a good grace* for liberty until we shall have enfranchised our slaves."

Enslaving people was inhumane and inherently unjust. "We have sunk the Africans & their descendants below the Standard of Humanity, and almost render'd them incapable of that Blessing which equal Heaven bestow'd upon us all."

Congress rejected Laurens's first attempt to integrate the army. In the spring of 1779, though, he left Washington's family to help defend his home state of South Carolina, which didn't have enough white residents to constitute a militia. Offering up black men to fight would solve that problem— and Laurens was the most logical leader for those battalions.

ABOVE: *GEORGE WASHINGTON OPPOSED LETTING ENSLAVED MEN FIGHT IN THE ARMY, THOUGH HIS ENSLAVED MAN WILLIAM LEE (AT RIGHT) AIDED HIM THROUGHOUT THE REVOLUTION.*

Alexander acknowledged it would be a tough sell for some people, but letting enslaved people fight and earn their freedom was not only morally just, it was also practical. So he wrote a letter in support of Laurens as the leader of a battalion of black men.

"I have not the least doubt, that [they] will make very excellent soldiers," he wrote to John Jay, who was then president of Congress. "I will venture to pronounce that they cannot be put in better hands than those of Mr. Laurens."

The odds against this plan were long. Even Washington opposed letting enslaved men into the army, although his enslaved man—Billy Lee, who'd left a wife and child to serve Washington during the war—accompanied him everywhere on the battlefield.

THE ODDS AGAINST THIS PLAN WERE LONG.

Washington's position was especially puzzling given his tendency to argue that British taxation on colonists was tantamount to slavery. He wasn't usually given to hyperbole. But when it came to enslaved people, he could be callously so.

Conflicted as he was, Washington had agreed in 1778 to let Rhode Island form a black regiment at the urging of Colonel James Mitchell Varnum. With the promise of freedom, Rhode Island recruited a regiment of more than two hundred black soldiers, as well as some Narragansett Indians. The men served for five years, much longer than the standard nine-month militia stint. One observer called them the sharpest-looking, most precise soldiers in the war.

In all, more than six thousand tribal citizens and enslaved black people fought on the side of the patriots. An additional five hundred free Haitian men fought for the states as well. (Many enslaved people and Indians fought for the Crown, betting they'd fare better with the king than with the colonials, particularly after Virginia's royal governor issued a 1775 proclamation promising freedom for all slaves who fought for the Crown.) Despite Varnum's success, and despite the great numbers of black men who fought, the case for arming enslaved men was especially tough to make in the South.

Alexander wasn't naïve. "I foresee that this project will have to combat much opposition from prejudice and self-interest. The contempt we have been taught to entertain for the blacks, makes us fancy many things that are founded neither in reason nor experience; and an unwillingness to part with property of so valuable a kind will furnish a thousand arguments to show the impracticability or pernicious tendency of a scheme which requires such a sacrifice."

But it was the rational and moral thing to do. "If we do not make use of them in this way, the enemy probably will; and that the best way to counteract the temptations they will hold out will be to offer them ourselves. An essential part of the plan is to give them their freedom with their muskets. This will secure their fidelity, animate their courage, and I believe will have a good influence upon those who remain, by opening a door to their emancipation. This circumstance, I confess, has no small weight in inducing me to wish the success of the project; for the dictates of humanity and true policy equally interest me in favour of this unfortunate class of men."

It was no small thing to argue in favor of giving an enslaved person a gun. Alexander, who'd grown up watching acts of resistance by enslaved people and the gruesome means used to crush them, knew the risks of arming people who'd been enslaved and abused.

With the weight of Alexander's argument, Laurens received conditional approval to arm three thousand black men. If the recruits performed faithfully, they'd be rewarded with their freedom and $50, though they could not keep their guns. The condition was challenging, though. The legislatures of South Carolina and Georgia, whose economies depended on slavery, had to approve.

They emphatically did not.

"We are much disgusted here at Congress recommending us to arm our slaves," wrote a member of the South Carolina government. "It was received with great resentment, as a very dangerous and impolitic step."

The South Carolina legislature threatened to surrender Charleston to the British over the matter. It didn't come to this, but the plan was defeated. On June 30, 1779, British General Henry Clinton issued a proclamation that freed any enslaved person who sought refuge with the British Army. Alexander was discouraged. "Prejudice and private interest will be antagonists too powerful for public spirit and public good," he wrote to Laurens.

There was not much to love about war. Alexander had endured starvation. Injuries and illness. Freezing temperatures. Death. The crushing boredom of writing routine letters and military orders. The terror and confusion of the battlefield. The outrage and frustration of conspiracies. And always there was the uncertain outcome of combat against a bigger, better-equipped, more experienced enemy.

But there was friendship in the midst of the dark days. Alexander and Laurens had become the dearest of friends in the trenches of war and at Washington's table. They were alike as brothers—smart, proud, and brave to the point of madness. Hamilton had other friends. But this bond was like no other in his life, and when Laurens went home to South Carolina to defend his state from the redcoats, Alexander missed him.

"I wish, my Dear Laurens, it might be in my power, by action rather than words, to convince you that I love you," he wrote in April 1779. "You know . . . how much it is my desire to preserve myself free from particular attachments, and to keep my happiness independent on the caprice of others. You should not have taken advantage of my sensibility to steal into my affections without my consent. But you have done it and as we are generally indulged to those we love, I shall not scruple to pardon the fraud you have committed, on condition that for my sake, if not for your own, you will always continue to merit the partiality, which you have so awfully instilled into me."

Laurens was in command of a battalion, something Alexander dearly wished for himself. But he was proud of his friend and happy, just as he was pleased to forward letters that had arrived back at Washington's headquarters after Laurens's departure. One was from Laurens's wife and contained news of his baby daughter, who had been born during the war and whom he'd never seen.

That was another thing Alexander wanted for himself: a woman to love. *A family.* He suggested Laurens might find a wife for him in South Carolina. It would be hard work, he joked, but a great way for Laurens to prove his friendship.

Alexander had a checklist. "She must be young, handsome (I lay most stress upon a good shape) sensible (a little learning will do), well bred (but she must have an aversion to the word *ton*) chaste and tender (I am an enthusiast in my notions of fidelity and fondness) of some good nature, a great deal of generosity (she must neither love money nor scolding, for I dislike equally a termagant and an economist). In politics, I am indifferent what side she may be of; I think I have arguments that will easily convert her to mine. As to religion a moderate stock will satisfy me. She must believe in god and hate a saint. But as to fortune, the larger stock of that the better."

It was hard to be happy without money, he knew. He wasn't likely to earn much, so he hoped his future wife would have some, or at least enough to cover her own extravagances. "If you should not readily meet with a lady that you think answers my description you can only advertise in the public papers and doubtless you will hear of many competitors for most of the qualifications required, who will be glad to become candidates for such a prize as I am. To excite their emulation, it will be necessary for you to give an account of the lover—his *size*, make, quality of mind and *body*, achievements, expectations, fortune, &c."

And in case Laurens sketched Alexander's portrait for a prospective bride, he wanted to make sure Laurens did justice to the length of his nose—by which Alexander actually meant a part somewhat lower down.

He was kidding, of course. In truth, he was not *really* in want of a wife, not then anyway. "I have plagues enough without desiring to add to the number that *greatest of all*. . . . Did I mean to show my wit? If I did, I am sure I have missed my aim."

Alexander might not have been ready to marry, but he loved being around women. He'd written several flirtatious letters to Kitty Livingston, one of his friend William Livingston's daughters, and after he figured out she wasn't interested, he let her know that he'd be all right, and that "ALL FOR LOVE is my motto."

All for love.

It wasn't just about having an itchy nose, though there was that. Alexander hungered for something deeper. Laurens was with his parents in South Carolina, and Alexander hadn't been permitted to go. The military family wasn't the same without Laurens. And after the war ended—however it ended—Washington's surrogate family would disperse, and Hamilton would once again be alone in the world.

"ALL FOR LOVE IS MY MOTTO."

And it wasn't a wonderful world to feel alone in. The war weighed like an ocean on his shoulders, enough to sink him into depression. In one dark moment, he confessed, "I am chagrined and unhappy, but I submit. In short, Laurens, I am disgusted with everything in this world but yourself and *very* few more honest fellows and I have no other wish than as soon as possible to make a brilliant exit. 'Tis a weakness; but I feel I am not fit for this terrestreal Country."

FOLLOWING SPREAD: *Washington's headquarters in Morristown, New Jersey, were much more comfortable than those in Valley Forge.*

J. Andrews, from a pencil Sketch.

Washington's Headquarters, Morristown

Present residence of Hon. Judge Ford .

But there was light in the midst of despair as Washington's family established winter camp once more in Morristown. This second encampment was much better than the first, and the presence of families nearby gave opportunities for socializing, even joy. There were dinners and music and dress-up and dancing. The officers—Alexander chief among them—chipped in money to put on dances at a storehouse near headquarters. They served food and drink, and people hitched their horses to sleighs and drove through snowy, dark nights to bask in the warmth and cheer. A few women caught Alexander's hungry eye early in the winter, and his fellow officers teased him about them.

The arrival of Elizabeth Schuyler changed everything. Dark-haired, dark-eyed, petite, and strong, she delighted him.

"Hamilton is a gone man," one of his roommates at headquarters observed.

Eliza was staying nearby with the Cochran family in their two-story clapboard house with a tiny front porch. The house was a quarter mile from headquarters, and Alexander visited every night, bounding up the five steps to the front door.

One evening he returned to headquarters after a giddy night spent wooing Eliza. The sentry, who knew Alexander well, asked him for the password. He couldn't remember. Never mind that he was fluent in Greek, Latin, and French. Never mind that he understood complex principles of economics and warfare. That password, whatever it was, had flown out of his skull entirely. He stood at the door, hand to his forehead, trying his best to pry it from the lobes of his brain. But a few hours in Eliza's intoxicating company had erased it. The sentinel wouldn't let Alexander pass. Finally, a fourteen-year-old boy, who was no doubt acquainted with

Elizabeth Schuyler

the spell of hormones, coughed up the password, along with the observation that "the soldier-lover was embarrassed."

Eliza had many charms at her disposal. She was the second daughter of a wealthy and powerful family. Her father was a general, and all the Schuyler daughters were intelligent, attractive, and musical. They were romantic, too—four out of five of them eloped, including one who escaped her bedroom on a rope ladder.

What's more, everybody loved Eliza. She was physically fit

ABOVE: *ELIZABETH SCHUYLER CAME FROM A FAMILY OF BEAUTIFUL AND TALENTED SISTERS.*

and energetic, and worldly in a way Alexander loved. She'd learned to play backgammon from none other than Benjamin Franklin. Her formal education was slight, but she had curiosity about the world in general. Her father had kept her informed about the war, and she had met many political leaders.

Alexander was so bent on impressing the family he sent a letter to Eliza's sister Peggy: "She is most unmercifully handsome and so perverse that she has none of those pretty affectations which are the prerogatives of beauty. Her good sense is destitute of that happy mixture of vanity and ostentation which would make it conspicuous to the whole tribe of fools and foplings. . . . In short, she is so strange a creature that she possess all the beauties virtues and graces of her sex without any of those amiable defects."

Eliza, who was equally smitten, had the time of her life that winter at her aunt and uncle's house. She once asked Alexander why he sighed. He wrote a poem in response, which she put in a little leather bag and wore around her neck for the rest of her life:

ANSWER TO THE INQUIRY WHY I SIGHED

BEFORE NO MORTAL EVER KNEW

A LOVE LIKE MINE SO TENDER—TRUE—

COMPLETELY WRETCHED—YOU AWAY—

AND BUT HALF BLESSED E'EN WHILE YOU STAY.

IF PRESENT LOVE [ILLEGIBLE] FACE

DENY YOU TO MY FOND EMBRACE

NO JOY UNMIXED MY BOSOM WARMS

BUT WHEN MY ANGEL'S IN MY ARMS

She and Martha Washington—Alexander's surrogate mother—rapidly developed a fondness for each other, too. The general's wife was almost fifty, small and plump, with frosty hair. Eliza loved her.

"She wore a plain, brown gown of homespun stuff, a large white handkerchief, a neat cap, and her plain gold wedding ring, which she had worn for more than twenty years," Eliza remembered. "She was always my ideal of a true woman."

Was Eliza also Alexander's ideal woman? In many ways.

ABOVE: *ELIZA HAMILTON THOUGHT MARTHA WASHINGTON WAS AN IDEAL WOMAN.*

But as much as he gushed about her, he also couldn't resist flirting with one of her sisters. Angelica was a year older. Beautiful, elegant, worldly, and vivacious. She spoke French, unlike Eliza. She had a husband already, businessman John Barker Church, or she might have been Alexander's first choice. The relationship fed a part of them that wasn't fully satisfied by their more stolid spouses, a part that needed a bit of intellectual fire and ambition.

"I LOVE YOU MORE AND MORE EVERY HOUR."

As spring came to Morristown, so did certainty about his future. Hamilton wrote to Eliza's parents asking permission to marry her. On April 8, 1780, they agreed. As soon as he had a free moment, he wrote to his future mother-in-law: "Though I have not the happiness of a personal acquaintance with you, I am no stranger to the qualities which distinguish your character and these make the relation in which I stand to you, not one of the least pleasing circumstances of my union with your daughter."

He didn't let Laurens know of his romance and engagement until June 30. Laurens had been taken prisoner by the British when Charleston was captured in May, and Alexander was thinking of that when he explained what had become of his heart.

"I give up my liberty to Miss Schuyler," he wrote. "She is a good-hearted girl who, I am sure, will never play the termagant. Though not a genius, she has good sense enough to be agreeable, and though not a beauty, she has fine black eyes, is rather handsome, and has every other requisite of the exterior to make a lover happy." The marriage, he promised Laurens, would not diminish their friendship.

All summer long, Hamilton poured his heart out through his pen to his fiancée. Some letters were so long he ran out of space—so he turned the page sideways and wrote up the margin.

"I love you more and more every hour. The sweet softness and delicacy of your mind and manners, the elevation of your sentiments, the real goodness of your heart, its tenderness to me, the beauties of your face and person, your unpretending good sense and that innocent simplicity and frankness which pervade your actions; all these appear to me with increasing amiableness and place you in my estimation above all the rest of your sex."

In another letter, he wrote, "My heart overflows with every thing for you, that admiration, esteem and love can inspire. *I would this moment give the world to be near you only to kiss your sweet hand.*"

He kept her up to date on her father's health, and he asked what she wanted him to wear to their wedding. He also worried. He once dreamed she was holding another man's hand, and he feared his poverty would be a burden.

"Tell me my pretty damsel have you made up your mind upon the subject of housekeeping? Do you soberly relish the pleasure of being a poor mans wife? Have you learned to think a home spun preferable to a brocade and the rumbling of a waggon wheel to the musical rattling of a coach and six? . . . If you cannot my Dear we are playing a comedy of all in the wrong, and you should correct the mistake before we begin to act the tragedy of the unhappy couple."

Eliza was certain Alexander was the man for her. She adored housekeeping and had been her mother's own chief of staff in tending the Schuyler home. Money didn't move her. His bravery and brilliance did. She believed in him, in the good he'd done for the world, and in all the good works he had yet to do. She would take care of his children and his home, and, as much as possible, be a partner to him in every endeavor.

Eliza and her family saw to the wedding planning while he was preoccupied with the business of war—which had taken dramatic turns over the summer and fall. At last the day came. The wedding, on December 14, 1780, was a small affair held in the southeast parlor of the Schuylers' two-story brick mansion. The room was cozy but high-ceilinged, with elaborate wood paneling, soaring windows, and a crackling fireplace.

Eliza's large family attended. Alexander's friend Major James McHenry was the only one able to accompany him from headquarters. Alexander had invited his brother and father, but neither was able to join. He promised Eliza he'd make sure she met his father someday. Alexander hadn't seen the man since he was a boy, but he hadn't given up on him.

"I shall again present him with his black-eyed daughter, and tell him how much her attention deserves his affection and will make the blessing of his gray hairs," he wrote.

George and Martha Washington also stayed behind, but the general sent congratulations. "Mrs. Washington most cordially joins me, in compliments of congratulations to Mrs. Hamilton & yourself, on the late happy event of your marriage & in wishes to see you both at head Quarters."

During the ceremony, Alexander carried a small, white linen handkerchief. Elizabeth's was larger and more ornate, its edges embroidered with flowers. The ring he gave her was

unusual: made of two slender gold bands that swung
open. One was engraved
with ALEXANDER 1780. The
other, ELIZABETH. This ring,
with its two finely wrought
halves, would stay on her
finger for nearly seventy-five

years, through times of happiness and times of heartbreak.

For now, though, there was joy. Hamilton's heart was full.
He had a family, a real one, large and lovely, at last.

BUT ALL WASN'T GLEE AND ROSES. AS ALEXAN-
der planned his life with Eliza, the irritating and overrated
General Horatio Gates continued to undermine Washington,
and by extension, Alexander. Washington was trying to play
nice with Gates. Gates had refused a command at the fort of
West Point, claiming he was too old, and even took a personal
leave for a few months. But by June 1780, the army needed
him back to lead a southern campaign.

Gates was nervous about the charge. He had a depleted
army and not enough funds, spirits were low, and he wouldn't
have Benedict Arnold, who'd made all the difference at Saratoga. Ultimately, Gates botched the job. He failed to deploy

ABOVE: *FOR THEIR WEDDING, ALEXANDER GAVE ELIZA A GIMMEL RING
MADE WITH INTERLOCKING BANDS INSCRIBED WITH BOTH OF THEIR
NAMES AND THE YEAR OF THEIR MARRIAGE.*

FOLLOWING SPREAD: *HORATIO GATES LED THE AMERICANS TO A BRUTAL
DEFEAT NEAR CAMDEN IN SOUTH CAROLINA.*

BATTLE OF CAMDE

DEATH OF DE KALB.

scouts, and his army of four thousand marched straight into two thousand British troops. At the Battle of Camden, 80 percent of the American forces were killed, hurt, or taken prisoner. Gates himself fled on horseback, abandoning his own troops.

Alexander wrote to Eliza about the debacle.

"Gates has had a total defeat near Cambden in South Carolina." The vigor of his retreat—he covered 180 miles in three days—proved he wasn't too old and weak to fight. Just too much of a poltroon. "He has confirmed in this instance the opinion I always had of him."

Meanwhile, Washington—often with Alexander as his scribe—navigated the twisty politics of war. It was true that Congress had denied Benedict Arnold a promotion in 1777 after a series of extraordinary deeds, which had left him with a leg shattered by a musket ball. Washington supported Arnold despite a court-martial and at last rewarded Arnold's leadership with a huge army command. He'd be in charge of the light infantry for a planned attack on New York. Using his leg as an excuse, Arnold surprised Washington by turning down the post. He asked, instead, for the command of West Point. Washington offered it without hesitation in June 1780.

Because of its location, West Point was a strategic fort. It was also a mess. There was no guard house, nowhere to store gunpowder, nowhere to keep prisoners. Arnold might be just the man to turn things around. Not long after Arnold took the post, Washington planned an inspection. Two aides rode ahead to let Arnold know the general was on his way to Robinson House, where Arnold and his wife, Peggy, were staying. Arnold, who'd been upstairs with Peggy, called for a horse. He galloped off, promising to return in an hour.

Benedict Arnold

Suspecting nothing, Washington, Alexander, and the others arrived. They ate breakfast. When they arrived at West Point for inspection, they found it in disarray. Strangely, they couldn't find Arnold. When they returned to Robinson House, the reason became clear.

A packet of letters had been discovered in the boot of a British officer who'd been caught in civilian clothes behind enemy lines—which made everyone suspect he was a spy. The papers, which were in Arnold's handwriting, made it

ABOVE: *BENEDICT ARNOLD WAS ONE OF THE BRAVEST AND BEST AMERICAN SOLDIERS . . . UNTIL HE BETRAYED THEM.*

clear he intended to sacrifice West Point to the British, and maybe even Washington and his military family in the process.

"Arnold has betrayed us!" Washington said.

It was unthinkable and yet undeniable.

Alexander set out immediately after him, but he was too late. Arnold was already on board the *Vulture* en route to British-held New York City. When Alexander returned, he found Arnold's young, attractive blond wife in a state of madness.

IT WAS UNTHINKABLE AND YET UNDENIABLE.

"It was the most affecting scene I ever was witness to," he told Eliza. "She for a considerable time intirely lost her senses. The General went up to see her and she upbraided him with being in a plot to murder her child; one moment she raved; another she melted into tears; sometimes she pressed her infant to her bosom and lamented its fate occasioned by the imprudence of its father in a manner that would have pierced insensibility itself."

She'd suckered him. Later, when Peggy Arnold was permitted to leave, she joined her old friend Theodosia Prevost, who was married to a British colonel stationed in the West Indies. Peggy told Theodosia she'd tricked Alexander and Washington with her performance—a tidbit Theodosia eventually passed on to her secret American lover, Aaron Burr.

In the midst of the drama, West Point was more vulnerable than ever. Alexander, taking charge, sent word to Nathanael Greene to send reinforcements.

Major John André

Meanwhile, the British officer, Major John André, was being held prisoner at a tavern in Tappan, New York. André was everything Alexander admired: handsome, educated, well traveled, a rising military star with refined manners and elegance. Tall and smart, with a gentle expression, he was a valued aide to a military leader. In many ways, he was Alexander's mirror image on the British side of the war.

André's general, Henry Clinton, made the case for his immediate return. Washington wouldn't hear of it. This was no common

ABOVE: *MAJOR JOHN ANDRÉ WAS EVERYTHING ALEXANDER ADMIRED.*

prisoner of war. He was out of uniform and on the wrong side of the front lines, which made him a spy. That meant he wasn't entitled to an officer's privileges. Above all, Washington was furious that the British had corrupted one of his most trusted and gifted men. André would pay the price.

André's plight hit Alexander hard. If André was in fact a spy, and not an unlucky man caught in the wrong clothes on the wrong side of the line, he'd swing from the gallows. But if he were to be treated as the officer he was, he'd get a more honorable death by gunfire.

Washington had Alexander write up the offense for a board of officers who'd sit in judgment. It pained Alexander to do so. "He came within our lines in the night on an interview

ABOVE: *An artist imagined John André's journey from the Vulture to the shore of Haverstraw Bay on the Hudson River.*

with Major General Arnold and in an assumed character; and was taken within our lines, in a disguised habit, with a pass under a feigned name and with the inclosed papers concealed upon him."

HE BEGGED FOR AN HONORABLE DEATH.

André admitted he'd done these things. He begged for an honorable death nonetheless. "Let me hope, Sir," he wrote to Washington, "that if ought in my character impresses you with esteem towards me, if ought in my Misfortunes marks me as the Victim of policy and not of Resentment, I shall experience the Operation of these Feelings in your Breast by being informed that I am not to die on a Gibbet."

He was found guilty by the board and sentenced to death by hanging, exactly the thing he feared.

Alexander was devastated. He'd been keeping André company in his confinement, chatting about art, poetry, music, and travel. He'd encouraged his friends at camp to do the same, to make André's last few days of life gentler. Some people wanted Alexander to propose a prisoner exchange— Arnold for André. Alexander knew André would say no, and he didn't want André to think he was dishonorable himself, so he didn't propose it. He did slip a letter, signed AB, to General Henry Clinton when a group of British officers came to Washington to plead for André's life.

Sir,

It has so happened in the course of events,
that Major André Adjutant General of your
army has fallen into our hands. He was
captured in such a way as will according to
the laws of war justly affect his life. Though
an enemy his virtues and his accomplishments
are admired. Perhaps he might be released
for General Arnold, delivered up without
restriction or condition, which is the prevailing
wish. Major André's character and situation
seem to demand this of your justice and
friendship. Arnold appears to have been
the guilty author of the mischief; and ought
more properly to be the victim, as there is
great reason to believe he meditated a double
treachery, and had arranged the interview
in such a manner, that if discovered in the
first instance, he might have it in his power to
sacrifice Major André to his own safety.

I have the honor to be &c

A B

Alexander wasn't naïve about the political challenges of prisoner exchanges. For two years, he'd negotiated these exchanges
with the British, a frustrating exercise. He complained about
these men to Eliza. "One of their principal excellencies consists
in swallowing a large quantity of wine every day."

Nonetheless, he hoped André's life could be spared by
intervention from the man at the top. Clinton refused. It

would have meant death for Arnold and an end to the possibility of turning patriots into spies. He was willing to exchange other prisoners and was outraged that Washington was considering André a spy when he was simply a messenger.

Others, including Benedict Arnold, wrote on André's behalf. "I shall think myself bound by every tie of Duty and honor to retaliate on such unhappy Persons of Your Army as may fall within my power." Arnold was livid. As part of this retaliation, he outed Hercules Mulligan as a spy to the British military in New York. Mulligan was jailed but eventually released for lack of evidence—his cover was that good.

The letters for André arrived too late to make a difference.

On October 2, 1780, André smiled, bowed his head, and strode to the hillside gallows wearing his officer's uniform. It was 5:00 p.m., one day after the board's decision. With dignity, André walked past Alexander and the rest of

ABOVE: *ANDRÉ HAD ONE LAST REQUEST: "YOU WILL WITNESS TO THE WORLD THAT I DIE LIKE A BRAVE MAN."*

Washington's men, including Benjamin Tallmadge, Washington's spymaster, who afterward wept.

When André saw the gallows, he hesitated. "*Must* I then die in this manner?"

It was unavoidable, he was told.

"I am reconciled to my fate," André said, "but not to the mode." Then he reassured himself. "It will be but a momentary pang." He sprang onto the cart that would lift him to the height of the hanging rope, and he made his final request: "You will witness to the world that I die like a brave man."

"*MUST I THEN DIE IN THIS MANNER?*"

A blindfold was tied. The cart moved. André swung. And then he was dead. Straightaway, his body was lowered into the nearby earth and covered in soil.

Alexander honored André's last request, writing a four-thousand-word letter to Laurens. "Among the extraordinary circumstances that attended him, in the midst of his enemies, he died universally esteemed and universally regretted."

He seethed that Washington had been so stubborn and that such a good man had died in dishonorable fashion. Nothing was more important than a man's honor. At this point, he wasn't sure how much more of the general he could bear.

Life had grown darker than ever in Washington's shadow. Alexander complained about it in a letter to Laurens. That depression he'd felt earlier was back with a vengeance. "I say this to you because you know it and will not charge me with vanity. I hate Congress—I hate the army—I hate the world—I hate myself. This whole is a mass of fools and knaves."

As much as Eliza made him glad to be alive, the idea of glory beckoned intensely. It was not enough to be George Washington's chief of staff. Alexander wanted to win the war with his own leadership skills and military know-how. He'd pay for glory with his own blood if need be. He was done with paper and ink.

In the months leading up to his wedding, he'd asked for a field command and Washington refused. Again. Winter was coming. So was a huge and life-altering fight between Alexander and the man who loved and frustrated him most: His Excellency, the leader of the Continental Army, George Washington.

CHAPTER SIX

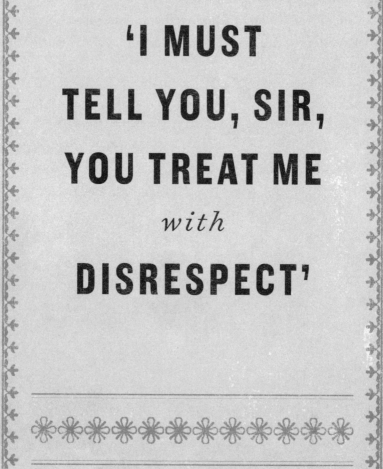

‘I MUST
TELL YOU, SIR,
YOU TREAT ME
with
DISRESPECT’

ALEXANDER HAD NEVER wanted to be an aide. He'd turned it down the first times he was offered, becoming an artillery captain instead. It was only the prestige and honor of George Washington's request, plus his lingering illness, that had made Alexander agree to it in the first place. He'd only ever wanted the chance to distinguish himself on the battlefield.

He'd been trapped behind a desk nearly four years. In that time, he rarely took days off, only for his wedding and when he was bedridden, and not always then. True, he had nowhere in particular to go. New York, his former home, was in the hands of the British. His school-era friends Elias Boudinot, William Livingston, Robert Troup, and others were engaged in the war effort. Hugh Knox and his family were reachable only by letter.

Washington and the rest of his aides had become Alexander's family. So he'd stuck with them. He'd made an enormous difference on behalf of the Continental Army and the revolutionary cause—everything from writing letters to recruiting and managing spies to making key decisions on behalf of Washington. He'd weighed in on military strategy, planned attacks, translated for foreign allies, and negotiated on behalf of prisoners of war.

But he was still just a lieutenant colonel. He'd have had a

higher rank if he hadn't taken a desk job. More people would have known his name and known his worth.

The politics of promotions were ridiculous, and they'd been part of the reason Benedict Arnold became a traitor. The letters Washington had sent to Arnold after he was denied a well-deserved promotion, urging Arnold not to make hasty judgments—Alexander Hamilton had written those on Washington's behalf. So he knew and felt the frustration of politics and the bumbling of Congress when it came to appointments. Even von Steuben hadn't been given the command he deserved after literally writing the book on how to run an army. How was Alexander, who had no family connections and no record of glory, ever supposed to be noticed?

THE FRUSTRATION WAS DEEP AND GROWING.

The frustration was deep and growing. Friends like John Laurens received field commands even though Alexander had better qualifications. And then Laurens was offered another post Alexander wanted: secretary to the minister plenipotentiary to France. It was a big diplomatic job, and he could have negotiated on behalf of America with the French.

Laurens had wanted the position to go to Alexander. "I am sorry that you are not better known to Congress; great stress is laid upon the probity and patriotism of the person to be employed in this commission. I have given my testimony of you in this and the other equally essential points."

After Laurens turned it down, Congress's votes were split between other candidates, and no one ended up in the post.

Eliza's father also lobbied on behalf of opportunities for Alexander. Lafayette was trying, too. He'd requested that Alexander help plan an offensive against Staten Island in October 1780. Washington refused. In November, Hamilton vented some of his frustration to Washington:

"There was a batalion without a field officer, the command of which I thought, as it was accidental, might be given to me without an inconvenience. I made an application for it through the Marquis, who informe me of your refusal on two principles—one that giving me a whole batalion might be a subject of dissatisfaction, the other that if an accident should happen to me in the present state of your family, you would be embarrassed for the necessary assistance."

When the Staten Island attack was called off, Alexander made the best case he could for command of the next one. And then Washington called off *that,* too. He didn't put Alexander up for promotions despite recommendations from Lafayette and Greene. When Congress was looking for a superintendent of finance, Congressman John Sullivan asked Washington whether Alexander knew anything about the subject.

Washington stayed mum. "I am unable to ansr because I have never entered upon a discussion of this post with him." Though he gave Alexander a recommendation, the general wildly undersold him. Not only did Alexander tote huge volumes of finance with him from camp to camp, but he'd written correspondence with Washington on the subject. They'd been in each other's company for nearly four years. Alexander burst with passion and knowledge on the topic. Washington just didn't want to let him go.

Laurens, meanwhile, got an even better job offer, to be an actual minister to France—which he took this time. Laurens

Tench Tilghman

had been gone for a while, of course, but other aides had departed in October 1780, forcing Alexander to postpone his wedding to handle the swelling workload. When Alexander did return after marrying Eliza, Washington's family had one aide left besides Alexander, Tench Tilghman, and he was too sick to work. So it was only Alexander and Washington, both of whom itched for the battlefield. They hadn't had any combat of note since Monmouth, and the months since had been awful.

ABOVE: *TENCH TILGHMAN WAS THE ONLY OTHER AIDE WORKING BESIDE ALEXANDER FOR A GRUMPY WASHINGTON DURING THE WINTER OF 1780–81.*

FIGHTING TENDED TO DIE DOWN DURING THE winter. As a result, tensions grew in the cramped quarters, which Washington found little better than those of Valley Forge. Washington was moody. He had whipped people on the battlefield with his cane when they'd disappointed him. He'd laced Charles Lee with an epic stream of castigation at Monmouth. One witness said his face during a rage looked like a thundercloud about to blast lightning. Now Alexander bore the brunt of the storms.

Pent-up frustrations came to a head in the middle of February 1781. Washington passed Alexander on the stairs and requested a meeting. Alexander promised he'd be right there, but first he dropped off a letter with Tench Tilghman. Before Alexander could make his way back to Washington, Lafayette held him by the button as they chatted.

When Alexander made his way back up the stairs, Washington loomed at the top, his face stormy.

"Colonel Hamilton," he said, "you have kept me waiting at the head of the stairs these ten minutes. I must tell you, Sir, you treat me with disrespect."

Disrespect. Alexander had been nothing but respectful. He'd served the man loyally for four years, postponing his own wedding in the process. He'd been denied promotions. Recognition. The chance to prove himself on the battlefield *and* to help win this frustrating, endless, awful war. He'd put up with Washington's moods and put off his dreams, and now he was done. This was exactly why he'd never wanted to be dependent on anyone but himself for his success in the first place.

As much as Alexander didn't want to cause an argument with the great man, when one presented itself, he seized the opportunity, and he quit. (But not without disputing Washington's perception of time. He hadn't kept him waiting ten minutes. It had been two at most.) He went home to Eliza immediately, leaving Lafayette and Tilghman to figure out the meaning of the argument they'd overheard in the cramped office.

ONCE AGAIN, A STORM—BUT THIS TIME A HUMAN one—changed Alexander's life. He was no longer part of Washington's family, but the loss was survivable because he'd been brought into another. He had his wife. He had her parents and sisters. He had somewhere to go. And even though Washington wanted to make up before even an hour had passed, Alexander held his ground.

This didn't mean he left headquarters for good straightaway. It also didn't mean his esteem for Washington was less. He admired the man's integrity and leadership abilities. Still, it was time Washington repented his terrible moods. Alexander would endure them no more.

He continued working at headquarters until the end of April 1781. He kept the rupture between himself and the general secret for the most part. It wouldn't do to have anyone question Washington's authority. Living elsewhere with Eliza, he started searching for a field command, sending out a discreet inquiry to Nathanael Greene. Lafayette, who wished Alexander would remain at headquarters, offered him command of a Virginia artillery unit, though Alexander didn't pursue it.

A few days after Lafayette's offer, Alexander wrote a letter to the general, asking him directly for a command.

"Your Excellency knows I have been in actual service since the beginning of 76. I began in the line and had I continued there, I ought in justice to have been more advanced in rank than I now am. I believe my conduct in the different capacities in which I have acted has appeared to the officers of the army in general such as to merit their confidence and esteem; and I cannot suppose them to be so ungenerous as not to see me with pleasure put into a situation still to exercise the disposition I have always had of being useful to the United States. I mention these things only to show that I do not apprehend, the same difficulties can exist in my case (which is peculiar) that have opposed the appointment to commands of some other officers not belonging to what is called the line."

WASHINGTON WASTED NO TIME IN SAYING NO.

Washington wasted no time in saying no. He didn't want to push his luck politically.

No one with sense would dispute Alexander's abilities. Washington had to balance the need to reward Alexander's work with the needs of the men in the field who also merited promotion.

"I beg you to be assured I am only influenced by the reasons which I have mentioned," Washington said.

Months passed. Alexander's father-in-law tried to get him

an appointment to Congress as a representative of New York. It fell through. Meanwhile, Alexander and Eliza had a baby on the way. He missed her terribly when circumstances forced them to be apart, and the only thing that made his frustrating existence at headquarters bearable as he waited for a field command was the letters she wrote.

"Indeed Betsey, I am intirely changed—changed for the worse I confess—lost to all the public and splendid passions and absorbed in you. Amiable woman! nature has given you a right to be esteemed to be cherished, to be beloved; but she has given you no right to monopolize a man, whom, to you I may say, she has endowed with qualities to be extensively useful to society. Yes my Betsey, I will encourage my reason to dispute your empire and restrain it within proper bounds, to restore me to myself and to the community. Assist me in this; reproach me for an unmanly surrender of that to love and teach me that your esteem will be the price of my acting well my part as a member of society."

YET HE YEARNED TO FIGHT.

As he waited for the right opportunity, he wrote a long letter to the man who had become the superintendent of finance, Robert Morris. The letter, some of which Eliza transcribed, addressed solutions to the problems that had crippled the war effort and would hamper the fledgling nation. Morris was impressed.

Alexander also wrote the first "Continentalist" essays published in the *New-York Packet*. In these essays, he examined

Robert Morris

the flaws in the United States' newly ratified Articles of Confederation and how the nation might shift from the power structure of war to peacetime governance. Civil war was a risk without a strong federal government. He was not quite twenty-seven, but he saw clearly the systems and structure the nation would need.

Yet he yearned to fight.

Finally, on the last day of July, orders from Washington came. Lieutenant Colonel Alexander Hamilton would lead

ABOVE: *ROBERT MORRIS, THE SUPERINTENDENT OF FINANCE FOR THE UNITED STATES, WAS IMPRESSED BY ALEXANDER'S KNOWLEDGE OF ECONOMICS.*

a battalion. He chose his college friend Nicholas Fish as his second in command. Then he made sure his men had shoes to wear, as well as tents, paper, kettles, and pails. Alexander would not be defeated for lack of shoes and gear. He'd learned those lessons of war well.

MEANWHILE, TERROR STRUCK ELIZA, WHO WAS in Albany. During an oppressively hot afternoon, three guards at the Schuyler mansion were napping in the cellar, and three more were lying on the lawn, trying to cool off. The family was gathered in the front hall when a servant announced that a stranger was at the gate.

He wanted to talk with Philip Schuyler.

Although Schuyler was retired from service, he was still helping the Continental Army. The British had put a bounty on his head, making him a target of kidnappers. Schuyler had been warned of this, and he was ready. The family barred the doors. Philip dashed upstairs to alert the guards with a shot outside his window. His family followed.

A group of twenty Tories and Indians burst into the house. Then Mrs. Schuyler remembered her baby—she'd left her asleep downstairs in her cradle. She rushed toward the stairs, but Philip held her back. Her life mattered more than their baby's.

The other Schuyler women wouldn't stand for it. Because Eliza and Angelica were pregnant, Peggy dashed down two flights of stairs to rescue her baby sister. The head of the raiders, thinking she was a servant, blocked her way.

Philip Schuyler

"Where's your master?"

"Gone to alarm the town," she lied.

Peggy rescued the girl, and as she was racing up the stairs, an Indian threw a tomahawk at her. The blade sank into the banister. Philip Schuyler called out the window to trick the raiders into thinking they were surrounded. They fled with three guards and some of the family's silver.

Alexander's heart pounded when he heard the tale. "It has felt all the horror and anguish attached to the idea of your

ABOVE: *ELIZA'S FATHER, PHILIP SCHUYLER, HAD A BRITISH BOUNTY ON HIS HEAD.*

being yourself and seeing your father in the power of ruffians as unfeeling as unprincipled; for such I dare say composed the band. I am inexpressably happy to learn that my [love] has suffered nothing in this disagreeable adventure, and equally so to find that you seem at presen[t] to be confirmed in your hopes."

This war had to end. He wanted only to be happy and alone with Eliza, his better angel. Forget the glories of public service. He wanted the comforts of private life. But first, he had to bring his battalion to the South. He had no time to say good-bye to her in person. The army had to race, stealthily, to Yorktown.

A sterling chance to win the war had arrived.

A LITTLE MORE THAN THREE YEARS BEFORE that fateful moment, an idea had struck. It was a risky notion—trading a sure thing for theoretical benefit down the road. But this was where Alexander shone: seeing the vast landscape of the future and understanding its contours.

The question at hand concerned the fate of General Henry Clinton, the British commander who'd made himself into a fat target. His predecessor, General Howe, had botched things for the British in Saratoga. The loss was devastating in other ways for the Crown. Chief among the blows: it had drawn the French to the American cause. As a result, the British had replaced General Howe with Clinton.

Howe had never impressed Alexander. Clinton impressed him even less. Clinton had taken over a house on Broadway in

General Henry Clinton

New York, one with an ample garden overlooking the Hudson River. Every afternoon, he trotted himself out to a backyard pavilion for a little nap. It would be so easy, one of Washington's men suggested, to sneak up at low tide and capture the general as he snoozed.

And it sounded like an excellent plan until Alexander voiced an objection. To capture Clinton "would be our misfortune, since the British government could not find another commander so incompetent to send in his place."

ABOVE: *BRITISH GENERAL SIR HENRY CLINTON WAS INCOMPETENT — AND ALEXANDER MADE GOOD USE OF THAT.*

Washington agreed they were, in fact, better off with a nincompoop in command. Now they were poised to see if this chess move would at last pay off.

Another British general, Charles Cornwallis, was nobody's nincompoop. Nathanael Greene called Cornwallis "a modern Hannibal." Lafayette considered him the best the British had. But Cornwallis was under the command of Clinton, and in June, Clinton ordered Cornwallis to set up a defensive post at either Williamsburg or Yorktown.

ABOVE: *THE BRITISH GENERAL CHARLES CORNWALLIS WAS KNOWN AS A "MODERN HANNIBAL."*

Cornwallis balked. These spots were vulnerable to attack by sea. But Clinton held firm, arguing that it was unlikely for the Americans and their allies to have a superior naval fleet any time soon.

Clinton recommended a spot between the York and James Rivers. Cornwallis did as ordered. He took his nine thousand troops—loyalists, redcoats, and Hessians—and occupied York-town and Gloucester Point, the same spot Washington had considered dangerous because soldiers stationed there could be trapped between a naval force and an army. All it would take was a few temporary fortifications to block a retreat.

Cornwallis got unlucky. As he established a fort at York-town, the French fleet from the West Indies was on its way to nearby Chesapeake Bay. That meant the Americans had access to the naval force they needed—the one Clinton doubted would arrive.

Washington leapt at the opportunity. Everything depended on speed and secrecy. Alexander, his loyalties now with his pregnant wife, let Eliza know where he was headed, and how hard it would be for him to be away from her:

"I cannot announce the fatal necessity without feeling every thing that a fond husband can feel. I am unhappy my Betsey. I am unhappy beyond expression, I am unhappy because I am to be so remote from you, because I am to hear from you less frequently than I have been accustomed to do."

There was a chance Cornwallis would slip out of the trap. Over the next fifteen days, Alexander and his well-shod men marched two hundred miles to the swift beat established by the fife and drum. They penetrated forests. They crossed

FOLLOWING SPREAD: *THE CHESAPEAKE BAY AND THE YORK AND JAMES RIVERS MEET NEAR WHERE CORNWALLIS WAS TRAPPED.*

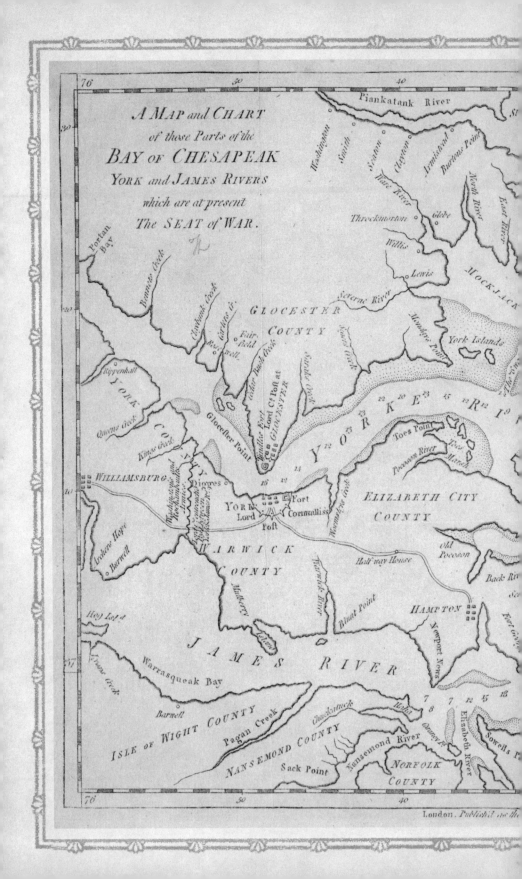

A Map and Chart of those Parts of the BAY of CHESAPEAK YORK and JAMES RIVERS which are at present The SEAT of WAR.

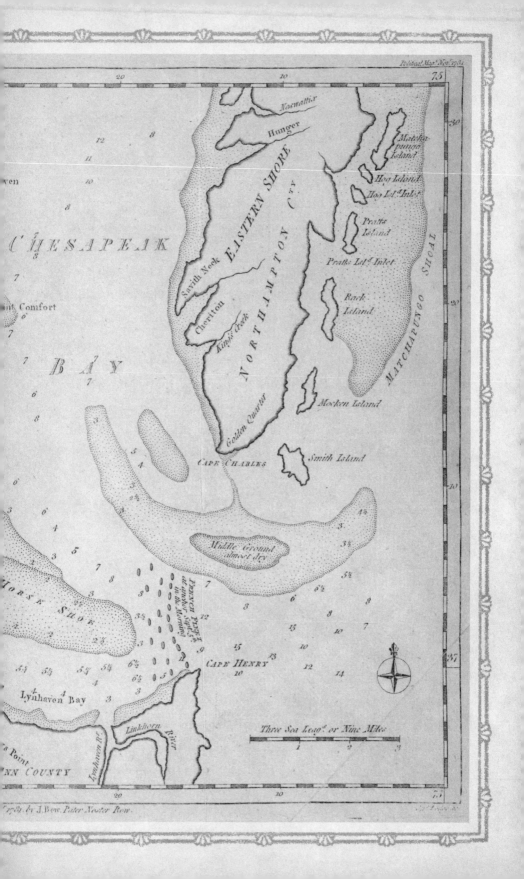

20   20

30

Naswattix

Hunger

Matchapungo
Island

12   8

Hog Island

11

Hog I.d Inlet

10

C'HESAPEAK

Pratts
Island

8

Pratts Isd Inlet

7

it Comfort

Rack
Island

6

7

B A Y

Savith Neck   EASTERN SHORE

7

Cheriton

Kings Creek

Mocken Island

6

8

NORTHAMPTON C.ty

MATCHAPUNGO SHOAL

Golden Quarter

CAPE CHARLES   Smith Island

3

5

4

Middle Ground
almost dry

4½

3

3¾

2¾

3½

3

HORSE SHOE

7

FRENCH FLEET
at anchor Sight
in the Morning

5½

6½

8

12

8

8

7

4

15

10

7

3½

9

15

10

Lynhaven Bay

13

CAPE HENRY

12

14

Lynhaven R.r

Linkhorn River

's Point

NN COUNTY

Three Sea Leag.s or Nine Miles

1   2   3

20   10

1781 by J.Bew, Pater Noster Row.

rivers. They passed through cities while inhabitants watched from the open windows of their houses.

By September 10, the French fleet had reached Chesapeake Bay with dozens of ships and three thousand troops—even after holding off the British fleet during the Battle of Capes on September 5. Cornwallis was trapped—the British navy could not get through now and needed to return to New York to repair damaged ships. The usually gloomy Washington was so giddy he waved his hat and handkerchief like a happy child. The stars had aligned themselves beyond his dreams.

Alexander wrote to Eliza: "Circumstances that have just come to my knowledge, assure me that our operations will be expeditious, as well as our success certain."

Cornwallis fortified his defenses, rationed food, and waited for Clinton's reinforcements. They were on their way, Clinton promised.

THE USUALLY GLOOMY WASHINGTON WAS GIDDY.

But all was not well for the Continental Army. The soldiers hadn't been paid and refused to go farther. Robert Morris and Washington had to make an appeal to the French commander, Comte de Rochambeau, for a loan. Rochambeau gave Washington half of what he had. Cash in hand, the troops continued.

Alexander and his men marched a few miles on September 9 to Chesapeake Bay, where they boarded ships and sailed south. Days into their journey, the weather turned stormy. High winds whipped at the rain drumming from cloud-darkened skies.

Alexander's mood darkened. He wrote Eliza, "How chequered is human life! How precarious is happiness! How easily do we often part with it for a shadow! These are the reflections that frequently intrude themselves upon me, with a painful application. I am going to do my duty. Our operations will be so conducted, as to economize the lives of men. Exert your fortitude and rely upon heaven."

The skies cleared. They sailed a period of days until they came ashore south of Williamsburg and began to march once more. At last, by September 24, they were within miles of the British hunkered down in Yorktown—450 long miles from where they'd begun.

The next day, the French admiral, Comte de Grasse, got cold feet. British ships were sailing toward him, and he began to doubt his chances in battle. What's more, should a gale strike, they would be exposed. He let Washington know he planned to set sail as soon as a favorable wind arrived.

Washington couldn't believe it. Victory was at hand, and his ally was throwing it away.

But then, de Grasse found his courage and decided to stay. The game was back on.

Meanwhile, the French and American allies crept toward their quarry, trading shots with the enemy every so often. On September 29, Alexander and his men crossed a muddy bog. The British launched cannonballs, blasting off one man's leg and killing three others, before retreating that night to their inner defenses. Washington tasted victory. They'd need to move quickly. "The present moment offers in prospect the epoch which will decide American Independence and the Glory and superiority of the Allies."

For six days, Alexander and the rest of the army feverishly bundled sticks to reinforce earthwork fortifications, all while British and Hessian forces blasted cannons at them.

Things could not have looked worse for Cornwallis. On October 2, Clinton wrote to let him know the fleet was delayed a few days for repairs. Cornwallis was trapped with no way out and no immediate salvation. To complicate matters, enslaved people eager for freedom had escaped their masters and come down the river to the British encampment in Portsmouth. Many were infected by smallpox and were dying by the scores. Cornwallis regretfully had to abandon them in Portsmouth when he evacuated for Yorktown.

Many of his troops were sick and hungry, too, having no food but rotting meat and wormy biscuits. Doctors who bled the ill found pink blood, indicating the men were anemic. One in four had typhoid fever. Even though the ill black men had been left behind, smallpox found its way to Yorktown, infecting white loyalists and black recruits alike. Cornwallis was down to thirty-five hundred men fit for combat.

The French and American forces were sixteen thousand strong. The Continental Army, which had once been a collection of poorly trained men who drank more than they ought and sometimes wandered away from duty, worked through the night on October 2, digging parallel trenches and dragging cannons and loaded wagons behind horses. They'd distracted the British by sending a detachment to fire elsewhere, and while the enemy took aim, they'd prepared a two-mile line and laid foundations for a pair of redoubts within six hundred yards of enemy lines. It

was an astonishing feat of productivity, coordination, and determination.

On October 7, after days of hard labor, Alexander moved his infantry into place. They planted flags and, accompanied by the drums of war, Alexander gave his men orders to rise out of the trench and run through ceremonial steps of soldiery. This was madness. He was risking his men's lives for no reason. But in doing so, he stunned the British so soundly that they didn't fire a shot. (They also happened to be out of range.)

On October 12, still emotionally feverish, he wrote Eliza. He scolded her lightly for not sending him more letters and teased that she should make it up to him by giving birth to

ABOVE: *THE CONTINENTAL ARMY WORKED DAY AND NIGHT TO PIN THE BRITISH IN PLACE AT YORKTOWN.*

a son, because he wouldn't be able to resist the charms of a daughter. His heart melted at the thought of a baby in his wife's arms. He knew it was distracting him from the business of soldiering. Not for long, though. Not for long.

"Five days more the enemy must capitulate or abandon their present position; if they do the latter it will detain us ten days longer; and then I fly to you. Prepare to receive me in your bosom. Prepare to receive me decked in all your beauty, fondness and goodness. With reluctance I bid you adieu."

Firing against the British had begun in earnest three days earlier. The dead and the wounded lay everywhere, minus arms, legs, and even heads. The wounded who lived cried out into air made thick with the smoke of burning houses.

Clinton had never imagined the Americans could do such damage in so short a time. Cornwallis, meanwhile, reeled to learn reinforcements were again delayed. There was no way he could last until the middle of November. His only chance was to escape via the York River, but his men were dropping swiftly under blazing artillery fire, and the French and American troops kept digging closer by the hour.

By October 14, the second trench was done. The patriots needed only to take over a pair of British defensive redoubts to win. Washington put Lafayette in charge of one force. Lafayette put one of his aides in charge of the other. Alexander was incensed. He had seniority over Lafayette's man, but Lafayette wouldn't change his mind, so Alexander fired off a letter to Washington making his case.

For once, Washington agreed. No doubt he didn't want the most thrilling campaign of the war to be led entirely by the French. But it also might have been time to give Alexander the command he'd craved for years.

Alexander, jubilant, ran to his tent to tell Nicholas Fish. "We have it! We have it!"

Washington ordered a swift and silent bayonet attack, made with unloaded guns that could not accidentally discharge and alert the enemy. Lafayette and his French troops would rush the redoubt on the left. Alexander and his infantry would take the one on the right.

WASHINGTON ORDERED A SWIFT AND SILENT BAYONET ATTACK.

That night, the French and American allies lit the sky with mortar fire. Under the glare of rockets, Alexander's men rose from the trenches. A quarter mile of earth separated them from the tenth redoubt, soil that had been churned for days by cannon blasts and blood. Bayonets in hand, they sprinted through heavy enemy fire. With no more need for silence, they screamed like wild men. Soldiers specializing in engineering ran in front to clear a path for the bayonets, barely staying ahead of Alexander and his bellowing soldiers.

When they reached the enemy stronghold, Alexander launched himself atop the parapet. He waved his men onward. Within ten minutes, they'd lined up in formation and captured the enemy. The attack had been perfectly executed. There were no more than eight casualties. Alexander was fit to burst with pride. He ensured the British prisoners were treated with honor and justice, even when one American infantry captain threatened to kill an officer.

Lafayette's brigade suffered more losses from a stronger resistance, but they too succeeded. Meanwhile, Cornwallis told Clinton his situation was critical. Their defenses were destroyed and their soldiers, weakened. The York River beckoned. Night fell on October 16, and Cornwallis tried to guide his men safely to the sea through the pounding of artillery. Stormy weather held them back.

The battle was over.

A warm sun rose on October 17. A British officer climbed atop the parapet to the rhythm set by a boy with a drum. He removed a white handkerchief from his coat and waved it.

Cornwallis was too ill to take part in the ceremony of surrender that followed. His stand-in, Charles O'Hara, had met Alexander in 1778 when Alexander negotiated prisoner exchanges. The two men had made a promise then: they'd take care of each other should either be taken prisoner. Now O'Hara was asking him to make good on his word. Alexander did.

ABOVE: *CORNWALLIS OFFICIALLY SURRENDERED ON OCTOBER 19, 1781, AS A MILITARY BAND PLAYED "THE WORLD TURNED UPSIDE DOWN."*

In their victory, the Americans captured 7,247 soldiers and 840 sailors. The triumph effectively ended the war, though some fighting continued. Alexander, astride his horse, watched the British leave the city accompanied by the ballad "The World Turned Upside Down."

He wrote to Eliza the next day.

"Your father will tell you the news. Tomorrow Cornwallis and his army are ours. In two days after I shall in all probability set out for Albany, and I hope to embrace you in three weeks from this time. Conceive my love by your own feelings, how delightful this prospect is to me. Only in your heart and in my own can any image be found of my happiness upon the occasion. I have no time to enlarge. Let the intelligence I give compensate for the shortness of my letter. Give my love to your Mama to Mrs. Carter to Peggy and to all the family.

"Adieu My Charming beloved wife, I kiss you a thousand times, Adieu."

He tore home so swiftly he wore out his first set of horses. When he arrived in Albany, his exhaustion gave way to illness. Once more, he was bedridden.

When he arose months later, he was a new man. The one-time orphan was a husband. A hero. A man of honor. On January 22, 1782, he added something else to his list: father.

He and Eliza named their newborn son Philip, after Eliza's father.

"You cannot imagine how entirely domestic I am growing," he told a friend from Washington's staff. "I lose all taste for the pursuits of ambition."

He quit the military and waived his wartime pay—five years' worth. He wanted nothing but the company of his wife and son. Or so he thought.

Fortune had plans of her own.

CHAPTER SEVEN

'ROCKING THE CRADLE and . . . FLEECING MY NEIGHBOURS'

FROM THE START, ALEXander threw himself into fatherhood with the same ardor and discipline he'd shown as a student and soldier. After seven months of close study, he had come to an opinion about his baby.

Philip was perfect. Well, nearly so. He was a bright-eyed looker. Good at sitting. Already, he was smart and an excellent babbler, who waved his tiny hand like a seasoned orator. His flaws were slight. He had chubby thighs, which might portend awkward dancing. Also, he tended to laugh too much.

Part of Alexander wanted only to bask in the glow of love for his wife and boy. His sad childhood still caused him pain. Just after Yorktown, Alexander had learned of the death of his half brother, Peter Lavien, who'd taken Alexander's books after their mother died. In his will, the wealthy Peter left Alexander and James a pittance: 150 pounds sterling. He even got James's name wrong, calling him Robert.

Alexander wrote about it to Eliza: "You know the circumstances that abate my distress, yet my heart acknowledges the rights of a brother. He dies rich, but has disposed of the bulk of his fortune to strangers. I am told he has left me a legacy. I did not inquire how much."

He wanted to do better by his own family, saying many times he was ready to put public service aside for private life. But his ambition was unquenchable. Since Yorktown and his convalescence, he'd thrown himself into activity.

Picking up where he'd left off at King's College, he crammed years of work into six months, during which he also wrote a 177-page law manual called *Practical Proceedings in the Supreme Court of the State of New York*, which was so good that law students in New York State would use it for decades.

In part, he had Aaron Burr to thank for the swiftness of his law degree. While Alexander was recuperating after York-town, Burr petitioned the New York Supreme Court to allow veterans who'd started studying law before the war to skip the customary three-year apprenticeship.

HE SIGNED IT, *"YRS FOR EVER."*

There was reason to rush. Alexander had waived his military pay, and he needed money to support his family. There would be many clients eager for representation once the dust of war had settled, and he intended to be ready.

He also wrote more "Continentalist" essays, continuing to explain how a federal government should look. At the outset of the war, no one had any idea how to establish a governing body for a new, independent nation. Anyone who said otherwise was kidding themselves. People were used to living life as colonists. They had to be led into a new world—one that embraced the reality of taxation by people who'd gone to war in protest of the same thing.

In June, he'd been appointed tax collector for New York, and it was an exercise in frustration. The nation had war debt to pay, both to soldiers and other countries. There was no independent source of revenue for the federal government, and some people were operating under the delusion that taxes were optional. The Articles of Confederation, which had been developed by Congress in 1777, made no provision for taxes and needed deep revision. He'd realized as much during the war and wished others would as well.

But that wasn't the extent of his public service. He'd also been elected to represent his state in Congress. His friend John Laurens was thrilled to see Alexander take office. The nation needed his services. For his part, Laurens had resumed "the black project," as he called his efforts to integrate the army, as a stepping-stone to emancipation. He didn't prevail, but he was heartened by his progress in the cause:

"I was out-voted, having only reason on my side, and being opposed by a triple-headed monster that shed the baneful influence of Avarice, prejudice, and pusillanimity in all our Assemblies. It was some consolation to me, however, to find that philosophy and truth had made some little progress since my last effort, as I obtained twice as many suffrages as before."

Alexander wrote back with an idea: Laurens could join him in politics. Together, they'd build a new nation that would withstand every challenge:

"Quit your sword my friend, put on the *toga*, come to Congress. We know each other's sentiments, our views are the same: we have fought side by side to make America free, let us hand in hand struggle to make her happy."

He signed it, "Yrs for ever."

Twelve days after he wrote it, a handful of British soldiers were scavenging rice growing near the Combahee River in South Carolina's low country. Laurens wanted to go after them but was ordered to stand down. Laurens's reckless heart wouldn't listen. The British, who'd been tipped off, were waiting. As Laurens raced forward in attack, he was shot and killed. He was one of the last Americans to die in the Revolution. One of the last, and one of the best.

"Intrepidity bordering on rashness," Washington said of him.

Laurens probably never received Alexander's letter.

Alexander wrote of his grief to Lafayette in Paris. "You know how truly I loved him and will judge how much I regret him."

He wrote to Nathanael Greene, too. "How strangely are human affairs conducted, that so many excellent qualities could not ensure a more happy fate? The world will feel the loss of a man who has left few like him behind, and America of a citizen whose heart realized that patriotism of which others only talk."

By November, now forever without his political soulmate, Alexander made his way to Philadelphia for his first term in Congress. Alexander hated how the delegates pandered to their constituents, trying to please them rather than doing the right thing for the nation as a whole. Even before he'd taken office, he vented his frustration in a letter to Robert Morris, who was still the superintendent of finance.

"The more I see, the more I find reason for those who love this country to weep over its blindness," he wrote.

His first order of business was to see that the federal government, as weak as it was, had revenue. Walking away from America's debts, as some wanted to do, would be disastrous. A nation had to pay what it owed. A fellow congressman, James Madison, agreed that a 5 percent federal duty on imported goods was the best way to raise funds.

It would be a tough idea to rally people around. Taxes were unpopular, to say the least. An import duty also meant the federal government could write laws that applied to citizens of all the states. To grant the federal government this much power worried some. It felt too much like a monarchy for the newly independent revolutionaries.

Despite the political challenges, they had no time to waste. As the Revolutionary War drew to an end, the terms of peace with England were being hammered out. This alarmed officers of the Continental Army, who feared they'd never be paid if the treaty was signed first. Violence was a real possibility.

VIOLENCE WAS A REAL POSSIBILITY.

As Alexander allied with Madison on the matter of taxes, he looked to another man for an alliance on leadership: George Washington. For the first time since he'd sent his resignation letter in March, Alexander wrote to Washington, informing him that Congress and the army were headed for a showdown. Alexander asked—confidentially—for Washington to lend his wisdom and influence to the task of settling this for the good of all. He let Washington know the country's finances were in terrible shape. The nation had to establish a fund to pay the country's debts. To do this, he wanted Washington to secretly use his influence to have the army apply pressure to Congress.

Washington, grateful, wrote back a few weeks later. He wished Congress had told him things were dire. That said, he insisted it would be a terrible idea for the army to take on the government directly. That overstepped the army's authority in a dangerous way. And it wasn't necessary: The army's claims were just, and sensible legislators would see the facts once they'd been presented. What's more, Congress needed more centralized authority, or all the blood they'd spilled over the eight years of war would achieve nothing.

With that, the two men were allies again—this time not to defeat a foreign enemy but to figure out how to build an enduring nation out of hopes, dreams, and difficult realities. The alliance was still tentative. Much had passed between them. But the nation needed them, just as they needed each other.

BUT THE NATION NEEDED THEM, JUST AS THEY NEEDED EACH OTHER.

A few days later, Alexander received more news from Washington. An anonymous letter circulating around an army camp in Newburgh, New York, demanded a military solution to the financial problems of Congress—in other words, a coup. Washington called for a meeting on March 15, where he urged his army officers to act with honor, dignity, and transparency:

"You will give one more distinguished proof of unexampled patriotism and patient virtue, rising superior to the pressure of the most complicated sufferings."

The men weren't persuaded. They wanted their money. Facing the failure of his prepared speech, Washington gambled. He unfolded a letter from a Virginia congressman explaining the financial straits of the government. And then he squinted and reached for a pair of eyeglasses.

"I have not only grown gray but almost blind in the service of my country," he disclosed. It wasn't like him to reveal vulnerabilities, especially ones of such a personal nature. The gesture shamed the men into listening.

Washington's delivery was positively Hamiltonian. Later, Washington made the soldiers' case before Congress, and Alexander led the committee that agreed to pay the officers a pension worth five years' salary. Congress didn't yet have the money, but the government had made clear its intentions to honor the country's financial obligations.

Alexander was relieved. He saw now that if the army had used force, it could have started a civil war that would ruin the military, if not the country.

Meanwhile, much was unsettled. The peace treaty with England had not yet been signed. There were still matters of international debt to hammer out. The war had been won, yes. But it seemed as though the real work was only beginning.

DURING THE SPRING AND SUMMER OF 1783, Alexander's shoulders sagged with challenges. Congress had officially ended the fighting in April. But this didn't mean the need for military protection had evaporated. On the contrary, troops were needed to keep the peace and protect the borders and harbors, and Alexander had to figure out how a peacetime army would work, and how state militias would coordinate.

Meanwhile, the unpaid army was running out of patience. On June 19, Congress learned that eighty angry soldiers from a Lancaster regiment were marching toward the capital in Philadelphia. They were going to get their money or else—and other soldiers were joining them on the way.

By the time the angry rabble arrived in Philadelphia and seized a military barracks, Congress had already adjourned for the weekend. Elias Boudinot, the president of Congress, called for a Saturday session. Before the congressmen had fully gathered, about four hundred soldiers—who vastly outnumbered the loyal guards—surrounded the State House. The mutineers sent in a note that gave the politicians twenty minutes to respond. If their grievances weren't heard in that time, they'd set the soldiers loose.

Many of the soldiers were drunk and getting drunker. Rumors flew that the furious men might also seize control of the city's bank. Congress refused to negotiate under such a menace, and by three thirty in the afternoon, the mutineers were persuaded to return to the barracks.

ABOVE: *A ROW OF PHILADELPHIA'S PUBLIC BUILDINGS CIRCA 1790.*

That night, Alexander and the rest of Congress met at Boudinot's home. Alexander, furious to be threatened by a mob, dashed off a resolution. The attempted military coup had been disorderly, menacing, and grossly insulting, "and the peace of this City being endangered by the mutinous disposition of the said troops now in the barracks, it is, in the opinion of Congress, necessary that effectual measures be immediately taken for supporting the public authority."

Either Pennsylvania would act to protect the authority of government, or Congress would leave town. Pennsylvania failed to respond fast enough. By Thursday, Congress had set up shop temporarily in Princeton. The mutiny ended when state leaders finally called up five hundred militiamen.

Afterward, Congress wouldn't have a stable home again for two years. It moved from Princeton to Annapolis to Trenton

ABOVE: *THE TREATY OF PARIS, SIGNED IN 1783, ESTABLISHED NEW BORDERS FOR THE UNITED STATES OF AMERICA.*

and finally New York in 1785. The frustration rankled. The states had too much power and influence and tended to hoard it rather than look to the needs of the nation.

Fed up, Alexander wrote a resolution in July, calling the Articles of Confederation "defective." He outlined its many broken elements: Its powers were too limited. Legislative, executive, and judicial powers needed to be separated. State and local regulations were impeding international treaties. Money was needed to provide for the common defense, but states weren't willing to uniformly contribute. Congress could borrow money without having the means to repay it. Printed money was rapidly shrinking in value, and the public credit of the infant nation was being destroyed. Leaving defense to states led to inequities, confusion, and conflict. Likewise, the economy would grow better with centralized oversight of taxes and regulations.

In short, the United States had to start acting like a nation and not a flimsy confederation of states. Revising the Articles of Confederation, which had taken four years to ratify, would be difficult. Even so, Alexander intended to submit his vision for a new nation to Congress.

Despite his best efforts, he couldn't rally enough support. Indeed, some people thought Congress *too* powerful already. Thomas Jefferson, who'd written the Declaration of Independence, thought the work of the federal government could be done by a committee.

Alexander and Jefferson could not have been cut from more different bolts of cloth.

Jefferson had thought the war would be over quickly. Unlike Alexander, he had not thrown himself into the study of military principles and learned to become a soldier and

Thomas Jefferson

leader when war broke out. Jefferson had behaved timidly on the battlefield, running from danger when he'd served as Virginia's governor and enabling Benedict Arnold to capture Richmond. Jefferson was in many ways Alexander's opposite: born to privilege, an owner of slaves, someone who envisioned an agrarian rather than a modern United States.

The first battle lines between them were drawn—and it would be a long war with surprising turns.

After beating his head against a wall for months,

ABOVE: *UNLIKE ALEXANDER, THOMAS JEFFERSON WAS BORN TO PRIVILEGE AND PERFORMED POORLY IN BATTLE.*

Alexander wanted only to be home with his wife and son. On July 22, he wrote to his beloved, hoping that in four days' time he'd be headed her way.

"I am strongly urged to stay a few days for the ratification of the treaty; at all events however I will not be long from My Betsey. I give you joy my angel of the happy conclusion of the important work in which your country has been engaged. Now in a very short time I hope we shall be happily settled in New York. My love to your father. Kiss my boy a thousand times. A thousand loves to yourself."

HE WAS AT HOME ON NOVEMBER 25, 1783, WHEN the British finally left New York. Alexander's former military commander Henry Knox secured the city with his troops. Meanwhile, George Washington and the state's governor, George Clinton, rode into the jubilant town on horseback. A parade of soldiers marched the general from the Bowery to Wall Street, where Alexander, Eliza, and Philip lived.

The bedraggled patriots looked nothing like the departing British soldiers, who had scarlet uniforms and polished weapons. The American troops wore mismatched uniforms tattered by weather and use. But New York felt pride in these men and loathing for the British soldiers, who were such sore losers they greased the liberty pole on their way out, making it hard for the Americans to hang their Stars and Stripes.

Patriots resented the British and their Tory sympathizers. Even Hercules Mulligan was endangered by it. So many

people believed he was a traitor that Washington needed to have breakfast with him after the parade, to show the nation whose side Mulligan had really been on.

It didn't help the Tories that New York was a shambles. Much of the city had been destroyed by a fire in September 1776, and the British had not repaired things during their seven-year occupation. They'd burned fences and trees to keep warm. The wharves were falling apart, and shanties had popped up everywhere.

Alexander had grand ideas for how the city could be restored and how carpenters and masons could be put to work building large and elegant structures, and he would make the case for his fellow citizens in the months and years to come.

But the city couldn't be rebuilt on a foundation of resentment. Alexander was outraged at the treatment of Tories and the way it was causing them—and their money and business ties—to leave in waves for Canada. These were not the values

ABOVE: *WALL STREET IN NEW YORK, HERE CIRCA 1785, STARTED AS A DEFENSIVE BOUNDARY, BECAME A SLAVE MARKET, AND TURNED INTO THE FINANCIAL CAPITAL OF THE UNITED STATES.*

he'd risked his life for, and it was putting the economic health of the city in jeopardy.

As ardently as he'd fought and managed the Revolution, he took up the cause of the loyalists who remained. Yes, they'd stood for the wrong values and aligned with the wrong forces. But they still had rights. The country would need to be stitched together of friends and former foes alike—and new laws restricting civil and property rights struck Alexander as being counter to the spirit of the country's founding principles. The way America treated its citizens—even the ones who'd been on the wrong side of history—would affect its standing internationally.

HE WASN'T MOTIVATED BY POPULARITY. NOT EVEN BY PROFIT.

He welcomed downtrodden loyalists as his clients, and soon, he was one of the most respected lawyers in the city. But he didn't limit his efforts on their behalf to the courtroom. In early 1784, he adopted the pen name Phocion, arguing in print against retribution and unjust treatment of sympathizers to the Crown.

"Nothing is more common than for a free people, in times of heat and violence, to gratify momentary passions, by letting into the government, principles and precedents which afterwards prove fatal to themselves," he wrote. This included disenfranchisement of broad classes of citizens, which could lead to aristocracy or oligarchy. Only due process—trial and conviction in a court of law—justified taking away a person's rights.

He wasn't motivated by popularity. Not even by profit. Though he joked to Lafayette that he was rocking the cradle and studying the art of fleecing his neighbors, if anything, he undercharged for his services. Alexander's passion was for principles, not profits. He once declined a client's promise to pay a $1,000 retainer because it was too much money.

Alexander challenged state laws that violated the treaty with England. He argued for justice systematically, passionately, and at length. (His college friend and study partner Robert Troup teased that Alexander never settled for delivering a blow to his opponent's head when he could slap down the insects buzzing around his fallen enemy's ears.) He kept his eyes on his long-term goal: creating a strong central government. Challenging laws that broke the international treaty was crucial. A state should not be able to pass laws that would violate those of the country as a whole. There was no more important way to establish the hierarchy between individual states and the nation. Nation first.

Not everybody saw it this way, and the fight for power between the states and the federal government would only grow.

As Alexander ascended the ranks of the city's lawyers, he was joined at the top by Aaron Burr. On the surface, the men had much in common. Both had been orphaned early. Both were ambitious students and ardent admirers of women. Both fell in love during the war. Both had become lawyers on a fast path, and both were doting fathers, though only one of the children Burr had with his wife survived.

But their paths began to diverge during the war and split widely afterward. Burr and Washington didn't care for each

Aaron Burr

other, and Burr had been one of Charles Lee's defenders after his reckless retreat at Monmouth. Alexander and Burr differed in the courtroom, too. Where the blue-eyed Alexander spoke volumes and sometimes got himself into trouble with his mouth, black-eyed Burr was more guarded. He cultivated this obscurity and described himself in the third person, as if he were talking about someone else: "He is a grave, silent strange sort of animal, inasmuch that we know not what to make of him."

ABOVE: *AARON BURR AND ALEXANDER WERE FRIENDS, THEN RIVALS, THEN BITTER ENEMIES.*

Burr even obscured body parts he didn't want people to see. He styled his dark hair so that it hid his small ears and, when he started going bald on top, arranged an elaborate comb-over to conceal his visible scalp.

Unlike Alexander, he charged steep fees and lived lavishly. Where Alexander cleaved to principles, Burr clutched at power.

They sometimes worked the same side of cases in the courtroom, though not always happily. Once, when they argued a case together, Alexander wanted to take the lead. Burr, irritated at this, anticipated all Alexander's arguments, leaving him no spotlight to stand in. Alexander sat down without arguing a single point.

WHERE ALEXANDER CLEAVED TO PRINCIPLES, BURR CLUTCHED AT POWER.

But they weren't always rivals. Burr helped Alexander become a homeowner in 1785—he was the one who tipped Alexander off that 57 Wall Street was for sale. In the distant future, they would work as allies defending a man in a sex-tinged murder-mystery trial, the first murder trial ever to be recorded in the United States. But no alliance between them would ever last, and neither could have predicted how dark their rivalry would become, or how deadly.

ALEXANDER WAS TOO BUSY EVEN TO CONSIDER such things. The year before he bought that first house, he'd transformed the financial prospects of his fellow New Yorkers.

It all started as a favor to his brother-in-law John B. Church. Church had made a fortune overseas and had invested some of that capital in the Bank of North America, the first such bank in the nation, established in 1781 in Philadelphia. Church wanted similar investment opportunity, so he and his business partner asked Alexander to set up a private bank in New York.

At the time, there were two ways to fund a bank: with land or with money (paper or coins made of silver and gold). Land was the more conservative option. But it's not a very flexible one. You can't turn it into cash immediately. So, when a rival proposed a land-based bank to merchants, Alexander used his deep knowledge of finance to persuade the merchants that it was the wrong route to take. He made such a compelling case that the merchants asked him to set up a money bank on their behalf. And so he did, feeling slightly chagrined at having overstepped his initial goal.

HAMILTON HAD PLANTED THE SEEDS FOR THE MODERN AMERICAN BANKING SYSTEM.

A newspaper advertisement invited interested people to meet on February 24, 1784, at the Merchant's Coffee House.

Before the Revolution, the Sons of Liberty sometimes met there. Now it was the founding place for the city's first bank.

Alexander was named a director. General Alexander McDougall, an army colleague, was chairman. Over the next three weeks, Alexander threw himself into the challenge of how the bank would work. He single-handedly created a constitution that outlined, in twenty crisply written articles, how the bank would run. It was so good that other banks used it as their model. And so, without really meaning to do anything other than help his brother-in-law, Alexander Hamilton had planted the seeds for the modern American banking system.

ALEXANDER HAD A KNACK FOR INSERTING HIM-self into controversial debates without fearing or even always anticipating the consequences. Because he represented loyalists in court, people wondered whether he was secretly one of them. He also believed that institutions like banks would be an integral part of a modern nation, and people accused him, falsely, of profiting from the one he had set up. He thought there should be a strong, centralized federal government, and people thought he was a closet monarchist. He retained his disgust at the practice of enslaving other human beings, and later some people claimed he was Creole himself.

With the matter of slavery, Alexander was compromised. Not only did associates like Washington keep many people enslaved, his wife's parents bought enslaved people and put them to work on their estate and in their fields and mills. Angelica and her husband owned people. What's more,

Alexander helped negotiate human purchases on behalf of his in-laws. He had their blood and sweat on his hands.

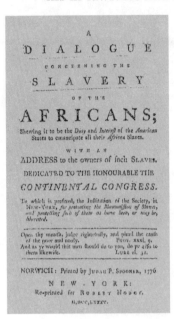

A

D I A L O G U E

CONCERNING THE

S L A V E R Y

OF THE

AFRICANS;

Shewing it to be the Duty and Interest of the American States to emancipate all their African Slaves.

WITH AN

ADDRESS to the owners of such Slaves.

DEDICATED TO THE HONOURABLE THE CONTINENTAL CONGRESS.

To which is prefixed, the Institution of the Society, in New-York, for promoting the Manumission of Slaves, and protecting such of them as have been, or may be, liberated.

Open thy mouth, judge righteously, and plead the cause of the poor and needy.   Prov. xxxi. 9.
And as ye would that men should do to you, do ye also to them likewise.   Luke vi. 31.

NORWICH: Printed by Judah P. Spooner, 1776

N E W - Y O R K:
Re-printed for Robert Hoder.
M,DCC,LXXXV.

On the surface, it was a clear issue morally for Alexander. A nation founded on principles of equality and liberty had no place forcing human beings into slavery. Human freedom also trumped the principle of property ownership that Alexander held dear. Enslaved people who'd been promised their freedom in exchange for fighting were entitled to their liberty. It didn't matter whose side they'd fought on.

Some people objected to ratifying the peace treaty with England unless the king reimbursed enslaved people's former owners for their loss of human "property." But Alexander disagreed. The enslaved people, once freed, were no longer property. No one was owed anything.

"The abandonment of [enslaved black people], who had been induced to quit their Masters on the faith of Official proclamations promising them liberty, to fall again under the yoke of their masters and into slavery is as *odious* and *immoral* a thing as can be conceived."

This didn't stop enslavers from traveling to New York and other cities and snatching black people off the streets, regardless of whether they had been given their freedom or had freed themselves. Partly out of outrage for this practice of abduction, the New York Society for Promoting the

ABOVE: *Alexander continued to oppose slavery by joining the New York Society for Promoting the Manumission of Slaves.*

Manumission of Slaves formed on January 25, 1785.

Robert Troup—who owned two enslaved people himself—was one of the founders, more than half of whom owned enslaved people. Soon afterward, Alexander joined the society, attending a meeting at the Merchant's Coffee House. Everyone agreed that the corrupt practice of enslaving other human beings needed to end, but how and when?

Alexander, Troup, and a fellow volunteer worked together on a solution, which they presented in November 1785 with details about timing and methods. As happened so often with Alexander, he was too ardent and aggressive with his ideas and couldn't rally people behind them. He kept at it, though. A few months later, he helped lobby the state legislature to stop the trade of enslaved people in New York, who were being treated like cattle as they were exported to the West Indies and the southern states.

The society would later found the New York African Free School in 1787. It wasn't the only school Alexander would have a hand in starting. He also became a trustee of a school for Oneida Indians and the children of white settlers, although few members of the tribe chose to go to the school, whose purpose was to help them assimilate into the culture of their colonizers.

IN THE FLURRY OF COURT CASES AND CIVIC activity, his role as family man was growing ever larger. Little Philip got a sister, Angelica, on September 25, 1784. More children would follow. In 1787, the Hamiltons also took in a two-year-old girl named Fanny after her mother died and her father was overwhelmed. Alexander doted on his family. When Eliza had a cold, he'd urge her to take good care of herself, lest she suffer pain and lose out on life's pleasures. He listened to little Angelica play the piano and sing. And he included his extended family, especially Eliza's sister Angelica, in his deep affections. When Angelica moved overseas, he mourned the loss:

"I confess for my own part I see one great source of happiness snatched away. My affection for Church and yourself made me anticipate much enjoyment in your friendship and neighbourhood. But an ocean is now to separate us."

As his understanding of what it meant to have a family grew, the memory of his childhood experience ached. He'd neglected to write Hugh Knox and felt the shame of that. Worse, he hadn't heard from his brother, James, in years. Maybe James had a wife and family—Alexander had no idea. It was his dream someday to set his brother up on a farm in the United States, but the postwar economic chaos was too great to make that possible at the moment.

When he finally did hear from James on June 22, 1785, the letter made him sad. He responded with an offer of help and love: "The situation you describe yourself to be in gives me much pain, and nothing will make me happier than, as far as may be in my power, to contribute to your relief. I will cheerfully pay your draft upon me for fifty pounds sterling, whenever it shall appear. I wish it was in my power to desire you to enlarge the sum; but though my future prospects are of the most flattering kind my present engagements would render it inconvenient to me to advance you a larger sum. My affection for you, however, will not permit me to be inattentive to your welfare, and I hope time will prove to you that I feel all the sentiment of a brother."

Becoming a father had made him miss his own, even though he hadn't seen the man in decades. His father still hadn't met Eliza, as Alexander had promised on their wedding day. The man hadn't seen any of his grandchildren. He didn't even know of their existence. Alexander worried his father was dead, and the thought of it, and how difficult his father's life had been, weighed on his heart like lead. He liked to fantasize that his uncles had helped lift his father's prospects, but feared that had not been the case.

He told James, "Let me know how or where he is, if alive, if dead, how and where he died. Should he be alive inform him of my inquiries, beg him to write to me, and tell him how ready I shall be to devote myself and all I have to his accommodation and happiness."

As for his own children, he hated to be away.

"I feel that nothing can ever compensate for the loss of the enjoyments I leave at home, or can ever put my heart at tolerable ease," he told Eliza. "In the bosom of my family alone must my happiness be sought, and in that of my Betsey is every thing that is charming to me. Would to heaven I were there!"

But he couldn't be home on Wall Street all the time. The young father was needed not just as father of his children, but as father of a nation. His fighting with musket and bayonet was done. But his most powerful weapon—his mind—was about to be unleashed.

It would be unlike anything the world had ever seen.

CHAPTER EIGHT

The

FEDERALIST

I N 1780, ALEXANDER HAD written a letter to his fiancée. The war was not yet won, its outcome not yet certain. Indeed, South Carolina had just been lost. His best friend was a prisoner of war, and Alexander—who'd wanted to fight by Laurens's side but couldn't—was overwhelmed with paperwork instead. The French fleet had arrived, and Alexander was charged with figuring out three different approaches for how the two nations might combine their militaries.

The workload left him gloomy. But he did find some sources of hope. There was the glow of Eliza's love, and his gut instinct that the political challenges the war had revealed could be fixed with reform of the Articles of Confederation. He was embarrassed to be musing on such matters in a love letter, but he couldn't help it.

"Pardon me my love for talking politics to you. What have we to do with any thing but love? Go the world as it will, in each others arms we cannot but be happy."

That said, if things didn't work out with the war, he had other ideas. "What think you of Geneva as a retreat? 'Tis a charming place; where nature and society are in their greatest perfection. I was once determined to let my existence and American liberty end together. My Betsey has given me a motive to outlive my pride."

Eventually, the war did end. He'd married the girl. But the work remained unfinished, including repairing all that was broken with the Articles of Confederation. By 1786, the rest of the nation was finally catching up with Alexander's understanding of the situation.

Tensions crackled between the states. In New York, Governor Clinton had imposed import taxes that local merchants despised. What's more, other states receiving parts of those shipments—like nearby New Jersey—*weren't* receiving income from the taxes. Maryland and Virginia were squabbling over the Potomac River—the conflicts went on and on. Every state was acting in its own interests, and the nation was suffering.

Alexander could see the scope of the disaster as it unfolded on every level. The countries that had loaned America money during the war weren't sure they'd be paid back, which was destroying America's credit potential overseas. States were hoarding tax revenue for themselves instead of fulfilling their commitment to make voluntary payments to the federal treasury. States were also taking advantage of each other, which was a recipe for civil war and an open door to meddling from foreign powers.

In the summer of 1786, thousands of farmers overwhelmed by bad crops, a depressed economy, and oppressive taxes put on their army uniforms and rebelled. Alexander sympathized with their cause, but mob violence wasn't the solution.

The truth was, people were suffering because Congress couldn't get the nation's finances in order. It wasn't just on a national level. Alexander felt it personally. Good people suffered. Baron von Steuben was to have been paid if the patriots won. And yet he was forced to come to Alexander for personal loans. Ralph Earl was an artist who'd painted bat-tlefield scenes. He went to debtors' prison in 1786. Alexander and Eliza helped Earl earn his way out the next year, when Eliza sat for Earl *in jail* as he painted her portrait.

Sometimes it felt as if the pub-lic's appetite for his services was endless. He'd fought in the war. He'd surrendered his pay. He'd collected taxes. He'd served in the Continental Congress. And then, in September 1, 1786, he was asked again to take time away from his law practice. The states were fighting among themselves, and he and delegates from other states needed to resolve it.

So, he set off for Annapolis. He fell ill on the road and was in low spirits as a result. What's more, he was one of only a few who responded to the call of duty. Just a dozen delegates from five states gathered in the city, chosen because it was small and far away from Congress, so no one would accuse them of being biased.

In a way, this relative apathy was good. Alexander was among friends, including James Madison. Alexander's fellow New Yorker, Egbert Benson, took notes, and before long, they'd all agreed that the real problem was this: the bal-ance between state and national influence had not yet been resolved. The Articles of Confederation needed revision. Alexander was so excited by the prospect that he unloaded

ABOVE: *ELIZA SAT FOR THIS PORTRAIT, BY RALPH EARL, IN DEBTORS' PRISON.*

the verbal equivalent of a howitzer as he made the case to Congress. His enthusiasm didn't go over well. The quiet, scholarly Madison had to walk him back to reality.

With Madison's influence, the revised document took a gentler tone, letting Congress know it was time to revise the Articles of Confederation. The situation was critical. The proposal set a date and a place. Philadelphia, the second Monday of May in 1787. They would devise a constitution adequate to the needs of the nation. They'd get Congress to approve it, and then take it to the states for ratification.

ALEXANDER'S GLEE DIDN'T LAST LONG. WHEN he returned home, his own governor, George Clinton, opposed the reform plan. Clinton, a political rival of Alexander's father-in-law and resolute believer in the rights of states over the federal government, made sure Alexander was surrounded by oppositional New Yorkers at the Constitutional Convention. It was the worst possible sort of baggage for him to carry to Philadelphia.

Delegates began to arrive in Philadelphia in early May. Delayed by weather, like so many other delegates, Alexander arrived on Friday, May 18, wearing a three-piece wool suit in the midst of a heat wave. A visiting Frenchman said of the weather, "The heat of the day makes one long for bedtime because of weariness, and a single fly which has gained entrance to your room in spite of all precautions, drives you from your bed."

As the days passed, the city swelled with delegates, and it wasn't always easy to find inns to accommodate them.

Washington, now fifty-five years old, had aching joints and had only attended at the urging of friends. He hated idling away his time when he had a plantation to run.

Finally, on May 25, enough men had arrived that work could begin. It was an "assembly of demigods," in the view of Thomas Jefferson, whose duties kept him in France. Alexander knew many: Washington, James McHenry, Robert Morris, James Madison, and Gouverneur Morris, a fellow lawyer and the friend he'd talked into slapping Washington's back that one time. Even Ben Franklin was there. Alexander hadn't met the legend yet but was eager to.

They met in the Pennsylvania State House—later known as Independence Hall—where the Declaration of Independence had been signed eleven years earlier, when Alexander had been a bright-eyed artillery captain, eager for war and glory. He was more than that now. He'd had his war. He'd

ABOVE: *THE CONSTITUTION WAS WRITTEN IN INDEPENDENCE HALL, PHILADELPHIA, DEPICTED HERE IN 1778.*

achieved his glory. In the midst, he had suffered and seen good men die. He had watched the army struggle because of defects with the Articles of Confederation and selfishness on the part of the states. This was his chance to change everything.

In some ways, the Revolution had been the easier part. Now they had to create a functioning government, a complex, high-stakes challenge that would determine the happiness or misery of millions of unborn people, as one senior delegate, sixty-one-year-old George Mason, observed.

WHAT WAS SAID IN THE ROOM STAYED IN THE ROOM.

Alexander was one of three men in charge of coming up with rules for the convention. An early and controversial rule established confidentiality: what was said in the room stayed in the room. This was to let the participants freely share their thoughts and arrive at the best possible conclusions. The secrecy was so vital that the doors and windows remained closed despite the heat.

Washington, elected leader, presided from a table at the front of the room. His mahogany chair featured a brilliantly painted golden sun carved into its crest rail. Facing him, the fifty-five delegates sat in plain Windsor chairs at tables topped with green cloths, inkwells, quills, writing paper, and books of philosophy and history they could consult as they worked. Men stood to face Washington as they spoke, and no

Edmund Randolph

one was permitted to interrupt or read from books or pamphlets when someone had the floor. Another rule required the men to stand at the end of each day, waiting to leave until Washington had passed.

To Alexander's relief, it quickly became clear that the Articles of Confederation were up for more than revision. He kept mostly mum as other men proposed their plans. Alexander had some dramatic ideas to reveal, but he was biding his time for the right moment.

ABOVE: *EDMUND RANDOLPH WAS ONE OF THE YOUNGEST FOUNDING FATHERS. HE AND JAMES MADISON PROPOSED A GOVERNMENT WITH A TWO-PART CONGRESS.*

Edmund Randolph of Virginia, at thirty-three years old one of the youngest men in the room along with Alexander, presented a plan he and Madison had devised. Their Virginia plan envisioned a two-part congress, the first part elected by the people and the second elected by the first, out of nominees provided by the state legislatures. Congress would choose the single executive. Representation would be based on state population. Virginia, as the largest state, had a vested interest in the sort of power it would give.

Delegates debated the plan, article by article, for days. Alexander remained silent as he observed the others. He had reservations about democracy and its potential for excesses. Tyranny was dangerous, but so were mobs. He'd seen them again and again—in the West Indies, at the outbreak of the Revolution, and afterward, with the soldiers who'd surrounded Congress with their guns, demanding money the government did not have.

Thinking about how he could make his case, Alexander spoke only rarely in the early days of the convention—once to second a motion by Ben Franklin that the executive of the federal government do the job for free. It wasn't a practical idea, and the delegates didn't vote on it, but Alexander especially wanted to honor the man, who was old and sick.

An alternative to Randolph's plan came from New Jersey delegate William Paterson, an Irish immigrant who'd studied law in Princeton. It represented a revision to the Articles of Confederation instead of a wholesale new constitution. His plan would establish one legislative house, allow the federal government to raise money with tariffs and stamp taxes, and establish an executive council elected by the Congress and subject to removal by a majority of the state governors. A

William Paterson

primary goal was to balance the power between large and small states.

Debate over the two plans highlighted the biggest points of contention: the hierarchy of the national and state governments and the balance of power between states of different sizes.

Alexander believed passionately in the importance of a strong federal government. Weak federal power had nearly cost them the war. After listening to both plans and considering

ABOVE: *WILLIAM PATERSON FROM NEW JERSEY ARGUED FOR REVISION OF THE ARTICLES OF CONFEDERATION.*

the wisdom of men with more experience—feeling reluctant to disagree with them—he could no longer hold back.

On June 18, he filled his lungs with a great deal of air, stood to face Washington, and for the next six hours outlined his bold vision for a new nation. He didn't care at all for the New Jersey plan. Proposals for popular governments were the same old pork, "with a little change of sauce." What the nation needed, he argued, was a balance between tyranny and the excesses of democracy. His plan included a two-part legislative body. The assembly would be elected to three-year terms. The senate would be chosen by electors voted on by the people. Senators would serve for life, barring misbehavior. This would provide necessary continuity. Judges on a supreme court would serve similar lifetime appointments.

"I AM SORRY YOU WENT AWAY—I WISH YOU WERE BACK."

Meanwhile, the United States legislature could appoint courts in each state. Any state laws that contradicted national ones or the constitution would be void. And no state would have its own army or navy; there would be just one for the nation as a whole.

A supreme executive authority, which some listeners heard as "monarch," would be a governor elected by electors chosen by the people. He would serve for life, except in cases of misbehavior. He'd have veto power over the legislature and command the navy and militia.

Alexander probably couldn't have uttered a more controversial notion than one that smacked of monarchy. He also praised the British system of government, another unwise move.

A Georgia delegate named William Pierce took notes on Alexander's performance. "Colo. Hamilton is deservedly celebrated for his talents. . . . Yet there is something too feeble in his voice to be equal to the strains of oratory. . . . His manners are tinctured with stifness, and sometimes with a degree of vanity that is highly disagreable."

When Alexander's marathon speech ended, the overheated audience clapped politely. No one bothered to dignify it with a rebuttal. The men were getting nowhere. Alexander, discouraged that the miracle of the convention was being squandered in a stalemate, slouched back to New York to take care of business.

He wrote to Washington: "I own to you Sir that I am seriously and deeply distressed at the aspect of the Councils which prevailed when I left Philadelphia. . . . I shall of necessity remain here ten or twelve days; if I have reason to believe that my attendance at Philadelphia will not be mere waste of time, I shall after that period rejoin the Convention."

Without bringing up Alexander's impolitic ideas, Washington commiserated: "The Men who oppose a strong & energetic government are, in my opinion, narrow minded politicians, or are under the influence of local views."

What's more, Washington missed his protégé. "I am sorry you went away—I wish you were back."

The convention lasted four long months. Alexander's fellow New York representatives left on principle in early July. They wouldn't agree to surrender their state's power to federal authority. They also no longer felt bound to keep confidential what had been said. In the middle of July, while Alexander was in New York, the Connecticut Compromise helped break the stalemate, which had become snagged on the balance of power between the states. To that end, each state would have the same number of senators, and votes in the House of Representatives would be proportionate to their populations. It was a delicate but necessary compromise.

There were other demanding issues to resolve, not the least of which was slavery. It was a bitterly divisive issue between the North and South. Rather than pick at the wounds, some delegates used euphemisms when talking about the institution, calling enslaved people "persons held to Service or Labour" and the slave trade "migrations," which suggested a natural or elective pattern of movement at odds with reality.

The debate wasn't about liberty for enslaved people, though. It was about power for their masters. Delegates from the slave states wanted their representation in the House to reflect their human property, increasing their clout in the legislature. A compromise was struck: enslaved people would count as three-fifths of a person (though they would not be allowed to vote).

The compromise depressed Alexander, who deepened his commitment to the Manumission Society.

Here, Alexander walked a difficult line. He had on occasion compromised his principles for political or personal reasons. Acting on orders during the war, for example, he participated in efforts to track down an enslaved man who'd joined the British and been taken captive. In Congress shortly after the war ended, he put forward a motion to protest General Guy Carleton's refusal to return formerly enslaved people who'd sought refuge behind British lines. Some of his friends in the Manumission Society continued to enslave people, even after joining. Alexander determined how those society members should treat their human property—a different tack from arguing for immediate freedom. And then there were the enslaved people owned by his relatives.

The union trumped all other beliefs, though. Without the three-fifths compromise, the whole enterprise would have been sunk. Some considered it unjust to give even partial representation to men who had no vote. But it was worth the compromise to keep the South and North together. The South grew staple crops, some of which were exported, and all of which benefited the nation as a whole. And then there was the argument that representation should go to property owners; enslaved men counted as property.

"THEY ARE MEN, THOUGH DEGRADED TO THE CONDITION OF SLAVERY."

This didn't make it just, he said later. "It will however by no means be admitted, that the slaves are considered altogether as property. They are men, though degraded to the condition of slavery."

Another contentious issue concerned the rights immigrants had to hold office. This rankled Alexander, who'd done more than many natural-born citizens to assure the nation's independence. Why should he be considered lesser because of the circumstances of his birth? But many in the

South were wary of "foreign" interference in the nation's business. When Alexander briefly returned to the convention on August 13, he advocated for immigrants to be able to serve in Congress or as president after spending four years in the country. Ultimately, the Constitution permitted someone who was a citizen at the time the document was signed to serve as president. Otherwise, the candidate had to be native born—which seemed a fair compromise.

Compromise became a theme toward the end of the convention. Alexander had been devoted to the idea of a strong federal government. The stronger the better, to guard against democracy run amok. He was even willing to let someone be the leader for life, if his behavior was good. And yet the notion of checks and balances among the branches of government had become reassuring enough that Alexander was fully behind the compromises that were adopted, including term limits. He even seconded a resolution by Madison on a method for amending the Constitution that required consent from the states—something he never would have agreed to in the early days of the convention. It wasn't about achieving perfection, but rather, something *closer* to perfection than the Articles of Confederation had reached.

By September 8, there was enough agreement on the principles that Alexander and four other men, including Madison, sat down to capture all the articles that had been agreed to and write them in a style the subject deserved. Gouverneur Morris penned introductory words that captured the intent of the men who'd gathered:

"We the People of the United States, in Order to form a more perfect Union, establish Justice, insure domestic

Tranquility, provide for the common defense, promote the general Welfare, and secure the Blessings of Liberty to ourselves and our Posterity, do ordain and establish this Constitution for the United States of America."

Seven articles followed, outlining the contours of the federal government that would balance power among three branches: the legislative, executive, and judicial. The Constitution detailed who could run for office and how appointments to the Supreme Court would work. It set up a financial

ABOVE: *THE CONSTITUTION OF THE UNITED STATES WAS SIGNED ON SEPTEMBER 17, 1787.*

system, and its articles outlined the relationships states would have with one another and how new states would join the union. They explained how the Constitution would be amended in the future and said that the debts that existed under the Articles of Confederation were still valid. The final article established how many states would have to say yes to make the Constitution the law of the land: nine out of thirteen.

In the end, not everyone was able to see the value of political compromise and balance of powers. Edmund Randolph, who'd proposed the Virginia plan, couldn't stomach the final document; there was too much power in the federal government.

On September 17, the Constitution was signed by thirty-nine men from twelve states. (Rhode Island hadn't sent delegates.) Alexander was the only signer from New York. As the last names were being set to parchment, Ben Franklin, the oldest signer, made an observation about the sun carved into Washington's chair: "I have the happiness to know that it is a rising and not a setting Sun."

He was so pleased with the document he sent it to his friends in Europe, anticipating the day when Europe might form a similar union of its different states and kingdoms.

But it was not yet a done deal, and Randolph made a bitter prediction: "Nine states will fail to ratify the plan, and confusion must ensue."

The official business over, Alexander and the rest of the men who'd managed to create a government without force or fraud went to the nearby City Tavern for a drink. A lot of drinks, actually. Beer, punch, madeira, cider, ale, porter, and claret, which they consumed by the light of candles made from crystallized whale oil.

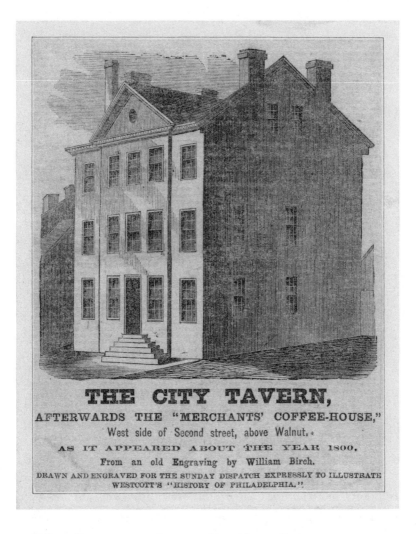

THE CITY TAVERN,
AFTERWARDS THE "MERCHANTS' COFFEE-HOUSE,"
West side of Second street, above Walnut.
AS IT APPEARED ABOUT THE YEAR 1800.
From an old Engraving by William Birch.
DRAWN AND ENGRAVED FOR THE SUNDAY DISPATCH EXPRESSLY TO ILLUSTRATE
WESTCOTT'S "HISTORY OF PHILADELPHIA."

When the sun rose the next day, Alexander set out to prove Randolph and other doubters wrong. On his trips home during the convention, he had faced outrageous rumors, including one that claimed the delegates had a plan to bring the second son of King George to rule America. His fellow New York delegates had also disclosed the secrets of the convention to Governor Clinton, whom Alexander accused of poisoning

ABOVE: *TO CELEBRATE THE NEW CONSTITUTION, THE FOUNDERS DRANK LOTS OF WINE AND BEER AT THE CITY TAVERN.*

James M. Madison

the electorate against the document before anyone had even read it. The battle ahead to ratify the Constitution would take every resource he had.

Things turned vicious fast. Clinton had cronies write newspaper articles criticizing Alexander. One piece suggested that Alexander had weaseled his way into Washington's family and then been fired.

"This I confess hurts my feelings," Alexander told Washington.

ABOVE: *JAMES MADISON AND ALEXANDER WERE, AT FIRST, ALLIES.*

Washington, who liked both Clinton and Alexander, sent a reassuring reply. "I do therefore, explicitly declare, that both charges are entirely unfounded."

These men had no business spewing lies about what Alexander accomplished and how. They had no business undermining the work of every man in that sweltering room. What's more, their reckless words threatened the nation. And they were an insult to his honor.

Within a few weeks, an outraged Alexander had assembled an elite intellectual and political fighting force to take on those naysayers in writing.

There was James Madison, who, while young, was a public fixture. He'd exhausted himself with study in college, and his health wasn't robust enough for him to have been a soldier in the Revolution. He sometimes had seizures. As a congressman, Madison was widely respected for his knowledge, thoughtfulness, and persuasive speaking manner. What's more, he was modest and sweet-tempered and an excellent conversationalist.

And then there was John Jay, a foreign-policy expert who'd helped negotiate the Treaty of Paris after the war. He'd married Sarah Livingston, whom Alexander knew from his prep school days. Jay hadn't attended the Constitutional Convention, but he was a former president of Congress and had worked on the constitution of New York state.

Alexander hoped his friend Gouverneur Morris would join them after his star turn in Independence Hall, but Morris was swamped with work. Another friend, William Duer, wrote pieces that didn't suit.

Meanwhile, he and Washington swapped intelligence with each other on how the proposed Constitution was faring.

Parts of Virginia were enthusiastic, Washington reported. "In Alexandria . . . and some of the adjacent Counties, it has been embraced with an enthusiastic warmth of which I had no conception. I expect notwithstanding, violent opposition will be given to it by *some* characters of weight & influence, in the State."

Alexander found the same. "The constitution proposed has in this state warm friends and warm enemies. . . . The event cannot yet be foreseen. The inclosed is the first number of a series of papers to be written in its defence."

FOR THE TRIO OF WRITERS, TIME WAS OF THE ESSENCE.

The enclosure was a newspaper clipping from October 27, 1787. It was the first in a series of written salvos his team had fired back at opponents to the new Constitution. It was based on an outline he'd drafted on board a sloop sailing up the North River on his way to his wife's family in Albany.

"To the People of the State of New York," he'd written.

He signed it "Publius," meant to indicate he was a friend of the people.

Each of the *Federalist* essays began this way, and each was a letter of sorts: a mixture of love, invective, lectures, hopes, and fears for America. He threw himself into the task, juggling this with his law practice and growing family. Eliza had another baby on the way, conceived during one of his visits home from Philadelphia.

It was the perfect writing challenge for Alexander. He had an opposing force on which he could leverage his arguments—the antifederalists who wanted states to reign supreme. He dipped quills into oceans of ink, intending to drown these men in words. Just as he walked and talked to memorize his studies when he was a student, he paced around his study while conjuring his arguments in his head. And then he sat at his desk for six to seven hours at a time to write, fueled by strong coffee. He first took down the Articles

ABOVE: *JOHN JAY ROUNDED OUT THE TEAM OF AUTHORS BEHIND THE FEDERALIST ESSAYS.*

of Confederation. Then he built up the document written to replace it. In just one week, he produced several essays on a subject close to his heart: taxation.

For the trio of writers, time was of the essence. The haste was partly to overwhelm opponents with words. But partly it was to beat the ratification process, which began in November.

Madison and Alexander, who wrote most of the letters, made something of an odd couple. Madison was much shorter than Alexander, whom no one ever called tall. Where Alexander loved parties and socializing and women, Madison was quiet and solitary. Where Alexander had, despite his busyness, managed to woo and marry during the clang of war, Madison would marry late. Where Alexander was stylish and meticulously groomed, Madison preferred simple black clothing.

They did have some things in common, and this helped them write so cohesively in the *Federalist* papers that some people couldn't tell their writing apart. Both were realists about human flaws. "If men were angels, no government would be necessary," Madison wrote.

Alexander always feared the excesses of the mob. This is where the devil emerged. The best safeguard against this was something he called "an aristocracy of merit": people who were intelligent, honorable, and experienced.

A better word for this might have been meritocracy. After all, Alexander wasn't an aristocrat by birth. He'd become one by effort. Any man could earn the same by giving as much. It was an *earned* aristocracy.

In all, amid the fullness of his life, he would write fifty-one of these essays. With Madison, he collaborated on three more. Madison took on twenty-six himself. Jay, who'd suffered ill health, managed to contribute five. In seven months, the three men wrote 175,000 words, which were eventually bound into two volumes totaling six hundred pages. It would become one of the most influential works of political philosophy and practical governing the world had ever seen.

Those who worried America would install a king and dissolve the separate states began watching him closely and collecting evidence that fit their paranoia. But Alexander never was a monarchist. And in *Federalist* No. 22, he wrote, "The fabric of American Empire out to rest on the solid basis of THE CONSENT OF THE PEOPLE." It didn't matter to some, though. Alexander made lifelong enemies as readily as he made lifelong friends.

IT WAS AN OPEN SECRET WHO'D WRITTEN IT.

He didn't let it worry him. He had only one aim: to persuade his fellow New Yorkers to ratify the Constitution. Nine states had to ratify the document for it to take effect. In December 1787, Delaware, Pennsylvania, and New Jersey voted to accept the document. The next month brought approval from two more states: Georgia and Connecticut. Massachusetts squeaked an approval through in February. That made six.

By March, Alexander, Jay, and Madison had bound their first *Federalist* book. It was an open secret who'd written it. Alexander and Madison sent hundreds of copies to delegates in New York and Virginia, two large states that had not yet voted. After Madison traveled back to Virginia from

New York, where he'd been working as a delegate, the two exchanged dozens of letters.

Alexander signed his affectionately. No one could ever replace Laurens's spot in his heart. But he and Madison had become close allies who shared similar antipathy to slavery and a commitment to holding the union together with passionately reasoned principle. Alexander relished the connection.

Meanwhile, the clock ticked. Maryland ratified in April, followed by South Carolina in May. That made eight. North Carolina and Rhode Island seemed like lost causes. New Hampshire was a toss-up. It would come down to Virginia and New York, Madison's and Alexander's home states.

The vote in Virginia would happen two weeks before the vote in New York. Alexander knew he couldn't beat Clinton and his faction by reason. The only hope was to use momentum from other states to bring New York into the fold. He kept in close contact with Madison, leaving nothing to chance.

"We think here that the situation of your State is critical," he wrote on May 19. "Let me know what you now think of it. I believe you meet nearly at the time we do."

He asked Madison to send word by express rider the moment things were decided. The stakes could not be higher. Without ratification, the nation could devolve into civil war.

Things looked grim in New York, despite Alexander's best efforts. He was one of the state's delegates, and his side was in the minority. Just nineteen federalists favored ratification. Clinton and his cronies had forty-six antifederalists.

New York's convention began June 17 in Poughkeepsie. Alexander traveled there with John Jay and Robert Livingston, cheered on by the city's merchants, who favored ratification and the way it would improve their business prospects. Once he arrived in Poughkeepsie, though, he was on hostile turf.

"Our adversaries greatly outnumber us," he wrote to Madison on June 19.

Clinton was elected chairman of the convention, which took place in the city's courthouse. Each clause of the Constitution would be debated point by point, as had happened during the Constitutional Convention. This rule was Alexander's doing, and it was a clever gambit meant to buy enough time for results from Virginia to come in.

Things looked far from certain in the South. "I am very sorry to find by your letter of the 13th that your prospects are so critical," Alexander wrote Madison on June 25. "Our chance of success here is infinitely slender, and none at all if you go wrong."

As New York's convention progressed, Alexander spoke dozens of times, once at such length that he had to sit down midspeech. That was on June 20. The next day, New Hampshire became the ninth state to ratify. The Constitution was now the governing document of the nation. But the fates of New York and Virginia still hung in the balance. Either could secede from the union.

The Clintonians shifted their tactics. They could not defeat the Constitution. But they could tie it up in strings—anything to preserve their power as a state.

The next week, on June 28, Alexander's own words from the Constitutional Convention were used against him as he was trying to show how the states' power would check federal overreach. John Lansing, who'd been there as one of New York's three delegates, accused Alexander of talking out of both sides of his mouth when it came to the viability of the states' power.

Alexander was incensed. The accusation was "improper and uncandid."

Lansing fired back and asked Robert Yates, the third delegate, to show the notes he'd taken of the secret proceedings as proof. Yates pulled them out. The crowd erupted, and Clinton had to call them to order before they adjourned for the day.

When they met again on Monday, June 30, the debate continued—much in the way of a courtroom cross-examination, with both Alexander and Jay grilling Yates, who never did read his notes. Two days passed, and a rider galloped to the courthouse with a letter for Alexander. It was from James Madison: Virginia had ratified the Constitution. They'd done it! Madison had triumphed!

Reinvigorated, Alexander turned up the heat on New York until, one by one, the antifederalists came around. Tempers flared like rockets. On July 4, a fight broke out in Albany. A group of antifederalists attacked a larger group of federalists. One person was killed and eighteen wounded.

Others were ready to celebrate. On July 23, giddy New York City residents anticipating victory staged a rally. Five thousand merchants and tradesmen paraded down Broadway in the rain. Mixed in with the floats and banners were a ten-foot-long loaf of bread, a three-hundred-gallon barrel of ale, and old friends of Alexander Hamilton, including Robert Troup and Nicholas Cruger, who'd dressed as a farmer with a half-dozen oxen.

The best of all, though, was a twenty-seven-foot miniature frigate christened the *Federal Ship Hamilton*. It rolled through town on hidden wheels. A cart followed, carrying a banner proclaiming a message in rhyme as cannons blasted the end of the Articles of Confederation and the birth of the new Constitution:

BEHOLD THE FEDERAL SHIP OF FAME,

THE HAMILTON WE CALL HER NAME;

TO EVERY CRAFT SHE GIVES EMPLOY,

SURE CARTMEN HAVE THEIR SHARE OF JOY.

The vote on July 26 was close, the closest in the nation, at thirty to twenty-seven. Alexander, against all odds, had won.

His next task, undertaken in September, was less daunting if no less vital. He had to persuade George Washington to do the last thing he wanted to do: leave his beloved farm behind and become the nation's first president.

ABOVE: *"BEHOLD THE FEDERAL SHIP OF FAME, THE HAMILTON WE CALL HER NAME!"*

CHAPTER NINE

MR. SECRETARY

IT WOULDN'T DO ANY GOOD to set up a system of government without the right man leading the nation. Washington had managed to lead an unprepared, overmatched army to victory despite obstacles flying at him from every direction; he could do the same with the nation. No other man could.

Alexander sent him a copy of both volumes of *The Federalist*, along with a nudging letter. "I take it for granted, Sir, you have concluded to comply with what will no doubt be the general call of your country in relation to the new government."

Washington wrote back. The work of Publius—he knew who the three authors were—would be a classic, he predicted, "because in it are candidly discussed the principles of freedom & the topics of government, which will be always interesting to mankind so long as they shall be connected in Civil Society."

At the end of his letter, he addressed the awkward matter of his candidacy. For one thing, people might not want him to be president. For another, he needed to wait for more information to know whether it was the right thing. He also wasn't sure he had the ambition for the job.

"I would not wish to conceal my prevailing sentiment from you," Washington wrote. "For you know me well enough, my good Sir, to be persuaded that I am not guilty of affectation, when I tell you, it is my great and sole desire to live and die, in peace and retirement, on my own farm."

Alexander, not a slow thinker like Washington, replied immediately. Washington *needed* to answer this call to duty. The system set up by the Constitution *depended* on Washington's approval and leadership. If things went awry because the wrong man was in the office, people would blame the system and the men who'd created it. Only Washington could deliver the faith of the people and the necessary wisdom.

Washington sent an appreciative response a few days later. "I am particularly glad, in the present instance, you have dealt thus freely and like a friend. . . . I thought it best to maintain a guarded silence and to lack the *counsel* of my best friends."

Washington remained humble but disclosed he would take the job for the good of the public, and then he would retire to his steady dream: "to pass an unclouded evening, after the stormy day of life, in the bosom of domestic tranquility."

Modest as he was, Washington was no fool. If he was the key to bringing the Constitution to life, then those who opposed the Constitution would prefer a president who'd kill it. He anticipated challenging days ahead and signed the letter "with sentiments of sincere regard and esteem."

The years had bent their bond. But they had not broken it.

ONCE THE GENERAL HAD BEEN PERSUADED TO run, Alexander left nothing to chance. If any other man should get the votes, Alexander predicted mayhem, and he wasn't shy about saying so.

Alexander saw a defect in the new Constitution, and he worried that even as admired as Washington was, it would lead to the inadvertent election of antifederalist John Adams. Under the Constitution, the person who got the most votes in the Electoral College would be president, and the runner-up, vice president. If federalists and antifederalists were divided about Washington but agreed on Adams, Adams would get the most votes and the top job. This must not happen.

Alexander kept tabs on who the electors were and whom they were leaning toward. He concluded it would be prudent to siphon away a few of Adams's votes, so he engaged in back-room politicking. In January 1789, he wrote to James Wilson, one of the few men who'd signed both the Declaration and Constitution, as well as friends in Connecticut, New Jersey, and Pennsylvania. He wanted a few people to throw away their votes, lowering Adams's count.

"Your advices from the South will serve you as the best guide; but for God's sake let not our zeal for a secondary object defeat or endanger a first."

Alexander also wanted Clinton's long reign as governor to end. So he campaigned for Robert Yates. Yes, the man had been an albatross around Alexander's neck during New York's ratifying convention, but he'd come around after the Constitution was ratified. Alexander's attempts to muck with state politics backfired. Clinton was reelected. Then he dismantled the coalition Alexander was trying to build by appointing a close friend of Yates's to the attorney general spot. That man was none other than Alexander's courtroom rival Aaron Burr.

IN THE FIRST U.S. PRESIDENTIAL ELECTION, ON
February 4, 1789, electors from ten states cast ballots. New
York hadn't put together its group, and North Carolina and
Rhode Island still hadn't ratified the Constitution. The ballots were to be unsealed and counted in March, but snowy
weather in New York meant that not enough congressmen
and senators could get to the capital until April 6.

The ballots were unsealed and tallied then, and the results
were stunning: every single elector had cast one of his two
ballots for George Washington. John Adams came in second
place with thirty-four votes. John Jay came in third place
with nine votes.

Washington, reluctant even with a unanimous victory,
traveled from Virginia to New York, where he was met by
Alexander's political enemy Governor Clinton. They led a
parade of soldiers and merchants through the city. The inauguration ceremony took place on the second-floor balcony of

ABOVE: *WASHINGTON WAS INAUGURATED ON THE BALCONY OF
FEDERAL HALL, ON WALL STREET.*

Federal Hall, a grand brick building with four stone columns holding up a pediment with an eagle. He wore a brown suit made of homespun cloth—to send a distinctly American message. The organizers, still finding their way, had forgotten a Bible, so Washington swore his oath on a thick and elegant

ABOVE: *ORGANIZERS BORROWED A BIBLE FROM THE NEARBY MASONIC LODGE FOR THE CEREMONY.*

one borrowed from a nearby Masonic lodge. His hands shook as he delivered an address, written by Madison, to both the House of Representatives and the Senate.

Straightaway, Washington turned to Alexander for advice on how to manage the public aspects of the presidency. Taking cues from European protocol, Alexander specified how often Washington should receive visitors and for how long. He said the president should accept no invitations, and he should throw parties a few times a year on important anniversaries of the Revolutionary War. He gave Washington permission to keep his weekly get-togethers small and brief.

THE STALWART WASHINGTON BORE THE PAIN.

The goal wasn't just keeping Washington's nerves intact. It was to make sure he didn't seem to show favoritism. Alexander wanted Washington to be happy *and* successful as he spun a new government from nothing. The nation wasn't just a glossy weave of abstract ideas. It would be durable: woven from tiny details into a fabric unlike anything the world had ever seen.

Not every detail was as small as the politics of a home-spun suit or the frequency and duration of dinner parties. One of the larger details Washington had to work out was his cabinet. The makeup of it hadn't been specified in the Constitution.

Before Washington could officially round out his cabinet, though, he got sick. It was June. He lay in bed with a fever and a painful growth, caused by a bacterial infection, in his left thigh. A physician cut it out without anesthesia, and the stalwart Washington bore the pain. But he was perilously sick. Bedridden for six weeks, he could not sit up or attend the public Fourth of July celebration. But he'd already quietly offered Alexander a position in the cabinet as the nation's first Treasury secretary. Thomas Jefferson would be secretary of state, and Henry Knox would be secretary of war.

Other men wanted the Treasury job, but Alexander came with a recommendation from Robert Morris, who had been in charge of finance during the Revolution.

Alexander gleefully accepted the challenge, though the $3,500 salary was far less than he made as a lawyer, and he and Eliza were supporting five children. Alexander turned his law practice over to Robert Troup. In early September, Washington officially established the Treasury Department, and on September 11, 1789, he appointed Alexander its head. The Senate confirmed the appointment immediately, and on the next day—a Saturday—Alexander set to work dragging the United States from the deep financial hole it had slid into. He arranged for a $50,000 loan from the bank he'd helped found in New York, then another the next day from the Bank of North America.

Congress passed a resolution on September 21, 1789, requesting that Alexander provide a full report on the nation's financial state. They wanted the details in less than four months. In his *Report Relative to a Provision for the Support of Public Credit* on January 9, 1790, he revealed in great detail what the country owed for its liberty: $79 million. Some money was owed to other countries, and some to U.S. citizens. The states' portion of the debt was $25 million; the rest belonged to the federal government. His report addressed how the debt would be paid and how the country would be able to take on additional debt in the future.

Alexander had a more sophisticated understanding of debt than most people at the time, who viewed it as an evil. The truth was, debt could sometimes be a useful and even necessary tool for a nation. The Revolutionary War was an example (as was the French and Indian War earlier). The Continental Congress had had no means of paying for the supplies, weapons, clothing, food, and salaries the war demanded, but they'd bet on the future fortunes of the nation that they would. There were also other reasons to go into debt. Without liquid capital—money that can be spent—an economy can't grow to its full potential. This is true for individuals and for governments, merchants, and property owners. Strategic debt can revive a struggling economy.

When governments can borrow at a reasonable interest rate and generate the tax revenue to pay off the principal and interest of the loan, that activity boosts the economy in many ways. What's more, states that pay their debts—just like people—earn the trust of their partners. Liberty depends on the integrity and security of property—this principle was utterly clear to Alexander.

Americans had been burned when it came to debt from the U.S. government, including soldiers who had been paid in government bonds. After the war, no one was sure if these IOU slips would be paid. Some soldiers, desperate for money, had even sold them for a fraction of their stated value. Others wagered that selling low was better than waiting for money that might never come. Speculators were happy to risk a few cents on the dollar for potential huge payout later.

Guaranteeing the value of those bonds would give people trust in the government and keep their value steady. There was one tricky aspect of this: what to do about the veterans who'd already sold theirs. Weren't they owed something from the nation they'd fought to build?

Alexander argued against compensating veterans. For one thing, it would be nearly impossible to track down every man who'd sold his bonds to speculators, determine the rate, and make up the difference. What's more, the ones who had sold out of desperation had chosen to bet against their own government. The speculators hadn't. Therefore, people who'd taken the risk deserved the rewards. This argument became the keystone of the securities market in the United States. The risk is on the buyers and sellers to manage their choices without government interference.

LIBERTY DEPENDS ON THE INTEGRITY AND SECURITY OF PROPERTY.

Alexander made another controversial argument: the federal government should take responsibility for debt incurred by individual states, even when some states had already repaid their portion. He had two reasons: The Constitution permitted only the federal government to collect duties on imported goods, a major source of revenue. Also, one repayment scheme was better than as many as thirteen separate ones.

His plan proposed taking out a $12 million loan in the form of government securities to repay the wartime debt and interest. People who bought the securities could choose among several payment plans, and the interest rate would be favorable compared to rates in Europe.

As for paying back the debt, revenue had to be generated somehow, both for past and future interest. The first step was to establish a system for taxing imports. To manage this, he proposed a national customs service, which would receive duties from goods brought into the country from the nations exporting them.

ALEXANDER WAS NERVOUS ABOUT HIS REPORT.

For revenue generated from American citizens, Alexander flagged items like tea, coffee, and alcohol. These might be luxuries, but people liked to indulge, so he anticipated it would be a relatively stable source of funds. And if people stopped drinking as much? All the better for their health.

Alexander was nervous about his report. The night before it was read to Congress, he wrote to Angelica. He'd seen Eliza's sister again during Washington's inauguration, but she had to return to England to take care of her children, and he missed her. They'd exchanged several letters in the interim, flirting wildly with each other as always. But this note was largely about his anxiety.

"Tomorrow I open the budget & you may imagine that today I am very busy and not a little anxious. I could not however let the Packet sail without giving you a proof, that no degree of occupation can make me forget you."

His fears were well placed. Some despised his report and its plans. What took him utterly by surprise, though, was the vehemence of opposition from his friend Madison, who'd supported his nomination as Treasury secretary. Yes, they'd had disagreements after their work together on *The Federalist*. Take the necessity of the Bill of Rights, for example. Alexander hadn't thought the ten amendments to the Constitution were necessary, but Madison was adamant about protecting individual liberties in the face of a powerful federal government. Even so, the last thing Alexander expected was that this difference would widen into a chasm.

Madison rolled out the verbal artillery against Alexander's plan with the IOUs on February 11, 1790. Madison thought speculators who'd bought the now-valuable public debt weren't morally entitled to the profits. It was meant for the original holders, who'd only sold out of desperation. What's more, he viewed public debt not as the blessing Alexander described, but as a curse.

Madison's argument didn't win the day, but the loss of the alliance crushed Alexander. They'd worked hard, inspired brilliance in each other, and jointly written a political masterpiece. There had been such warmth in their letters. Not as much as in the ones he'd exchanged with Ned Stevens, Lafayette, and especially John Laurens. But still the bond was there. He'd cherished it. And then it vanished.

Growing in its place was something hard and bitter, a division between federalists and antifederalists, echoed in the ever-widening rift between the North and South. The North would follow Alexander's plan and diversify its economy with manufacturing, banks, stocks, and bonds, while the

South would continue to rely on the labor of enslaved people. The great irony was that the South and its antifederalists claimed their path was the one of liberty.

The next big fight was whether the federal government would assume the states' individual debts. States that had paid their debts opposed assumption. Alexander and Washington favored it. After all, every state benefited from the war, and some had suffered more than others. By spring, Washington was ill again, and Alexander had to campaign for assumption on his own. He had a rough go of it, and on April 12, the House rejected it by a two-vote margin.

It spelled disaster. What's more, Alexander's political foes turned on him in pointed ways, especially Aedanus Burke, a silver-haired, eagle-nosed representative from John Laurens's state of South Carolina. Burke had been offended back in July when Alexander gave a eulogy for Nathanael Greene, who'd died on his Georgia plantation in 1786.

Alexander had called Greene "a general without an army—aided or rather embarrassed by small fugitive bodies of volunteer militia, the mimicry of soldiership!" The line was meant to highlight what Greene had accomplished with an ill-equipped militia against well-trained professional soldiers. It mortified Burke.

He stewed over this characterization and unleashed it on Alexander in March on the floor of the House. He called Alexander a liar, a blow to his always vulnerable honor. When Alexander heard about Burke's charge, he penned the first salvo of a duel, telling Burke he'd misinterpreted the eulogy.

Burke fired off a nearly immediate reply. "The attack which I conceived you made on the southern Militia, was, in my opinion a most unprovoked and cruel one. . . . You may

Aedanus Burke

have forgot it, but some of your Friends and all your acquaintances have not forgot it. . . . Thus I have very candidly, in this disagreeable business explained my feelings and motives." His last line was ominous, saying that men "of Sensibility and honor" would approve of his conduct.

That word choice was provocative. More letters were exchanged in accordance with the rules for affairs of honor. Resolving the matter without bloodshed required intervention from several congressmen. And in it, Alexander revealed

ABOVE: *AEDANUS BURKE ACCUSED ALEXANDER OF MAKING A CRUEL ATTACK ON SOUTHERN SOLDIERS.*

his fatal flaw: a willingness to throw away everything he had—his wife, his home, his children, his ascending career, and even his own life—for the sake of his reputation.

He wasn't just tempting death. He was actively inviting it to visit. It was romantic. It was daring. But it did nothing to solve the pressing problem at hand: how to get support for a federal assumption of the states' debt.

Not far from Alexander's residence at 57 Wall Street, Thomas Jefferson had rented a home of his own once he'd returned from Paris to become secretary of state. Accompanied by his enslaved chef, James Hemings, who'd had culinary training in Paris, Jefferson had moved to New York in March 1790, after Alexander's initial report was delivered. Like Madison, Jefferson hated it and the idea of assumption. But this issue wasn't the only big one stalled in Congress. The other: where the federal government should have its permanent home.

ALEXANDER LOOKED "SOMBRE, HAGGARD, AND DEJECTED BEYOND COMPARISON."

Alexander wanted New York, the temporary home of Congress, to have the honor. Then, like London and Paris, New York would be both a financial and political hub. Southerners like Jefferson and Madison disagreed. Not only was New York far from their states, it was also distinctly urban—the opposite of the agricultural South. Congress was stymied.

By June, it looked as though the plan for assumption was doomed as well.

Alexander, frustrated to the point of wanting to quit, ran into Jefferson outside Washington's office. In his journal, Jefferson wrote that Alexander looked "sombre, haggard, and dejected beyond comparison." Sensing an opportunity, Jefferson invited him to a dinner at his house to talk it over with Madison.

At the Sunday, June 20, dinner, which also included Tench Coxe from the Treasury, it became clear that Madison and Jefferson were in the mood to make a deal to wrap up the many conversations they'd had on the topic. If Alexander would agree to make a few changes to his debt plan *and* place the nation's capital in the South, they would agree to drum up votes on behalf of assumption.

The dining-room deal was struck, and by the end of summer, the votes had been cast. The federal government would assume the debt, ensuring the enactment of Alexander's vision for the nation's finances. And the capital would be in the South, on the banks of the Potomac and Anacostia Rivers. Land that had been taken from the Algonquian-speaking Nacotchtank tribe after they'd been decimated by European diseases would now be given up by Maryland and Virginia. It would take years to design and

ABOVE: *JEFFERSON AND ALEXANDER MADE THE DEAL THAT TURNED WASHINGTON, D.C., INTO THE NATION'S CAPITAL IN A HOUSE ON MAIDEN LANE IN NEW YORK.*

build the new capital. In the interim, the government would leave New York and move to Philadelphia.

The summer of 1790 was busy. Not only did Alexander work out the compromise with Jefferson and Madison, but he also noticed that tax collectors in the Customs Department were bringing in suspiciously low revenues. Based on his experience as a shipping clerk, he suspected smugglers.

MADISON AND JEFFERSON HATED THE PROPOSAL.

In response, Congress passed the Tariff Act, which established a ten-ship fleet of revenue cutters, working under the Treasury Department to enforce import duties. (Alexander had found time the year before to research ships, their construction, and the makeup and salary requirements of their crews; the fleet was the forerunner of the U.S. Coast Guard.) As head of the Treasury, he was also managing a growing system of lighthouses, beacons, buoys, and piers, dealing with employees who thought they weren't getting paid enough, and continuing to wrestle the constitutional intricacies of paying soldiers for their service in the war.

By the end of that year, however, his work was beginning to pay off. Not only had Alexander saved the nation from bankruptcy, but the government had generated a revenue surplus. This didn't mean he could let up; the next step was to begin repaying the debt of the states, which would require direct taxation on whiskey.

What's more, there were complications with England and France. Although France had been an ally during the war, the trade terms with England were better for America, and this commerce brought in three-quarters of the Treasury Department's revenue. France also was in the midst of a revolution of its own, which meant it was no longer the same government that had been allied with the states.

Alexander didn't let up for a minute, and on December 15, he made his most controversial proposal yet: to found a Bank of the United States. The Constitution said nothing about banks, and this would become an issue with his opponents. But the country needed one. The nation's finances were so haphazard that some debt payments from the states had been made in Spanish dollars and tobacco receipts.

He'd been pondering a national bank for years. It would do much for the nation. Not only would a bank give America a uniform currency, but it would also provide the credit that businesses needed to grow. The government could take loans and hold deposits, too.

He'd locate it in Philadelphia, a good choice because it was a big city with lots of business activity. And he'd need $10 million to get the wagon rolling, $8 million of which would come from private investors, with the last $2 million being the government's share. He'd long thought a mix of public and private funding made sense.

Madison and Jefferson hated the proposal, which passed in the House of Representatives anyway in February 1791. The vote was lopsided, with the urban North heavily in favor and the agricultural South staunchly opposed. Jefferson even sniped to Madison that the idea was treasonous—essentially saying anybody who so much as worked as a bank teller should be put to death for it.

The crux of their objections: it was unconstitutional for the nation to form a bank because the Constitution hadn't given the federal government this power explicitly. Madison hadn't always thought this way. In fact, *Federalist* No. 44, which he wrote, said, "No axiom is more clearly established in law, or in reason, than wherever the end is required, the means are authorised; wherever a general power to do a thing is given, every particular power for doing it, is included."

There wouldn't be any more dinner parties at Jefferson's house. Madison and Jefferson were united in bitter rivalry with Alexander. Madison wanted Washington to use the presidential veto power for the first time. Washington gathered opinions from Jefferson and his attorney general, Edmund Randolph, the author of the Virginia plan. They opposed the national bank.

When Washington asked Alexander for his opinion of Jefferson's and Randolph's arguments, Alexander rubbed his hands together, rolled up his sleeves, and went to work.

In a matter of days, he'd written a short book on the topic, staying up all night to meet the president's deadline. Eliza worked through the wee hours with him, copying his writing. When he walked out the door the next morning, he delivered the document to Washington. He'd demolished Jefferson's and Randolph's arguments, and Washington signed the bill.

With that, Alexander Hamilton had created a bank.

In the meantime, he'd also written a *Report on the Establishment of a Mint* that contained a plan for creating and managing coins of varying denominations that would be useful and accessible to the rich and to the poor. By July 1791, the public had an opportunity to buy stock in Alexander's bank. The venture was wildly successful, selling out much more quickly than the week he'd anticipated. Madison and

Jefferson muttered about a den of corruption, a place where "stock-jobbers" gambled their morality away instead of putting in an honest day's work. So feverish was the buying and selling of bank stock scrip that in August, prices expanded into a bubble. Alexander instinctively had the government buy up some shares to ease the pain of the pop.

AROUND THE SAME TIME, ANOTHER MATTER OF money—this time, a pocketful of bills—would occupy Alexander's time. Like his rivalry with Jefferson and Madison, it would grow to ruinous proportions.

It all started with a knock on the door at his home in Philadelphia.

A woman stood before him. She had dark eyes and pale skin and a cloud of curls around her heart-shaped face. She was young. She was beautiful. She was in trouble. Alexander couldn't resist her. He told her that she'd come at a difficult time for him—Eliza and the children were still home—but that he'd visit her that night, bringing a small supply of money.

Much to his regret, he did.

CHAPTER TEN

GENIUS

and

FOOL

THE WOMAN AT THE DOOR was young, just twenty-three. She said her husband had abused her and left her for another woman, and she didn't have the money to return to New York. She knew, of course, that Alexander was a New Yorker. Perhaps he could help?

Alexander wanted to be of service ever so badly. His heart was no match for a woman in need. His mother had been treated badly by her first husband and then abandoned by Alexander's father, after all. Men were meant to protect women. Honor—or something that felt like it—demanded it.

That night, he stashed money in his pocket and walked less than a quarter of a mile to her house at 154 South Fourth Street. He was shown upstairs, where Maria met him and led him into a bedroom. He fished the money out of his pocket. They chatted, and it became apparent to him quickly that she would be consoled by something a bit warmer than cash.

And so began an affair. He met with Maria Reynolds frequently. He even moved these trysts to his own house once Eliza and the children had traveled to Albany for the summer.

Little James, his three-year-old, was sick, and Alexander played up his concern in a letter to his wife. As usual, he had lots of medical advice for Eliza, urging her to keep flannel next to James's skin. She should feed him barley water with a dash of brandy and prevent him from eating any fruit whatsoever. What's more, he should drink water that had been boiled in an iron pot.

"I hope he will have had some rhubarb or antimonial wine," Alexander wrote. "Paregoric at night in moderation will do him good & a little bark will not do him harm."

Most important, she should stay away for a while. For her health, of course.

Meanwhile, he'd stay in Philadelphia. "I am so anxious for a perfect restoration of your health that I am willing to make a great sacrifice for it."

He wrote letter after letter urging her to stay away for the sake of her health. He even sent one to his son Philip, suggesting he delay visiting until school holidays, even though Alexander had promised to welcome the boy: "A promise must never be broken. . . . But it has occurred to me that the Christmas holidays are near at hand, and I suppose your school will then break up for some days and give you an opportunity of coming to stay with us for a longer time than if you should come on Saturday."

The affair didn't end when Maria told Alexander her husband wanted to reconcile. Meanwhile, she let Alexander know her husband had important information about a scoundrel in the Treasury Department. Alexander, wary, sent for James Reynolds. When Reynolds came to Alexander's office, he pretended to be reluctant to speak of corruption. But he rather quickly named William Duer as the rascal.

Duer was an old friend who'd married Alexander's former crush Kitty Livingston. He'd written *Federalist* essays that weren't up to snuff. He had in fact traded wildly in securities, but it was *after* he'd left the Treasury Department, and Alexander had already scolded him for it. A few months later, Duer had managed to ruin himself financially and go to jail,

William Duer

and Alexander refused to pull strings on his behalf, so adamant was he about the integrity of his department. Duer had been a disaster for Alexander, and more so for himself.

Still, to keep relations good with the husband of his mistress, Alexander pretended to care about the irrelevant disclosures. Not long afterward, Reynolds asked Alexander for a job in the Treasury Department. Much as Alexander wanted to keep the peace on account of his situation with Maria, he deflected Reynolds's request.

ABOVE: *WILLIAM DUER PROVED TO BE A DISASTROUS FRIEND TO ALEXANDER.*

As time passed, Alexander wanted out of this mess. But Maria held on. By December, she sent him letter after hysterical letter, sometimes using her maid to deliver them. Her heart was ready to "Burst with Greef," she wrote. "I can neither Eate or sleep I have Been on the point of doing the moast horrid acts at I shuder to think where I might been what will Become of me."

Her writing, atrocious as it was, tugged at his heartstrings. She loved him, or seemed to, and this pleased his vanity. Some

ABOVE: *ALEXANDER AND HIS LOVER HAD THEIR AFFAIR JUST STEPS FROM INDEPENDENCE HALL IN PHILADELPHIA.*

part of him always remained the boy abandoned by his father, the one who needed to prove himself in his adopted country, the one who was so often treated as an outsider. That part of him craved being loved. What's more, he thought it better to let her down easy than break it off all at once.

Disaster struck on December 15, not long after he'd presented a groundbreaking *Report on the Subject of Manufactures* to Congress. Maria let him know that they'd been discovered by her husband. Worse, he was going to tell Eliza.

"Oh my God I feel more for you than myself and wish I had never been born to give you so mutch unhappisness do not rite to him no not a Line but come here soon do not send or leave any thing in his power," she wrote.

The same day, Reynolds sent a letter of his own. He told Alexander that Maria had been weeping, and curious about the reason, he'd watched her hand a letter to a man on Market Street. Reynolds followed that man to Alexander's door. Alexander, not keen to admit guilt if he didn't have to, invited him to visit at the office.

Reynolds was cagey, and Alexander smelled a plot. He made an offer to help Reynolds find a job as best as he could. This mollified Reynolds, but only for a couple of days. That's when another letter arrived. "I find the wife always weeping and praying that I wont leve her. And its all on your account. for if you had not seekd for her Ruin it would not have happined."

The gist of Reynolds's letter was that Alexander had seduced Maria, made her fall in love with him, stolen her from Reynolds, and done him harm.

Alexander, fearing he was the subject of a most serious plot, visited Reynolds and demanded to know what the man really wanted. Two days later, Reynolds's answer came. He'd feel much better if Alexander gave him $1,000. Reynolds would take the money and his daughter, and leave Maria for Alexander.

Alexander, short on funds, had to pay Reynolds in two installments, the first, of $600 on December 22, and the second on January 3, 1792.

Reynolds didn't leave town, though. Two weeks after Alexander had paid the second lump, he received yet another letter, this one inviting him to start visiting Maria again—as a friend. Alexander didn't accept right away. Then Maria started begging.

"I have kept my Bed those tow dayes and now rise from My pillow wich your Neglect has filled with the sharpest thorns. . . . Let me Intreat you If you wont Come to send me a Line oh my head I can rite no more do something to Ease My heart or Els I no not what I shall do for so I cannot live Commit this to the care of my maid be not offended I beg."

James Reynolds followed two months later with a letter of his own, begging Alexander to visit, because his visits kept her cheerful. Reynolds mentioned he had no desire to cause Alexander's family pain, a doubtful claim. Maria, meanwhile, wrote again and again. Her bosom was tortured and she couldn't *believe* Alexander wasn't visiting. "If my dear freend has the Least Esteeme for the unhappy Maria whos grateest fault is Loveing him he will come as soon as he shall get this and till that time My breast will be the seate of pain and woe."

P.S., she wrote, with no subtlety whatsoever: her husband would be away that evening.

Meanwhile, James Reynolds hit Alexander up for more

money. For months, the couple continued to badger Alexander for money and visits, essentially blackmailing him, else they'd expose the affair.

Eventually, Alexander stopped paying Reynolds. The situation reeked of a setup. And it may well have been. Back in the days of the Constitutional Convention, someone had sent a letter suggesting that the delegates were conspiring to bring King George's second son to rule the United States. Alexander's political enemies consistently accused him of being a closet monarch, and that letter was no doubt meant to smear him in particular.

Its author? James Reynolds.

MEANWHILE, ALEXANDER'S CONTROVERSIAL whiskey tax had taken effect around the time Maria Reynolds first came to call. As he expected, it wasn't popular. But it was the government's best bet for revenue because it wasn't a direct tax on citizens. Instead, it taxed the producers of alcohol, who could pass the burden of the fees down the line by charging consumers a bit more.

Farmers didn't go for this, particularly the ones on the frontier who made whiskey from their surplus corn. They were short on actual money (a problem Alexander was also trying to solve), so they sometimes used whiskey as literal liquid currency. Federal taxes got in the way. What's more, frontier prices were lower, so the tax represented a greater portion of the product and felt unfair.

A rebellion began brewing.

And then there was his *Report on the Subject of Manufacturers*. He'd presented this in December 1791, as things with Maria were unraveling spectacularly. The report landed with a thud. This was the final major program he devised as Treasury secretary. He'd prevailed with his first two reports: the federal assumption of state debts and the creation of the Bank of the United States. His political foes, especially Jefferson and Madison, were itching to hand him a defeat.

The plan envisioned a manufacturing base that could compete with England's. This would diversify the American economy and leave the country less dependent on British imports. It wasn't a trivial matter. It was necessary. American soldiers had gone shoeless during the war because of a lack of American manufacturing—something Jefferson and Madison hadn't witnessed from their distant perches safe from combat.

The plan called for industries that produced necessities such as coal, wool, and cotton to be subsidized. It lowered tariffs on some imports used as raw materials. And it imposed import tariffs to give American manufacturers an edge against overseas competition, as well as government subsidies designed to boost production.

Alexander challenged Jefferson's vision of an agrarian economy, which depended on the labor of enslaved people. "It has been maintained, that Agriculture is, not only, the most productive, but the only productive species of industry. The reality of this suggestion . . . has, however, not been verified by any accurate detail of facts and calculations," he wrote.

What's more, manufacturing and agriculture weren't competitors. They were allies in creating a stronger national economy. Each segment would bolster the other.

No matter how forward-thinking his argument was, elected officials from slave states bristled. The idea of reorienting an economy away from slavery felt too threatening. Plus, the way speculation had roiled the economy left some people wary of more from Alexander.

Madison and Jefferson sharpened their rhetorical knives. For Madison, Alexander's influence from the executive branch over the legislature was eroding the separation of powers established in the Constitution. Jefferson also disliked the bounties for certain industries the report called for. He thought these subsidies were ripe for abuse.

Newspapers got into the fray. A Republican Party paper, the *National Gazette*, printed editorials by Madison that pummeled Alexander.

Madison also tried to edit some technical aspects of a speech of Washington's so that it would sound as though Washington supported Jefferson's views on the makeup of coins, and not Alexander's. The editing was subtle enough that Washington wasn't even aware until Alexander pointed it out to him.

Jefferson tried behind the scenes to turn Washington against Alexander using so-called evidence that Alexander was a monarchist. Jefferson hadn't been in Washington's family during the war, though, and couldn't fully appreciate the faith the president had in Alexander. Washington never wavered.

By May 1792, despite the support of Washington, Alexander's burdens felt heavy. The secret Reynolds business clotted his conscience, and he felt under siege from Jefferson and Madison. He never would have taken the Treasury job in the first place had he known Madison would not only abandon their partnership but set it ablaze with increasingly strident rhetoric.

Madison and Jefferson weren't Alexander's only political enemies. When political chatter suggested John Adams might lose the vice presidency, Aaron Burr's name came up as someone Jefferson might back for the job. Alexander couldn't stomach that prospect, especially after Burr had endorsed another Clinton governorship, so he started writing friends confidential letters eviscerating Burr. Alexander considered it a "religious duty" to oppose Burr's career.

One letter read, "As a public man he is one of the worst sort—a friend to nothing but as it suits his interest and ambition. . . . In a word, if we have an embryo-Cæsar in the United States 'tis Burr."

It was a restless, unhappy time for Alexander, and there was unrest and misery in the world as well. In August 1792, just as Eliza gave birth to a baby boy, radical French revolutionaries—the sort of mob Alexander loathed and feared—had ordered Lafayette's arrest. He fled France but was captured in Austria and thrown into a brutal prison.

Then, in mid-November, Reynolds and an associate were arrested on charges they'd defrauded the U.S. government of $400. It wasn't Reynolds's first run-in with the law. He'd been charged earlier in connection with speculating on the IOUs but was never convicted. This time, though, he'd had a friend perjure himself, and he got caught, along with a man named Jacob Clingman, who'd worked for Congressman Frederick Muhlenberg.

Oliver Wolcott Jr., the comptroller of Alexander's Treasury Department, brought the charges. As he did, Reynolds revealed he had information that could damage someone in the Treasury. Wolcott, having no idea what Reynolds was getting at, asked Alexander for advice. Though he knew the stakes, Alexander didn't hesitate: Reynolds should be held until the charge was investigated.

In a meeting on December 13, 1792, with Alexander, Muhlenberg, and Aaron Burr, Wolcott agreed to drop the charges if Clingman and Reynolds surrendered the list of names they'd used for their crimes, paid back the money, and turned over the person who'd given them the list in the first place.

If Alexander thought he'd dodged a bullet with this tidy resolution, he was wrong. Clingman had continued to pester Muhlenberg with the promise of scandalous information about someone in the Treasury. Finally, Muhlenberg consented to listen.

On December 15, the anniversary of Alexander's report on America's future as a manufacturing country, three congressmen presented themselves at his office: Muhlenberg, Abraham Venable, and James Monroe. The men were concerned about what seemed to be an improper connection between Alexander and James Reynolds.

When Alexander objected to a suggestion he'd violated the public trust, the men backpedaled. It wasn't that they thought he was guilty of such things. They wanted to let him know, though, that this information had come to them unsolicited. They'd even thought about telling President Washington, but they wanted to give Alexander a chance to explain first. This wasn't personal; it was their duty.

The men presented notes gathered while interviewing Reynolds, Clingman, and Maria. Alexander admitted he'd written them in disguised handwriting. But the situation wasn't what they thought. He hadn't committed *financial* impropriety, and he had proof of this at home.

They agreed to meet him there that evening along with Oliver Wolcott. When the men came to call, Alexander confessed the truth: He'd never engaged in speculation of any sort. He'd had an adulterous affair with Maria Reynolds.

At that mortifying disclosure, the men told him they'd heard enough. Any more detail would be unnecessary. But Alexander wanted to make an exhaustive case for himself, so he told them everything. After he concluded, all three men indicated that they understood the situation and believed him, even if Monroe acted coldly.

HE'D HAD AN ADULTEROUS AFFAIR WITH MARIA REYNOLDS.

Alexander hoped the thorough confession would be the last of this sordid business. He didn't realize Monroe had sent a copy of the documents to "a Friend in Virginia." That friend was Thomas Jefferson, who had shared their contents with Madison and a few other key Republicans. The fuse was long, but it was lit.

That same month, Washington was elected unanimously for a second term, and Adams beat out George Clinton for vice president. Washington usually aligned politically with Alexander, but now in his second term, he wanted his two most important cabinet members to lay off each other. Neither Jefferson nor Alexander complied. Longtime grudges with others erupted, too.

A Maryland politician who'd worked for General Charles Lee accused Alexander of all sorts of things, nearly provoking a duel.

Alexander was also hit by requests from Representative William Branch Giles to account for foreign loans. Even as he dealt with the Reynolds business, he labored under the pressure of producing report after report to meet the heavy demands of Giles and the House. The effort jeopardized his health. But the reports didn't satisfy Jefferson, who asked Washington for an official inquiry into Alexander's financial dealings. Washington declined, so Jefferson took the matter back to Giles, who advanced nine resolutions, one of which demanded Alexander's removal from office.

After investigation, eight of nine were shot down by the House, foiling the Republican plot. The House on March 1, 1793, did find that Hamilton had too much power to shift money from accounts when juggling interest payments, but there wasn't a shred of proof that he'd benefited personally from his office. His enemies pressed on, and into darker corners. His friend Henry Lee wrote him a sympathetic letter in May lamenting all that Alexander was going through, ending on an ominous note: "Was I with you I would talk an hour with doors bolted & windows shut, as my heart is much afflicted by some whispers which I have heard."

Alexander knew exactly what this cryptic message meant. Word of the Reynolds affair was out. But he couldn't stop to fret about this looming disaster; the world at large had demands of its own.

The revolution in France had taken a disturbing turn. Louis XVI, who'd helped the Americans in their revolution, was beheaded to the thudding of drums on January 21, 1793, and then his head was held up as a souvenir by a young guard, who

gestured rudely as he brandished it. This sort of barbarism gave some people pause.

After France declared war on much of Europe, Alexander recommended American neutrality. The president agreed. Madison and Jefferson grumbled, as they thought the revolution was a continuation of the American one.

Washington received a direct challenge to neutrality in European wars when France's new ambassador, Edmond Charles Genêt, arrived in April 1793, aiming to bring Americans into

ABOVE: *LOUIS XVI, AN ALLY DURING THE AMERICAN REVOLUTION, LOST HIS HEAD.*

Edmond Charles Genêt

the war. He recruited men to fight in French militias. He tried to recruit merchant ships to become pirates and attack British vessels—the polite name for them was privateers because they had written permission from France to plunder. When Genêt finally traveled north to Philadelphia, he officially asked for the United States to suspend its neutral stance and provide food and supplies.

He had little regard for Washington's answer. Genêt thought the president was a ceremonial position, as it had

ABOVE: *GENÊT MADE ENEMIES IN THE UNITED STATES—AND THEN SOUGHT ASYLUM THERE.*

been under the Articles of Confederation. This was not so. And even as Jefferson and Madison sympathized with the French revolution, Genêt's behavior was so outrageous that Jefferson, who loved France, was repulsed. Washington asked Alexander and Jefferson for advice, and the men for once set aside their differences and helped the president draft an extremely long letter.

Genêt remained obstinate, and Washington's cabinet asked France to recall him on August 23, 1793, about three months after he'd arrived. Things in France became more extreme, though, and Genêt ended up seeking asylum in the United States instead of going home—and his chief defender in that pursuit was Alexander.

As this was happening, a massive outbreak of yellow fever rolled through the nation's capital. The deadly sickness, which spread from the wharves across the city, turned its victims' skin yellow, caused black vomit, and sent waves of fear through the city. The State House itself had been empty since a door-man dropped dead there. Many perished, more fled.

One victim told his brother, "You can not immagin the situation of this city. . . . They are a Dieing on our right hand & on our Left. . . . great are the number that are Calld to the grave, and numbered with the silent Dead."

No one was certain what caused it. Rotting coffee beans on the dock were a leading suspect, but all the same, people avoided one another for fear it was catching, and they dosed themselves with pungent garlic and vinegar, hoping to ward off the menace.

By September, the most cosmopolitan and diverse city in the United States was a ghost town. When ships arrived at the docks, there was no one to sign for the goods. The only people walking the sweltering, late-summer streets were those looking for a doctor, a nurse, a bleeder, or someone to help bury the dead.

As many as a hundred people died each day. In all, at least five thousand of the city's forty-five thousand citizens perished, and another seventeen thousand fled. Corpses putrefied rapidly in the heat, so it was urgent that they be buried swiftly. All day and night, the bereaved wailed in graveyards. The city's two thousand black residents—incorrectly assumed to be immune to the fever—provided a great deal of care for the dying.

The traditional treatment for the disease, and one offered by the acclaimed physician Benjamin Rush, was severe. He bled his patients and dosed them with mercury to purge their bowels. He even treated himself this way when he fell ill.

His method was controversial, and when Alexander and Eliza contracted the fever in early September, they evacuated their children to Albany and turned elsewhere for treatment. Their physician was none other than Alexander's best friend from childhood, his lookalike Ned Stevens, who'd become a prominent doctor in town.

Instead of bleeding the Hamiltons, who were violently ill, Stevens treated them with cold baths, spirits, and quinine, and he gave them nightly sedatives. They recovered in five days. Alexander, thrilled, sent a letter about his treatment to the city's College of Physicians. This touched off a round of political sniping. Rush wasn't just a doctor; he was a signer of the Declaration, he'd attended the Constitutional Convention, and he was a friend of Jefferson and Madison.

Jefferson relished Alexander's suffering. On September 8, he wrote Madison: "Hamilton is ill of the fever as is said. He

Benjamin Rush

had two physicians out at his house the night before last. His family think him in danger, & he puts himself so by his excessive alarm. . . . A man as timid as he is on the water, as timid on horseback, as timid in sickness, would be a phaenomenon if his courage of which he has the reputation in military occasions were genuine. His friends, who have not seen him, suspect it is only an autumnal fever he has."

It was a ridiculous posture. Not only had Alexander survived a near drowning during the war while he was being fired

ABOVE: *BENJAMIN RUSH DIDN'T LIKE ALEXANDER QUESTIONING HIS TREATMENT METHODS.*

upon, he'd fought valiantly on horseback several times, and he'd had his horse shot out from under him. This was in contrast with Jefferson's own truly timid wartime performance.

Alexander *had* been infected, as had his wife. What's more, the city was in misery and panic, and Jefferson knew it. Only a few days later, the mayor warned that Philadelphia was close to anarchy. It would have been a good time to rise above politics, but Jefferson wasn't capable, perhaps because he was frequently bothered by diarrhea and migraines.

To make matters worse, Alexander and Eliza had a hard time reuniting with their children in Albany. Alexander and Eliza missed them horribly. Once the Hamiltons were well, they packed their bags, taking care to wash any linens that had been used while they were infected. They also brought winter clothes that hadn't come into contact with germs. Nonetheless, people in other towns didn't want to admit travelers from Philadelphia, and the Hamiltons were shunned as if they were carriers of the plague.

Across the river from Albany on September 23, doctors gave them a clean bill of health. But after the Hamiltons took a ferry to the other side, people went berserk. Someone even started a rumor that Eliza's father had swabbed his mouth with vinegar after he'd kissed her, implying he was afraid she'd make him ill.

The townspeople wanted to be certain that Eliza's father had taken the precautions he'd promised before their visit, and they ran the Hamiltons through a wringer. They wanted Schuyler to pay for another medical examination. They wanted the Hamiltons to bring no baggage, burn their clothes, ride only in an open carriage without servants, and engage in no communication with anyone in Albany. To make sure this happened, the town also wanted the Schuylers to pay for a guard outside their house. Insulted to the bone, Alexander fired off a scathing letter to the mayor. It felt as though the world were conspiring against him. Some people had even spread rumors that he'd died.

IT FELT AS THOUGH THE WORLD WERE CONSPIRING AGAINST HIM.

For months afterward, he suffered effects of the illness. In mid-December, still struggling and far from happy with his job, he asked the Speaker of the House, Frederick Muhlenberg, to conduct a full investigation into his conduct as Treasury secretary. Alexander had already been cleared, but he wanted to be cleared again, at length, to silence his critics at last.

He confided the frustrations of his situation to Angelica in a letter: "I am just where I do not wish to be. I know how I could be much happier; but circumstances enchain me. It is however determined that I will break the spell. Nothing can prevent it at the opening of the Spring, but the existence or the certainty of a war between this Country and some European Power—an event which I most sincerely deprecate but which reciprocal perversenessess, in a degree, endangers."

The year had brutalized him, and he would quit his post when he could do it with honor. Good news did come on the last day of the year, though: Thomas Jefferson resigned as secretary of state, ostensibly to retire to private life and philosophy. Alexander suspected Jefferson would be back someday to run for president. He was not wrong.

FOR THE FIRST FIVE MONTHS OF THE NEW YEAR, the House investigated Alexander. Ultimately, it found no wrongdoing. As for those frequent accusations that he'd used the Bank of New York and the Bank of the United States to enrich himself personally, the May 22, 1794, report said it looked as though "the Secretary of the Treasury never has, either directly or indirectly, for himself or any other person, procured any discount or credit, from either of the said Banks, upon the basis of any public monies which, at any time, have been deposited therein under his direction."

He didn't have time to savor his vindication. The war he worried about with Angelica had become a distinct possibility when the British fleet in the West Indies captured more than 250 American merchant ships, stole their goods, and claimed American sailors on board were British deserters.

"War may come upon us, whether we choose it or not," he told Washington in March.

He urged the fortification of ports and the raising of twenty thousand troops. The executive branch needed to take leadership in this first potential international conflict since the Revolution ended. For all the pains they'd taken to preserve peace, they had an equal responsibility to be prepared for war.

His political enemies loved to accuse him of being an incorrigible British puppet. In reality, he was hard at work pondering the best course of action against England. War was such a threat to the country's prosperity that it ought to be a last resort, he counseled Washington. The president knew this, of course. But Alexander wanted him to impress this on the country as well. Meanwhile, he also wanted to strike at England financially, cutting off direct and indirect imports.

Alexander relinquished his chance to be a special envoy to Britain—he was seen as being too political, and he knew it. He recommended John Jay, his *Federalist* coauthor and chief justice of the Supreme Court, instead. Jay left in May to hammer out a new treaty with England if at all possible.

The potential war abroad wasn't the only one that preoccupied Alexander. On the western frontier in Pennsylvania, men took up arms to protest Alexander's despised whiskey tax. And at home, one of his children was seriously ill, and Eliza was pregnant and struggling. Alexander asked Washington for some time off so he could take his ailing toddler to the country for fresh air. The president was sympathetic and urged Alexander to take care of his little son.

Alexander helped settle Eliza and some of their children in Albany, and he returned to Philadelphia with his older boys. He needed to be in the city to focus on the tax protests, which had turned violent. On July 16, a group of angry farmers marched on the home of a tax collector in western Pennsylvania, where they had a shootout with him and his slaves. The next day a force of five hundred returned, firing on the house and burning the buildings to the ground. What's more, an army of rebels several thousand strong had gathered on Braddock's Field near Pittsburgh by the end of July, threatening to vanquish any army that would take them on.

Alexander assembled a long list of heinous things tax protestors had done since 1791. They'd burned effigies. They'd broken into people's homes and terrorized their families. A mentally ill man who'd claimed to be a tax collector was stripped naked, tarred, and feathered. One witness said the incident "exceeded description and was sufficient to make human nature shudder."

It was lawful to protest a law. But it wasn't lawful to disregard one that had been enacted according to the Constitution. Alarm was high in the administration. The threat of overthrowing the government from the western frontier was palpable. Alexander intended to do everything he could to ensure that the government and the nation it served survived.

EVERY LETTER FROM ALBANY HE OPENED WITH TREMBLING HANDS.

Around this time, Henry Knox, the secretary of war, asked for a leave to take care of some real estate business in Maine. Washington let him go and put Alexander in charge of the army. As he managed the Treasury Department and the army, the health of his darling boy worried him to the extreme, and he fretted about Eliza's pregnancy. Every letter from Albany he opened with trembling hands.

He regretted he could only send her his best wishes. "They are all I can now offer—Hard hard situation."

After weeks of worry, he got good news at last about his darling Johnny in late August. A couple of weeks later, Washington decided it was time to send troops to Pennsylvania from New Jersey, Maryland, and Virginia. Alexander, still performing Knox's duties, set out to supply the militia with everything they'd need: clothing, blankets, weapons, kettles, medicine. Alexander decided that as the man who'd devised the tax strategy, he ought to be part of the expedition against the insurgents. He asked Washington's permission, taking it for granted that General Knox would be back on the job soon.

Reassuring his sons Philip and Alexander that he would face no danger, and possibly would even enjoy health benefits from the ride, Alexander set off with Washington on the last morning of September, reaching the militia troops in Carlisle, Pennsylvania, on October 4. After the 12,950 troops reached Bedford, the sixty-two-year-old president felt confident enough to return to Philadelphia, leaving Alexander and General Henry Lee, the governor of Virginia, to take the army through the mountains to the rebellious counties.

By October 23, it was clear to Alexander that the military outing was prudent, even as there were some stragglers and drinkers in the force. He sent Angelica a cheerful letter about his journey "to attack and subdue the wicked insurgents of the West.... A large army has cooled the courage of those madmen & the only question seems now how to guard best aganst the return of the phrenzy."

The arrival of nearly thirteen thousand troops was enough to squelch the Whiskey Rebellion, and by mid-November it was over. It was no small achievement. Bloodshed and death were minimal, and Washington pardoned the men who'd been found guilty of treason. Alexander didn't think the president should have gone soft on scofflaws, but Washington had wisdom and unbeatable political instincts. The public admired how the mess was handled by the new federal government, but Jefferson and Madison continued to grouse about Alexander, and now even Washington.

IN LATE NOVEMBER, AS HE WAS HEADING HOME, Alexander received an urgent letter from Henry Knox, sent ahead at the insistence of the president. Eliza was not well. She was either in danger of losing their baby or already had. Guarded by six soldiers, Alexander raced to his family in Philadelphia.

When he arrived, he found a family in great distress. He quit his job that day. He could simply take no more. His last day as Treasury secretary would be January 31. A week later, he wrote to Angelica with the news. He put a positive spin on his resignation:

"Don't let Mr. Church be alarmed at my retreat—all is well with the public. Our insurrection is most happily terminated. Government has gained by it reputation and strength, and our finances are in a most flourishing condition. *Having contributed to place those of the Nation on a good footing, I go to take a little care of my own; which need my care not a little.*"

He was circumspect when it came to the real reason he was quitting politics. He'd let Angelica know that Eliza had been very ill. She'd recovered but was still weak. What he did not tell his beloved sister-in-law was the truth that pained him most about his absence and its cost:

He wasn't there when Eliza needed him, and she'd lost their baby.

CHAPTER ELEVEN

HAMILTON'S HEART

HIS LAST FEW WEEKS IN office passed in a flurry. He sent reports, arranged for the payment of debts, and on his final workday, a Saturday, offered the president lengthy advice about the U.S. Mint. Alexander was eager to be free, but he didn't want to leave anything undone—or leave off influencing anything still in his power to influence.

The Monday after Alexander left, Washington wrote him a letter.

"After so long an experience of your public services, I am naturally led, at this moment of your departure from office—which it has always been my wish to prevent—to review them.

"In every relation, which you have borne to me, I have found that my confidence in your talents, exertions and integrity, has been well placed. . . . My most earnest wishes for your happiness will attend you in your retirement, and you may assure yourself of the sincere esteem, regard and friendship of Dear Sir.

"Your affectionate Go: Washington."

Together, these two men had won a war. Together, they'd built a nation. Now it was time for Alexander to build something for himself, starting with a fortune. Not a large one, but one that was large enough. He had $500 to his name and a family that cost quite a bit more. Public service had put him in a financial hole. It would take him four to six years of work to emerge. On the bright side, it would be less work than he'd been doing. And he'd be back in New York, a city that loved him, living at 26 Broadway, a short walk from the Battery, where he'd started as an artillery captain.

Not long after Alexander left office, Robert Troup made him an offer. Alexander could represent Dutch and English capitalists buying real estate in the old Northwest Territory. Troup saw no risk in the plan and intended to go ahead with the venture himself. Alexander could even take part anonymously. Troup reminded Alexander he could work as a lawyer for a decade and still not have enough money to support his brood.

"I DONT WANT TO BE RICH . . ."

As much as he appreciated his old friend's generosity, Alexander declined. His thought it better not to be involved in speculation, particularly with foreign citizens. He'd already had enough accusations that he was a British tool. What's more, relations with both England and France were fraught. Alexander wanted to remain uncompromised should the country once again be drawn into war.

But more to the point, money was not his master. "I dont want to be rich and if I cannot live *in splendor* in Town, with a moderate fortune moderately acquired, I can at least live *in comfort* in the country. . . . I know it is pride. But this pride makes it part of my plan to *appear truly what I am*."

And who was he?

Despite his intentions to be nothing more than a lawyer, a husband, and a father to five children, he could not scrub the public servant from his soul. In almost no time, he was back advising Washington on political matters, the most vital of which was ratification and funding of John Jay's treaty with England, which resolved some issues that had been left unsettled after the war.

Jay had sent the first draft back to Philadelphia before Alexander handed in his resignation, so Alexander was familiar with its points when the official version arrived on March 7, 1795. The treaty was greeted like a barrel of spoiled ham, especially by Republicans who looked at anything favorable to England as corrupt. They complained it didn't force the English to pay for slaves they'd removed. Worse, America had to treat England as a most-favored trading partner, but England didn't have to return the favor. The trade provisions at least allowed American manufacturers to sell to overseas markets. But there was one undeniable virtue of the imperfect treaty: Jay had averted a war with England when the United States was in no shape to fight one.

Even though Alexander didn't care for the trade restrictions in the treaty, it galled him to see the agreement under such fire from the Republicans. Aaron Burr—once a member of the New York Manumission Society—made quite the spectacle arguing that the value of slaves "and other property" should be reimbursed by the British government. At least the Senate overruled Burr's many objections and passed the treaty.

Washington had yet to sign. He first wanted Alexander's opinion, if time permitted. Alexander *made* the time. He wrote a long evaluation of the treaty's merits and flaws, sending it in installments the next week. There were problems with trade restrictions, yes. But on the whole, the treaty meant peace. The country was too fragile in every way for war.

Washington was delighted to have Alexander back in the fold, even at a distance. The president had yet to sign the document when opponents staged a protest on July 18. The rally at the same building where Washington had been sworn in incensed Alexander so much that he interrupted the first speaker. Hecklers went wild. When Alexander stood to defend the treaty in front of a mob, people threw rocks at him, one of which clocked him in the forehead.

Afterward, Alexander ran into a man on the street who'd recently disparaged his honor. They scuffled, and Alexander challenged him to a duel. He continued down the street, insulted a member of the powerful Livingston family, and offered to fight a series of men one by one. Before long, he'd issued his *second* challenge to a duel in a single day—and duels weren't even legal.

Any restraint he'd cultivated under Washington was gone. The first showdown would be with James Nicholson, a friend of Aaron Burr's. Nicholson had accused Alexander of squirreling away a hundred thousand pounds. The charge made no sense. Alexander had been a stalwart Revolutionary and an ardent defender of the Constitution. He'd waived his wartime pay. He would never take British bribes or abuse the public trust. What's more, he'd sacrificed his family's financial well-being in working as the Treasury secretary. The pay was a fraction of what he'd earned as a lawyer. He was in debt, for mercy's sake.

Determined to fight for his honor, Alexander wrote his will, which revealed he owed five thousand pounds to

Angelica's husband. He also drafted an apology that Nicholson could make to him, which would avert the duel. His second, Nicholas Fish, got Nicholson to sign it. Likewise, the second challenge ended with something of an apology to Alexander.

At last Alexander had decided who he was and what his priorities were.

Whatever it took, whatever it cost, even if his family should be left financially ruined, his honor was the sun around which his thoughts and actions orbited. He would work within the law to support his wife and children. But there were limits. For the sake of his honor, he would step outside the law.

Why did his honor matter so much to him, when he'd already accomplished more than most men in the world? The question would take years to answer.

THE JAY TREATY EVENTUALLY PASSED AND WAS funded a year later by the House of Representatives. In the midst of that charged fight, Lafayette's son arrived in town and stayed with Alexander and Eliza during the fall of 1795. Young Lafayette had wanted to see Washington, but politics made it impossible. His father languished still in an Austrian fortress, and the United States could do nothing. Although he was an American hero, Lafayette was considered a traitor in France. International relations were too fragile to permit intervention.

The young Lafayette was close in age to Alexander's oldest, Philip, who was thirteen and no longer the chubby baby Alexander found nearly perfect. He remained his family's pride, though.

"Philip inherits his father's talents," Angelica observed to Eliza. "What flattering prospects for a mother!"

Alexander's second child, Angelica, was eleven, a pianist who spoke French (something that pleased him so). And then there was Alexander, age nine. James, who was seven, and Johnny, age three. He adored each and every one. Chastened by the bullet he'd dodged with the Reynolds business, he was conspicuously devoted to them. He could have traveled the country he'd helped establish. He could have visited Europe. He did not, and when he had to leave town for a case, he'd write Eliza to let her know how much he missed them all. The more the world showed itself to be a hard and unjust place to him, the more he appreciated the steadfastness of his wife and family.

BY 1796, ANOTHER ERA HAD COME TO AN END. Washington wanted to step down from the presidency. He was growing old, and he'd never aspired to the post in the first place. What's more, he wanted to answer the increasingly bold critics who'd suggested he was flirting with monarchy.

Alignments had shifted from the days when Washington took office. Madison had written Washington's inaugural speech, but after Madison's carping about the Jay Treaty, Washington chose Alexander to write his farewell address. Alexander's role was secret, but he worked late into the night with Eliza by his side, reading her bit after bit so that she could tell him how the words came across.

With the retirement of President Washington, Alexander also could have removed himself from the public sphere. He'd given much, after all. He also could have been a fine candidate for president, and the job—which paid $25,000 a year—wouldn't have been a financial hardship. But there was the Maria Reynolds scandal. If he ran, there was a chance it could come to light. Someone had written the newspaper editor Noah Webster implying this would happen if Alexander dared run. And so he never pursued the presidency or any other office.

But he couldn't resist inserting himself into the game. In 1796, the political scene was rough. Factions—the federalists and antifederalists—had split firmly into opposing parties. Vice President John Adams and former Secretary of State Thomas Jefferson were the leading Federalist and Republican candidates, and they had opposing views on many things.

Adams wasn't part of Washington's cabinet and hadn't been in Washington's inner circle. What's more, he spent a lot of time in Quincy, Massachusetts, tending his sick wife, Abigail. Alexander and Adams therefore hadn't worked together much, but they weren't adversaries. Alexander had even hired Adams's son as his law clerk for a while.

Even so, Alexander had seen enough of the man to know he preferred Thomas Pinckney, a South Carolina war hero and former governor, for president. As he'd done before Washington's first election, he tried to influence other people's votes. That way, Pinckney would come out on top without anyone being the wiser. He might have managed, except that Aaron Burr—for now a Republican who wanted to be vice president—provided evidence of Alexander's meddling that reached Adams and his wife.

Adams was livid. He called Alexander conceited, debauched, and hypocritical. "I shall take no notice of his Puppyhood but retain the same Opinion of him I always had and maintain the Same Conduct towards him I always did, that is keep him at a distance."

Alexander also tried to sink Jefferson's campaign. Writing as Phocion, he suggested Jefferson was a coward, a dilettante, and a hypocrite. He quoted some of Jefferson's most obnoxious speculations about black people and then implied Jefferson was having a sexual relationship with one of his enslaved women. This wasn't a wild fantasy, as was the accusation that Alexander was sitting on a secret stash of English wealth. The rumor was every bit as true as Alexander's dalliance with Maria Reynolds. Alexander had heard from Angelica that the enslaved woman was Sally Hemings, the young sister of Jefferson's enslaved chef, James.

And as much as Jefferson liked to portray himself as the unadorned populist philosopher-farmer, the man had an appetite for luxury, and he enjoyed a European-style loose morality when it came to marriage. Jefferson had become enchanted with Angelica when he lived in Paris, for example. Although Angelica had a husband and four children, he wrote to her suggesting they travel together during the fine spring weather. She did not go, though she kept the letter. At that point, Jefferson had not yet worked with Alexander. He had no way to know that with Angelica, Alexander would always come first.

When Alexander made this reference to Jefferson's sex life in October 1796, the *Aurora*, a die-hard Republican paper, printed a response addressed to Treasury Secretary Oliver Wolcott. The response referenced his investigation of

Reynolds. Message received, Alexander dropped the public subject of Jefferson's intimate life.

Adams was elected president in February 1797. Jefferson got the second-most votes and became vice president—a result that put him closer to the top than ever. In the process, Alexander had earned himself a new enemy, Adams, and had further inflamed the wily Jefferson.

JEFFERSON WAS A COWARD, A DILETTANTE, AND A HYPOCRITE.

Where Alexander had been a welcome voice in the Washington administration, he was the opposite in President Adams's. When Alexander sent the new president a long letter after his inauguration, Adams did not appreciate it. His cabinet members often turned to Alexander for counsel, however. Alexander might not have had a position in government, but he was considered very much a leader of the Federalist Party. But the sorts of rivalries that had split the nation into two parties now began to fracture the Federalists.

Meanwhile, Angelica and her husband finally returned to New York in May 1797. It was a happy time. Philip was also distinguishing himself in his studies at Columbia, even if he was frustrated that his professor cut a favorite line from a speech he planned to give.

But the joy wouldn't last.

A month after Angelica's return, Alexander came across a newspaper advertisement for a book called *The History of the United States for 1796; Including a Variety of Interesting Particulars Relative to the Federal Government.* Its author was James Thomson Callender, who'd fled Scotland after the British government charged him with sedition.

Alexander picked up a copy of the book, which mocked his ideas and writing as hopelessly wordy: "He has such skill at beating out his guinea into an acre of gold leaf." After pummeling Alexander for his financial systems and taxes, Callender unloaded the major artillery and mentioned a packet of papers that had once been in the possession of three congressmen.

THE TIMING FOR THIS DISCLOSURE COULD NOT HAVE BEEN WORSE.

The papers Alexander knew well. They were the Reynolds letters. His secret was out. The timing for this disclosure could not have been worse. Eliza was eight months pregnant. She'd already lost one baby on his account. Now there was a chance she'd lose another in the aftermath of this public humiliation.

In the fifth and sixth volumes of his so-called history, Callender published signed notes from Monroe, Muhlenberg, and Venable. He also printed an accusation from Maria that "she rather *doubted*" Alexander was innocent of illegal speculation. Callender presented a signed affidavit from Jacob Clingman, Reynolds's accomplice in fraud, which said that he'd seen Alexander in the Reynolds's house more than once, including in the evening, and that Alexander had given Reynolds more than $1,100. What's more, Reynolds had told Clingman "that he had it in his power *to hang colonel Hamilton*; that if he wanted money, he was *obliged to let him have it*."

It looked damning. And the Callender history revealed something Alexander didn't know. Clingman had approached Monroe *after* the three legislators had met with Alexander. Clingman said Maria Reynolds appeared "much shocked" at the news she'd had an affair with Alexander. She'd wept and called it a fabrication. Her husband and Hamilton were conspiring together and using her as cover, and Clingman believed her.

To Callender, the claim of an affair was preposterous. It was a cover-up for financial fraud, and Reynolds was probably one of twenty people hired to speculate on Alexander's behalf. After all, Alexander had been the second-most powerful man in the nation. "In the secretary's bucket of chastity, a drop more or less was not to be perceived," he wrote.

This was Republican vengeance and then some. Alexander suspected the papers had been leaked by Monroe, if indirectly through a Republican aide. Monroe had been angry to be recalled from France by the Federalist government. Jefferson probably had a hand in the matter, too.

The publication was an outrage. But what really riled Alexander was that it implied Monroe, Venable, and Muhlenberg hadn't believed him, when they assured him they *had*. He immediately asked all three men to vouch for him. Muhlenberg did, as did Venable, who let Alexander know Monroe had been the one to hold the Reynolds documents and that the aide who'd copied them was probably the leak.

For his part, Monroe didn't respond immediately to Alexander's request. Alexander demanded a meeting. He advised Monroe to bring a witness. A meeting was set with Alexander, his brother-in-law John Church, Monroe, and Republican merchant David Gelston.

Alexander stormed into the meeting on July 11, reminding Monroe that he'd earlier said he believed Alexander guilty of adultery, not corruption. Monroe bristled. He didn't need a rehash of the history of their talk. He swore he didn't know about the papers being published—something he was sorry had occurred.

Refusing to be mollified, Alexander demanded to know what had delayed Monroe's reply. His character and reputation and the peace of his family had depended on it, after all.

This only pushed Monroe further toward the edge. He told Alexander to calm down and be quiet so he could explain the delay. Monroe then insisted the package of papers was still sealed with his friend in Virginia, as far as he knew.

"Your representation is totally false," Alexander said.

"Do you say I represented falsely?" Monroe said. "You are a scoundrel."

Both men leapt from their chairs.

"I will meet you like a gentleman," Alexander said.

"I am ready," Monroe said. "Get your pistols."

Church and Gelston separated the two men and tried to calm them down before all hell broke loose. Gelston said he had a proposal.

"By all means." Alexander was hot and agitated. Monroe, on the other hand, was cold and contemptuous.

Gelston suggested a compromise—that Alexander wait for Monroe to meet with Muhlenberg and Venable. The men would then write a joint letter. Alexander reluctantly agreed. The letter, written by Monroe and Muhlenberg because Venable was out of town, fell short of his expectations, so Alexander sent letters with fresh attacks on Monroe, who before long suggested the men have a duel. Monroe reached out to Aaron Burr and asked him to be their go-between. Burr, after reading the hostile exchanges, managed to quell the hostility temporarily.

"*I AM READY. GET YOUR PISTOLS.*"

Meanwhile, Alexander's friends thought he should say nothing further about the matter. They were no doubt thinking of dear, sweet Eliza, who'd been first wounded by Alexander's betrayal and then humiliated by the public airing of it. Eliza, who loved him so. Eliza, who'd cared for his children and taken in orphans and stayed up late with him, listening to him read his work and copying his pages in her own hand.

Her love proved stronger than her hurt. She reserved her outrage for Alexander's critics, and she held on to her pregnancy and bore a baby boy on August 4. They named him William Stephen Hamilton. A few weeks later, George Washington sent Alexander a letter and a present: a wine cooler for four bottles.

"I pray you to present my best wishes, in which Mrs Washington joins me, to Mrs Hamilton & the family," he wrote, "and that you would be persuaded, that with every sentiment of the highest regard, I remain your sincere friend, and Affectionate Hble Servant."

He said nothing of the scandal, a silence that spoke volumes in a way only Washington could.

It was not the sort of silence Alexander could muster. Instead of listening to his friends and being grateful that his humiliation had not cost him more, he decided to beat his guinea into an acre of gold leaf and, on August 25, published a ninety-five-page pamphlet vindicating himself of all charges. It was as graphic as its title was long: *Observations on Certain Documents Contained in No. V & VI of "The History of the United States for the Year 1796," in Which the Charge of Speculation Against Alexander Hamilton, Late Secretary of the Treasury, Is Fully Refuted.*

"My real crime," he confessed in that pamphlet on the Reynolds affair, "is an amorous connection with [Reynolds's] wife, for a considerable time with his privity and connivance, if not originally brought on by a combination between the husband and wife with the design to extort money from me.

"The confession is not made without a blush. I can never cease to condemn myself for the pang which it may inflict in a bosom eminently entitled to all my gratitude, fidelity, and love."

He'd once again chosen his honor over everything else, including Eliza's feelings. Certain that a thorough airing of the affair would prove to the world that he hadn't engaged in speculation, all he succeeded in doing was showing people that he'd been unfaithful. The *Aurora* wasted no time before mocking his faulty logic. "I have not broken the *eighth* commandment. It is only the *seventh* which I have violated."

Alexander's Reynolds pamphlet also riled Monroe, temporarily raising the specter of a duel again. Meanwhile, Alexander received an express message while he was in Connecticut for a court case. His son Philip had contracted an illness, and it appeared he would not survive. Alexander raced toward home.

Philip was feverish and nauseated. The doctor suspected typhus. The disease progressed rapidly, and his family began to lose hope. Philip was delirious, his pulse low. He suffered so greatly that the doctor sent Eliza from the room to spare her the sight of his last struggles. In a flash of inspiration, the doctor lowered Philip into a hot bath spiked with quinine and rum. He poured in spirits of hartshorn—ammonia—to increase the stimulating effect, and within a few minutes, Philip's delirium had passed. His pulse grew stronger, and he was able to swallow some strong sherry. After a fifteen-minute soak, he was wrapped in blankets and put back in bed. He slept.

But within hours, he relapsed. Despair returned. They tried two more baths, and at last, Philip was on the mend. Alexander arrived in the night, expecting to find his son dead. To his great joy the boy still lived. As Philip recovered, Alexander fed his son his meals and medicine by hand.

His son. His family. He loved them dearly. More losses on this front would be too much to bear.

HE'D CERTAINLY LET HIS FAMILY DOWN WITH the publication of the Reynolds pamphlet. The family bought as many copies as they could to minimize their embarrassment. It wasn't a surprise to them that Alexander had an eye for women. The subject had been something of a joke in Washington's headquarters, and with Eliza's knowledge, Alexander had flirted with Angelica for years. Angelica once dropped a garter at a party, and Alexander gallantly retrieved it. She joked about his not being a Knight of the Garter. Peggy, the sister outside the love triangle, zinged back that "He would be a Knight of the Bedchamber if he could."

The truth was, women energized Alexander, none more than Angelica. "I seldom write to a lady without fancying the relation of lover and mistress. It has a very inspiring effect," he told her. "And in your case the dullest materials could not help feeling that propensity."

In the same letter, he wondered about a stray comma between *Dear* and *Alexander*. Was it an accident? Or did she mean to tell him something about what he meant to her?

Their understanding was exquisite. She felt his ambition deeply, and she knew exactly how to talk with him to ignite his furnaces. She understood that his appetite could not be separated from his essence. After the scandal broke, she tried to explain it to her sister and shift the blame where it belonged.

"Tranquillize your kind and good heart, my dear Eliza, for I have the most positive assurance from Mr. Church that the dirty fellow who has caused us all some uneasiness and wounded your feelings, my dear love, is effectually silenced. Merit, virtue, and talents must have enemies . . . my Eliza, you see the penalties attending the position of so amiable a man. All this you would not have suffered if you had married into a family less *near the sun*." In other words, had she not married Alexander, she would have missed the pride, pleasure, and nameless satisfactions his brilliance provided.

His family rallied around him despite his transgressions. But would the Federalist Party? The president most definitely would not. Adams hated Alexander. His cabinet members

Napoleon Bonaparte

still leaned on Alexander's military and financial expertise, though. Alexander answered many questions for his former colleagues still in the cabinet—Oliver Wolcott, Timothy Pickering, and James McHenry—even as he worked long hours by candlelight in his law office.

Because of the Jay Treaty, the relationship between the United States and France was shaky. The military ruler Napoleon was especially fearsome. In negotiations, the French were shockingly aggressive, and Alexander believed it was

ABOVE: *NAPOLEON ROSE TO POWER DURING THE FRENCH REVOLUTION AND WREAKED HAVOC IN FRANCE.*

time for the United States to build an army. Congress agreed. But not one of fifty thousand men, as Alexander had envisioned. Adams ridiculed that ambition, saying Alexander wanted such a thing because only he had a "superabundance of secretions which he could not find Whores enough to draw off."

Mulling the army, Alexander wrote to Washington in May 1798, echoing the letter he'd written persuading him to become president. The Republicans in the South were so enamored of France that they weren't seeing the danger the country posed, Alexander said. Washington's influence was needed. What's more, if they went to war, the public would want Washington to lead its soldiers. "You will be compelled to make the sacrifice."

"YOU WILL BE COMPELLED TO MAKE THE SACRIFICE."

Washington was concerned, though he didn't think it would come to war. He wasn't sure he should be the leader of this army himself; perhaps that job should fall more to a man in his prime. And he was of course wondering who would serve with him. Alexander, he hoped.

Alexander was game. "If you command, the place in which I should hope to be most useful is that of Inspector General with a command in the line."

Adams, for his part, preferred others for the job of inspector general: the disgraced Horatio Gates, a nearly dead Daniel

Morgan, or a sleepy Benjamin Lincoln. "Anyone but Hamilton" might as well have been his motto. Alexander was a foreigner and an upstart, "the bastard brat of a Scotch Pedler"—never mind that he'd effectively been Washington's chief of staff *and* had distinguished himself on the battlefield.

In dragging his feet, Adams forced Washington to say the words that Alexander would most want to hear—and that most irritated Adams. "That he is ambitious I shall readily grant, but it is of that laudable kind which prompts a man to excel in whatever he takes in hand.—He is enterprising,—quick in his perceptions,—and his judgment intuitively great."

In July, Alexander was appointed inspector general of the U.S. Army, with the rank of major general. When Aaron Burr heard, he asked Alexander for a military appointment of his own. Alexander made the attempt but discovered there was still no love lost between Burr and Washington. Burr thought Washington was an illiterate hack. Washington thought Burr was perhaps better at intrigue than soldiering. So there was no chance for Burr, even as Adams tried to foist him on Washington.

Once again working for the public, but now for even less money than he'd made as Treasury secretary, Alexander found himself growing short on funds. His legal practice shrank as his to-do list for the army grew. They'd need uniforms, huts, training, hospitals—probably even something like a military academy. His mind raced forward like an out-of-control carriage as he even considered military ventures in Latin America.

Meanwhile, Federalists and Republicans continued to smack each other in Congress, in the newspapers, and in private letters. The dominant Federalists wanted to keep their political advantage. So they restricted two things: freedom of the press and immigration. (Many immigrants were Irish and despised England and, therefore, were more likely to sympathize with the French, just like the Republicans.) The Alien and Sedition Acts allowed the government to imprison or deport any immigrant deemed dangerous and to punish speech critical of the government. Alexander—an immigrant himself, who should have known better—favored them nonetheless.

In response, Jefferson and Madison secretly wrote legislation on behalf of state governments intended to undermine the federal acts. In doing so, they aimed to elevate states above the national government, undermining the Constitution in the process. It was a mess all around.

Alexander, hoping to swing Republicans to the Federalist side, tried to help Aaron Burr start a public water venture called the Manhattan Company. In addition to the political benefits, the venture would be good for the city. A year earlier, New York had suffered an outbreak of yellow fever, perhaps due to dirty water. A public water system would improve public health and the city's ability to fight fires. What's more, the venture would give Alexander's wealthy brother-in-law John Barker Church something to do.

Alexander threw himself into getting approval for Burr's plan from the state legislature. It came about, but the bill turned out to be a Trojan horse. Burr hadn't meant to found a water company at all. He'd inserted language that instead let him open a bank to compete with Alexander's.

Burr's slipperiness won him no fans and cost him his seat in the state assembly. Worse, no water was delivered to citizens, and in the summer of 1799, yellow fever returned. John

Church was so furious that he suggested Burr had taken bribes while he was in office. That statement provoked Burr into issuing a challenge for a duel. The week the Manhattan Company Bank opened, the two men and their seconds faced off in Hoboken, New Jersey. Church shot a button off Burr's coat. Burr, whose gun had been improperly loaded, missed. Church apologized for speaking indiscreetly, and the duel ended.

CHURCH SHOT A BUTTON OFF BURR'S COAT.

Smarting from being outmaneuvered by Burr, Alexander continued his civic works along with Eliza. In addition to trying to get funding and supplies for the army, Alexander pitched in with the New York Manumission Society, while Eliza worked with the Society for the Relief of Poor Widows with Small Children. The two had also patched up their relationship enough to have another child, Eliza, on November 26, 1799.

The newspapers hadn't let the adultery scandal drop, though. The Saturday, December 14, edition of the *Aurora* included these side-by-side bits:

"General Hamilton arrived in town yesterday and, it is said, means to *keep watch* in Philadelphia for the winter. He despairs doing anything with the 'Aurora' . . . but still considers it as the most cruel opposer of his views in the United States."

"Mrs. Reynolds, alias *Maria*, the sentimental heroine of the memorable *vindication*, is said to be in Philadelphia once more."

It had been a long, frustrating, and sad year. Alexander's father had died a few months earlier. The wedding-day promise that he would meet Eliza had never come to pass. In fact, Alexander hadn't seen the man since he'd run off decades earlier.

But this wasn't the hardest death for Alexander that year.

On the same day the *Aurora* implied Alexander was still carrying on with Maria Reynolds, George Washington died. Two days earlier, Washington had gone for a ride in nasty weather. Rather than be late for a meal, he dined in his wet clothing. He fell ill, and despite measures taken by three doctors, he died late Saturday evening, surrounded by his wife, his secretary Tobias Lear, and some of the slaves he owned.

"I DIE HARD; BUT I AM NOT AFRAID TO GO."

"Doctor," he said as his body was shutting down, "I die hard; but I am not afraid to go." His last request was that he be decently buried after three days had passed.

The day Washington took ill, he'd written to Alexander. The letter was brief, even mundane. He signed it, "With very great esteem & regard, I am, Sir, Your most Obedt. Servt."

Neither could have known those would be the last words exchanged between them.

More than anyone else, Washington had believed in Alexander, and his patronage had transformed him from orphaned immigrant to the second-most powerful man in the nation.

It wasn't just that Alexander's star had risen with Washington's. The man had also been more of a father to him than anyone else, with all the difficulty such relationships can contain.

They'd struggled and reconciled, and at the lowest moment of Alexander's life, Washington had been there for him. And now he was gone. There would be no replacing him.

What's more, as the quasi war with France was in the process of being resolved diplomatically by John Adams, there was no need for the army. Alexander had to walk away from the dream it represented.

Meanwhile, the courtroom beckoned. A week after Washington died, a twenty-two-year-old woman named Gulielma Sands disappeared. On January 2, 1800, her bruised and shoeless body was found in a Manhattan well.

The Manhattan Well Mystery riveted the city. Suspicion quickly swung around to a man named Levi Weeks, who'd been the last person seen with her. He was arrested. But the young man had rich and powerful relatives. To defend Levi, these relatives hired the city's best lawyers: Alexander Hamilton, Aaron Burr, and Brockholst Livingston. It was the first murder trial in the history of the United States to be captured on transcript.

Things looked terrible for Weeks. Elma had told people they were to be married. A housemate, Richard David Croucher, said he had seen the victim and Weeks engaged in intimate activity. Contrary to Weeks's claims that Elma had been depressed and had spoken of ending her life with a dose of laudanum, witnesses said she'd been cheerful when she borrowed the muff of another housemate. A one-horse sleigh similar to one owned by a relative of Weeks had been seen and had left tracks in the snow near the well. And of course, he'd been the last to see her.

In the candlelit courtroom, Alexander and Burr provided a formidable defense that culminated in Alexander's discrediting of Croucher, the housemate who claimed to have seen Elma and Levi having sex. Alexander lifted a candle to Croucher's face so another witness could identify him. "I have been acquainted with this Croucher for some time," the witness said, "but I never liked his looks."

The jury agreed. Their deliberation in the wee hours of April 2 lasted five minutes. Weeks was found not guilty. Though the public protested Weeks's acquittal, three months later Croucher was convicted of rape; his victim was a thirteen-year-old who'd been at the same troubled boardinghouse.

Around the same time, Philip graduated from college. Alexander wanted his son to follow in his footsteps, both in diligence and in the law. He sent instructions outlining when Philip would wake, when he would study, when he would eat, and when he had free time (every day between 5:00 and 7:00 p.m., and after noon on Saturdays).

"He must not Depart from any of these rules without my permission."

Without a father of his own to write such rules, Alexander became increasingly reckless, especially in his rivalry with Burr. The two campaigned fiercely during the spring elections in New York. Burr, better organized, brought out a Republican majority. That meant the upcoming presidential election looked even more promising for their side, with the detestable Burr positioned well to become vice president.

Alexander was depressed about the state of the world around him, and he was disgusted with Adams, who had not only brokered a treaty with France against Alexander's advice but also disbanded the army and removed two of Alexander's friends from the cabinet. What's more, his sister-in-law Peggy had fallen ill.

Dispirited and feeling his political influence wane, Alexander took steps to prevent Adams from winning a second term. He had to be careful—Adams's fiercest rival would be Jefferson, and Alexander wanted to save the nation from that man's fangs. Walking a precarious line, Alexander urged Federalists in May to throw equal weight behind Adams and Charles Cotesworth Pinckney. The idea was that enough electors from the South would vote for Pinckney and he'd wind up president.

ALEXANDER WAS DEPRESSED ABOUT THE STATE OF THE WORLD AROUND HIM.

By June, though, Alexander had changed his tune. Pinckney deserved *all* the votes. Alexander discussed writing a document that outlined Adams's unfitness to be president with Oliver Wolcott, who urged Alexander to abandon the idea altogether. "The poor old Man is sufficiently successful in undermining his own Credit and influence."

Alexander wrote a draft anyway, sending it to Wolcott for his comments. Alexander intended to print the pamphlet and publish it in South Carolina to a select audience of Federalist electors. But Aaron Burr and other Republicans got wind of it and leaked it to their newspapers, which gleefully publicized the internal meltdown of the Federalist Party. Madison snickered to Jefferson that the pamphlet would be a thunderbolt to both Hamilton's and Adams's careers.

Federalists were also dismayed. The *Gazette of the United*

States, & Daily Advertiser on November 24, 1800, printed a letter that said, "The undertaking discovers a degree of vanity, and the performance too much personal feeling, to persuade any one, that the design is solely *public good.*"

Adams was livid. "Of all the Libellers of me this was the most unprovoked, the most ungrateful and the most unprincipled."

As harsh as Hamilton's pamphlet was, it was far from the ugliest bit of the 1800 election. Callender, who'd leaked Alexander's affair with Maria Reynolds, said Adams had "hideous hermaphroditical character."

Meanwhile, a Federalist paper said that if Jefferson were elected, "murder, robbery, rape, adultery and incest will openly be taught and practiced."

By December, once all the states had chosen their electors for the presidential Electoral College, it was becoming clear that no winner was going to emerge when the votes were officially counted in February. Jefferson and Burr, the two Republicans, would be tied. The Constitution specified that the Federalist-controlled House of Representatives would have to choose.

Because Burr had flirted on occasion with federalism, many Federalists preferred him to Jefferson. This put Alexander between the devil and the deep blue sea. He couldn't stand either man, but he saw Jefferson as the lesser evil. Jefferson at least had principles.

Alexander wrote letter after letter to Federalists, trying to persuade them to throw their votes to Jefferson. Burr's election would be a disgrace. He was bankrupt beyond redemption. Worse, his financial distress made him a target for foreign bribes.

Sure enough, when the electoral votes were counted in the new capital of Washington, D.C., Jefferson and Burr each received seventy-three votes. Adams and Pinckney took third and fourth places, respectively. Alexander's influence was waning.

The vote then went to the House, where each state delegation had one vote. Nine states were needed to win. Jefferson had the support of eight, Burr six, with two states' delegations split and unable to cast a ballot. The legislators voted thirty-five times over six days, but the results remained the same. Finally, on the thirty-sixth ballot, Federalists in the Maryland and Vermont delegations abstained, giving those states to Jefferson, which put him into office as president.

In his inaugural speech on March 4, 1801, Jefferson tried to heal the painful party divisions. "We are all Republicans, we are all Federalists. If there be any among us who would wish to dissolve this Union or to change its republican form, let them stand undisturbed as monuments of the safety with which error of opinion may be tolerated where reason is left free to combat it."

A few days later, Eliza's sister Peggy passed away. "Viewing all that she had endured for so long a time, I could not but feel a relief in the termination of the scene," he told Eliza. "She was sensible to the last and resigned to the important change." But it was a crushing loss, and Alexander ached to console Eliza, who hadn't been there when the sad event happened.

In the midst of this grief, Alexander's public life felt extinguished. His son, the family's eldest and brightest hope, would have to carry on his work in that sphere. Meanwhile, Alexander sought refuge in his disappointment. As he meddled in the elections, he'd also acquired real estate. On

August 2, 1800, he'd invested $4,000 in a fifteen-acre lot on a hill overlooking the Hudson River and the Harlem Valley. The next month, he paid $750 for an additional three adjoining acres. Later, he'd buy seventeen more.

As he sank roots here with his family, he alluded to other family history and named the place the Grange, as both his ancestors in Scotland and relatives in Saint Croix had done. He hired Ezra Weeks, the brother of his client Levi, to build his family a home.

He also launched the *New-York Evening Post*, a Federalist newspaper, on November 16, 1801, hiring the man who'd written the court transcript of the Manhattan Well Mystery to be its editor. Its aims were high: "to diffuse among the people correct information on all interesting subjects, to inculcate just principles in religion, morals, and politics, and to cultivate a taste for sound literature."

It impressed people immediately. Even James Callender, who'd raked Alexander repeatedly through the muck, called it "the most elegant piece of workmanship that we have seen either in Europe or America."

A major story would soon land in the laps of editors at the *Post*. The story had its genesis in a Fourth of July address given by a Republican lawyer named George Eacker, who claimed Alexander's army had been secretly meant to suppress opposition to federalism.

A few months later, Philip Hamilton spied the dirty earwig at a theater. It was a Friday night, and a comedy called *The West-Indian* was on the boards. Philip and his friend barged into Eacker's box and harassed him. Eacker offered to take their dispute into the lobby, and as he did, he called Philip and the other boy "a set of rascals."

Rascal was an intentionally chosen word, and it had the intended effect of forcing a duel. John Church and a lawyer friend of Philip's tried to bring about a truce, but Eacker refused to drop the matter. Eacker and Philip would duel Monday afternoon in Paulus Hook, New Jersey.

When Alexander caught wind of it, he thought Philip could salvage his honor by throwing away his first shot. If he did this, his opponent wouldn't fire to kill; that would be tantamount to murder and the height of dishonor. The move would also keep the blood off Philip's hands, and it would keep his own honor intact.

The two young men faced off at three in the afternoon. The command to fire was given. For a long moment, they stared at each other. Eacker raised his pistol. Philip followed, and Eacker fired off a deadly shot. The bullet tore through Philip's right hip, ricocheted through his body, and landed in his left arm. Grievously injured, he sank to the earth. He had not fired a shot.

THE TWO YOUNG MEN FACED OFF AT THREE IN THE AFTERNOON.

Philip's terrified friends rowed him across the river and back into the city. A doctor had been summoned, but there was nothing to be done. Philip lay on a bed, delirious with pain. Alexander lay next to him, and on the other side, Eliza, who was expecting another baby. The family and friends in the room wept.

Philip died before dawn. He was buried in the rain at four in the afternoon. Many mourners attended, and Alexander needed someone to hold him upright as he approached the grave of his beloved firstborn, his perfect baby who'd grown to be such a promising young man and who was now gone forever.

The *New-York Evening Post*'s coverage urged the outlawing of dueling. But even in his son's death, Alexander's political enemies would not leave him alone. Rival papers thought the *Post* had been unfair to Eacker and advanced stories with a different slant.

THERE WAS ONE SMALL BIT OF GRACE IN THE AFTERMATH OF TRAGEDY.

Some old enemies of Alexander reached across the ocean of despair, though. The physician Benjamin Rush, whose son was friends with Philip, sent condolences. When he could muster the heart, Alexander wrote back. "The highest as well as the eldest hope of my family has been taken from me. You estimated him rightly—He was truly a fine youth. But why should I repine? It was the will of heaven; and he is now out of the reach of the seductions and calamities of a world, full of folly, full of vice, full of danger. . . . I firmly trust also that he has safely reached the haven of eternal repose and felicity."

The death traumatized Alexander's daughter Angelica so much that she had a mental breakdown and was only able to speak of him as if Philip were still alive.

Philip Hamilton

There was one small bit of grace in the aftermath of tragedy.

On June 2, 1802, at the Grange, Eliza gave birth to a healthy baby, a boy.

They named him Philip.

ABOVE: *PHILIP HAMILTON WAS ALEXANDER'S PRIDE AND JOY.*

CHAPTER TWELVE

'THIS IS

a

MORTAL

WOUND'

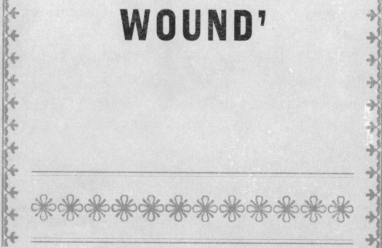

A LITTLE MORE THAN A year after Philip died, Alexander sat at his desk in his new country house and began a letter to a friend, the man he had wanted to become president.

"My Dear Sir," he wrote. "A garden, you know, is a very usual refuge of a disappointed politician. Accordingly I have purchased a few acres about 9 Miles from Town, have built a house, and am cultivating a Garden. The melons in your country are very fine. Will you have the goodness to send me some seed, both of the Water & Muss melons? My daughter adds another request, which is for three or four of your peroquets. She is very fond of birds."

His garden and his girl. He lavished love and energy into both. While the garden grew, Angelica had still not recovered from the trauma of Philip's murder. Would parakeets bring her back into her right mind? He could only hope as another year, 1802, was coming to a close.

During those sad months after Philip's death, Alexander threw himself into the construction of a solid home for his family. Built far from the bustle of the wharves where he'd first landed as a boy, far from the clatter of wagons through the financial center he'd helped establish, the Grange was two stories tall and painted white, with eight fireplaces. Guests entered on the west, while verandas graced the north and south sides. Near the southwest corner of the house stood a nod to the work of Alexander's life: a circle of thirteen smooth-barked, deciduous gum trees.

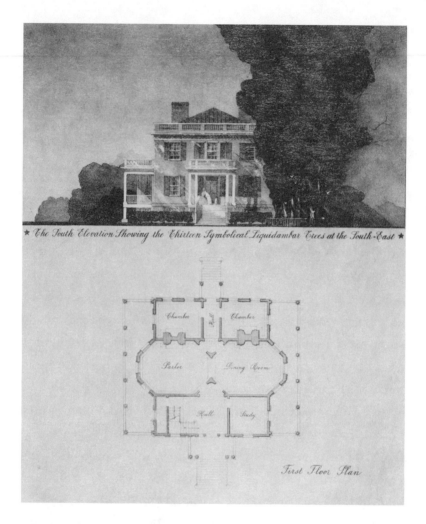

★ *The South Elevation Showing the Thirteen Symbolical Liquidambar Trees at the South-East* ★

First Floor Plan

He'd had plenty of advice on the project from Eliza's father, who provided clapboards for the siding and recommended design tips that would keep rodents at bay. Ezra Weeks completed the building. The construction and cultivation of his new home was costly, but nothing he would not be able to pay back with diligent work. Alexander was at last making a decent income, $12,000 a year.

ABOVE: *ALEXANDER BUILT THE GRANGE AS HIS RETREAT FROM THE WORLD.*

"To men who have been so much harassed in the busy world as myself," he wrote, "it is natural to look forward to complete retirement, in the circle of life as a perfect desideratum."

Alexander both needed and wanted to return to the earth, with its cycle of sprouting and blooming and harvest and decay.

Dr. David Hosack, who'd tried to save Philip after the duel, helped Alexander with the garden, offering cuttings, bulbs, and encouragement. Alexander was as specific about his flowers and vegetables as he was about uniforms and supplies for soldiers. English raspberries belonged by the orchard. In the center of his garden would bloom an eighteen-foot ring of tulips, hyacinths, and lilies, planted in alternating clusters of nine. These would be surrounded by wild roses and laurel. He wanted dogwoods scattered along the edges of things, but not before the fruit trees were moved to the front. It would take a while for much to be produced by the farm, but variety began to emerge from the soil: strawberries, cabbages, asparagus.

As Alexander and his family took root there in grief, they found happy times, too. Friends like Gouverneur Morris came to call. So did Eliza's family, and when her parents visited, they brought fruits and vegetables and even beef, although her father was growing too ill to visit often. Alexander and Eliza also attended plays, including the *Tragedy of Alexander the Great with a Grand Heroic Spectacle of the Siege of Oxydrace.*

In his solo moments, he walked through the woods of Harlem, where he'd once been a young soldier. This time, though, his quarry was not men but small game. Into the stock of his single-barreled gun, he'd carved A. HAMILTON, N.Y., a name that meant something in a city that had grown much under his leadership.

Work often brought him to Albany, a several-day journey by sloop or mail stage. During these trips, his thoughts traveled to his wife. Sometimes he sent her practical letters. The ice house might need a chimney, and he had ideas on how it should be constructed. Or there were compost beds to be built, which required a careful mix of clay (he knew just the sort), cow dung, and black mold.

Sometimes, though, he just wanted Eliza to know she was his own heart.

"For indeed my Eliza you are very essential to me. Your virtues more and more endear you to me and experience more and more convinces me that true happiness is only to be found in the bosom of ones own family."

Family. It was his refuge and his worry. Death had been greedy, stalking little Johnny, stealing Philip. He'd lost his father and George Washington. Philip Schuyler was ailing. Whenever Eliza took ill, Alexander's heart seized.

Friends noticed how solicitous Alexander had become. At the Grange in April 1804, "there was a furious and dreadful storm," a friend later wrote. "It blew almost a hurricane. His house stands high and was much exposed, and I am certain that in the second story, where I slept, it rocked like a cradle. . . . I was alone, and he treated me with a minute attention that I did not suppose he knew how to bestow."

For Alexander, whose life had found its direction through a hurricane, death itself was the inexorable storm that laid waste to everything he held dear, again and again. He lived in the shadow of this inevitability.

Theodosia Burr

This was another of the things he and Burr had in common. They'd been born far apart, Alexander on Nevis and Burr in New Jersey. But their lives had traveled parallel tracks toward each other since. Both were orphans. Both heroes in the Revolution. Both lawyers and statesmen. Both had wives they adored.

As Alexander doted on his children, Burr lavished his sole child, Theodosia, with love and attention. He ensured that she was educated with a rigor typically reserved for boys. Mary

ABOVE: *THEODOSIA BURR WAS EDUCATED AS RIGOROUSLY AS A BOY WOULD HAVE BEEN.*

Wollstonecraft's *A Vindication of the Rights of Woman* impressed him as a particular work of genius. Death had been greedy with both. Burr's wife suffered from cancer for all the time they knew each other. He'd wanted to quit the Senate to care for her, but she wouldn't let him. She died in 1794, and Burr devoted himself more fiercely than ever to his precious girl.

DEATH HAD BEEN GREEDY WITH BOTH.

As parallel as their lives had been, their key difference made collisions inevitable. Alexander believed in honor and the nobility of public service. Burr was about private gains. Politics was fun, not a matter of principle. George Washington had perceived this selfish core in Burr immediately. When Burr was briefly part of his military family in 1776, he did not impress the general. Burr was brave, yes, but he was fundamentally driven by the personal. Alexander shared Washington's fundamental drive, to serve the nation. Thus, even when Alexander and Washington quarreled, they were able to patch things up.

Where Alexander was careful not to benefit personally from his public service, giving up his military pension, charging modest fees to his legal clients, and avoiding business ventures that could give him a conflict of interest, Burr did the opposite. Despite charging higher legal fees and engaging in shady deals, Burr still ended up in financial straits.

This became the heart of one of the most devastating charges Alexander made against Burr. There had been rivalry all along. Burr had opposed Alexander's financial plans. He'd been a political opponent to Alexander's beloved father-in-law. But he was financially corrupt. Alexander had seen this with Burr's law clients. He'd felt the sting of it with the Manhattan Company.

This is why Alexander listed his opinions about the man in a private, nine-point letter to several friends—a letter that eventually found its way to Burr.

"1. He is in every sense a profligate; a voluptuary in the extreme, with uncommon habits of expence; in his profession extortionate to a proverb; suspected on strong grounds of having *corruptly* served the views of the Holland Company, in the capacity as a member of our legislature: and understood to have been guilty of several breaches of probity in his pecuniary transactions. His very friends don't insist on his integrity.

"2. He is without doubt insolvent for a large *deficit*. All his visible property is deeply mortgaged, and he is known to owe other large debts, for which there is no specific security. . . ."

No political office paid enough money to get Burr out of his financial trough. He would face the temptation of selling out the nation to a foreign country, abusing the public trust, or even causing a war. This made him dangerous.

Alexander wasn't the only one who despised Burr. James Monroe—no fan of Alexander's—said, "I consider Burr as a man to be shunned."

Even Jefferson disliked his vice president. In his private journal, he wrote, "His conduct very soon inspired me with distrust. I habitually cautioned Mr. Madison against trusting him too much."

IN JUNE 1804, ALEXANDER'S SON JAMES HAD asked for his father's help on a speech he'd written for a class at Columbia.

Alexander wrote back: "I have prepared for you a Thesis on Discretion. *You may need it.* God bless you."

His thesis for his son was infused with hard-won wisdom. Discretion would steer a man free from potential errors, Alexander wrote. "*Discretion* is the MENTOR which ought to accompany every Young *Telemachus* in his journey through life."

Telemachus was the son of the Greek warrior Odysseus, a man known for his cleverness. Odysseus ended the Trojan War, and then took ten years to return home to his son and long-suffering wife, enduring many trials along the way (and sometimes cheating on his wife). It was an odyssey not unlike Alexander's own.

That same month, Alexander received a letter from Burr, who demanded to know what Alexander had been saying about him. Two days later, Alexander replied. He'd tracked down the letter Burr had mentioned. The accusation in it was too vague to acknowledge. He trusted that Burr, after thinking about it, would agree. Otherwise, "I can only regret the circumstance, and must abide the consequences."

That line said everything: this long rivalry had ruptured into an affair of honor.

Burr turned to William P. Van Ness, his second, to craft a response. When Alexander received it, he dug in his heels and chose a second of his own, Nathaniel Pendleton. The two seconds tried to reach an agreement that would head off a duel. They could not.

As the sparks between Burr and Alexander began to smolder, a veterans' group called the Society of the Cincinnati met at the Fraunces Tavern to celebrate the Fourth of July. Both Alexander and Burr attended. Burr was gloomy and quiet, his gaze fixed on a cheerful Alexander as he sang along to "Why, Soldiers, Why," which was also known as "Wolfe's Song."

WHY, SOLDIERS, WHY?

WHY SHOULD WE BE MELANCHOLY BOYS,

WHY SOLDIERS WHY?

WHOSE BUSINESS 'TIS TO DIE;

WHAT? SIGHING? FYE!

DAMN FEAR, DRINK ON, BE JOLLY BOYS;

'TIS HE, YOU OR I,

COLD, HOT, WET, OR DRY;

WE'RE ALWAYS BOUND TO FOLLOW BOYS,

AND SCORN TO FLY.

THAT SAME DAY, A WEDNESDAY, ALEXANDER SAT down to write the first of two farewell letters to his wife. Through Pendleton, Alexander let Burr know he'd be available to duel any time after the following Sunday.

When that Sunday arrived, Alexander and Eliza set out before the summer heat became oppressive for a stroll through the grounds of the Grange. Then he gathered his family around and read through the morning service of the Episcopal Church. The family spent that afternoon together, and when twilight fell, Alexander gathered his children around him at the base of a tree. They lay together in the grass until the sky blackened and the stars emerged from the infinite darkness overhead.

The next day, the seconds worked out the particulars of the duel. In his office at 12 Garden Street, Alexander seemed tranquil, going about business as usual. He tended his clients' needs, and then he wrote his will and outlined his financial obligations, which weighed heavily on him. He worked until the setting sun's rays bent through the window, casting a glow on the mundane tools of work. One man remained in the office with Alexander, a clerk named Judah Hammond. The clerk noticed nothing amiss as his boss stood by his desk in the gently fading light. "These were his last moments in his place of business."

Alexander may have concealed his cares, but his heart groaned under the weight of them. Should he be killed, his wife and children would probably have to rely on the generosity of friends to escape poverty.

He didn't want to duel. Duels violated his religious and moral principles. His life was of the utmost importance to his dear family. He owed money to others, and he did not wish to harm them with unpaid debt. What's more, he didn't have ill will toward Burr. It was a political matter, not a personal one. He had nothing to gain from dueling.

But he had to do it, and he enumerated his reasons. Yes, he'd said bad things about Burr's political principles and private conduct, but he couldn't disavow statements he believed to be true. This made the duel unavoidable, even as dueling was wrong.

As he contemplated what was to come, Alexander reserved empathy for Burr. Alexander's words had no doubt been painful for his rival. What's more, some lies might have been thrown into the mix by people who passed the comments along. The best Alexander could hope was that Burr had satisfied his own conscience with his actions.

For his part, he hoped the world believed his words were just. "It is also my ardent wish that I may have been more mistaken than I think I have been, and that he by his future conduct may shew himself worthy of all confidence and esteem, and prove an ornament and blessing to his Country."

He had good reason to believe Burr would survive the duel and go on to shine. He planned to throw away his first shot, and maybe even his second, to give opportunity to Burr to pause and reflect.

THE DUEL WOULD HAPPEN JUST AFTER DAWN ON July 11. Alexander had been involved in many affairs of honor, but this was the first time he'd stare down a gun's dark barrel. He hoped Burr would be as halfhearted as he'd been with John Church, taking lazy aim with a misloaded weapon. Then he could put this unhappy business behind him and return to the work of tending his family, his home, and his law practice.

The night before the duel, he visited Robert Troup and spent an evening with Oliver Wolcott and friends at Wolcott's house. He put on his most cheerful face. Then he returned home and took to his desk. By the light of a candle, he wrote a final letter.

This one was to Eliza.

It was 10:00 p.m., almost time.

EARLY THE NEXT MORNING, ALEXANDER STEPPED outside. It was 5:00 a.m.—about a half hour before sunrise. He closed the door to his house behind him; he had an appointment to keep. Because dueling was illegal in New York, the seconds had arranged for Alexander and Burr to meet in Weehawken, New Jersey, at a spot beneath the pale, ridged cliffs of the Palisades that was secluded enough and reachable from Manhattan by water.

Alexander and Burr crossed the Hudson in separate boats rowed by four men each. These men would neither see the duel nor the weapons and thus could not stand as witnesses should there be a trial. Alexander brought Pendleton and Dr. David Hosack. Burr brought William P. Van Ness and his surgeon. Alexander had a pair of pistols concealed in a portmanteau.

The boats crossed the river in the first glints of daylight. Burr arrived first, at six thirty in the morning. When Alexander landed just before seven, he found Burr and Van Ness with their coats off, clearing brush and tree limbs so there was enough space to fight.

The men greeted each other. The seconds cast their lots. Alexander's won both, giving him the choice of where to stand. Pendleton would also call out the words to start the duel.

The seconds loaded the guns, the same pair used when a button was shot off Burr's coat. Manufactured by Wogdon of London, these walnut pistols had concealed hair triggers that made them prone to fire quickly. They had sights on the front and rear, as well as nine-inch barrels weighted with bronze. The bores were unusually large, big enough to accommodate a one-ounce ball of lead.

A gun from the same set had killed Alexander's son.

The men stood ten paces apart. Alexander faced south. The bright morning sun shot its rays through the surrounding brush and trees.

"Stop," he said. "In certain states of the light one requires glasses." He pulled spectacles from his pocket, put them on, and checked his weapon's sights. "This will do. Now you may proceed."

Pendleton confirmed the men were ready. The seconds stood with their backs to the duelers so they could swear they saw no shots fired.

Pendleton shouted, "Present!"

The men aimed. Shots rang out. One, from Alexander's gun, lodged itself in a cedar bough twelve feet off the ground and behind Burr. The other blasted through Alexander's abdomen, just above his right hip. It fractured a rib, ravaged his diaphragm and liver, and buried itself in his spine. The bullet's force lifted him up on his toes. Then he turned to the left and collapsed, landing on his face.

"Dr. Hosack!" Pendleton dropped into the dirt and pulled Alexander into his lap.

Burr took a step toward his victim, a regretful look on his face. Then, without saying a word, he turned and fled. Van Ness concealed Burr's face behind an umbrella so that neither the surgeon nor the bargemen could say they'd seen him.

Hosack raced to Alexander's side. Gazing up, Alexander said, "This is a mortal wound, Doctor."

The doctor stripped off Alexander's clothing and knew

immediately that the ball had struck a vital organ. Alexander stopped breathing, and when Hosack put his hand on Alexander's heart, he perceived no motion.

"His only chance of survival is to get him to the water," Hosack told Pendleton.

Pendleton carried Alexander out of the woods and to the riverbank. The bargemen loaded Alexander, pushed off, and raced toward Manhattan.

Hosack searched for signs of life. He rubbed Alexander's face, his lips, and his temples with spirits of hartshorn, the same fluid that had helped rouse Philip in the bath when he had typhus. Hosack also smeared it on Alexander's neck and chest, on his wrists, and palms, and even tried to pour a little into his mouth.

When the bargemen had rowed them some fifty yards from shore, Alexander sputtered a few breaths. Within minutes, he sighed, revived either by the hartshorn or the fresh air rising off the water.

"My vision is indistinct," he said.

But his pulse grew stronger and his breathing more regular. Soon, his vision returned.

Hosack checked the wound. Pressure caused pain, so he stopped.

Alexander glanced toward the gun case. "Take care of that pistol. It is undischarged, and still cocked; it may go off and do harm." He tried to turn toward his second. "Pendleton knows that I did not intend to fire at him."

"Yes," Pendleton said. "I have already made Dr. Hosack acquainted with your determination as to that."

Alexander, unaware his gun had indeed fired, closed his eyes and kept still. He asked the doctor once or twice how his pulse was, and informed him he couldn't feel his legs. Hosack adjusted Alexander's limbs, but it didn't help. He'd been paralyzed.

As they drew near the shore, Alexander thought of his wife. "Let Mrs. Hamilton be immediately sent for—let the event be gradually broken to her; but give her hopes."

When a messenger reached Eliza, she was told Alexander was suffering spasms.

From the shore, Alexander's friend William Bayard scanned the river for their return. As they drew nearer, Bayard saw only Pendleton and the doctor sitting. He clasped his hands in fear.

"Have a cot prepared," Hosack called out.

Bayard, spying Alexander lying in the bottom of the boat, wept. Alexander was the only one who remained composed. The men carried him to a large, square room on the second floor of Bayard's house in Greenwich Village.

"MY VISION IS INDISTINCT."

He'd grown faint when he was removed from the boat, so Hosack administered a weak mixture of wine and water. They undressed Alexander, laid him in bed, and darkened the room.

The pain increased. Hosack gave him laudanum and other painkillers. Another doctor was summoned, but he could only shake his head. The French consul sent a surgeon from a nearby frigate to see if his experience treating gunshot wounds might help, but he only confirmed the opinion of the other doctors: there was nothing to be done for Alexander.

"My beloved wife and children," Alexander said, over and over.

His family held on to hope.

Eliza's sister Angelica wrote from Bayard's house: "My dear Brother, I have the painful task to inform you that General Hamilton was this morning wouned by that *wretch Burr* but we have every reason to hope that he will recover.

ABOVE: *AFTER THE DUEL, A PARALYZED ALEXANDER WAS CARRIED TO THE BAYARD MANSION.*

May I advice that you repair immediately to my father, as perhaps he may wish to come down—My dear Sister bears with saintlike fortitude this affliction; The Town is in consternation, and there exists only *the expression of Grief* & Indignation."

At one in the afternoon, a clergyman arrived to give Alexander his last rites. Before receiving Communion one last time, Alexander lifted his hands and said, "I have no ill will against Colonel Burr. I met him with a fixed resolution to do him no harm. I forgive all that happened."

He was able to sleep a bit in the night, but by the next day, his symptoms worsened. His mind remained clear and focused on his family. When they arrived at his bedside, he opened his eyes and looked at the seven of them.

"Remember, my Eliza, you are a Christian." He kept his voice firm. Then he closed his eyes until the people he loved most were taken from the room.

At two o'clock in the afternoon, Alexander Hamilton died.

THE NEWS LEVELED HIS FAMILY.

"My Dear Dearly Beloved and Affectionate Child," Philip Schuyler wrote to Eliza, "If aught under heaven could aggravate the affliction I experience, it is that . . . I cannot fly to you to pour the balm of comfort into your afflicted bosom, to water it with my tears, to solace yours and mine in this depressing situation."

Oliver Wolcott, who'd shared some of Alexander's best and worst days as well as his last night, rushed over as soon as he heard the news. "Thus has perished one of the greatest men of this or any age," he told his wife.

In a second letter, Wolcott wrote, "Yesterday General Hamilton expired in the midst of his family, who are agonized beyond description. No person who witnessed their distress will ever be induced to fight a duel—unless he is a person wholly insensible to every sentiment of humanity."

Wolcott was in shock. Alexander had a brilliant mind. He was moral and decent. Devoted to his family. And here he'd been, secretly settling his affairs for days because a concern for justice over small matters had blinded him to the importance of his family obligations.

"It proves," he wrote, "that on certain points, the most enlightened men are governed by the most unsound reasons."

ALEXANDER'S FUNERAL TOOK PLACE JULY 14. New York City turned itself inside out for its favorite son. Starting at 10:00 a.m., a British warship dressed for mourning fired guns every five minutes for an hour. French frigates fired, too, and merchant vessels flew their flags at half-mast.

An enormous procession began at the Churches' house on Robinson Street. When the casket appeared, the military saluted, and a band struck up melancholy music as mourners headed through town toward the church. So many had turned out: The Society of the Cincinnati. A militia regiment. Army and navy officers. Lawyers. Government leaders and agents from foreign consuls. Bank officers. Port wardens and ships' captains. The entirety of Columbia College. Merchants, mechanics, and people from all walks of life followed the coffin as it was carried through the city to Trinity Church by a gray horse, filling the streets and doorways and standing on rooftops. Women everywhere wept.

Alexander's hat and sword rested on top of the coffin, and his empty boots and spurs rode backward in the stirrups. Two black servants in white clothing and black-and-white turbans led his horse. As the mourners made their way up Beekman, Pearl, and Whitehall Streets, and then along Broadway to Trinity Church, more guns fired from the Battery.

Gouverneur Morris, flanked by four of Alexander's boys, delivered the eulogy. He had given thought to what he'd say about his friend. He couldn't gloss over his embarrassing birth. What's more, Alexander had flaws: vanity, a lack of discretion, too many opinions. He'd died in a duel, an illegal practice. He'd been unfaithful to his wife. These truths had to be told, along with the other truths about him.

Slowly and clearly, Morris spoke his last words about his beloved, brilliant, complicated friend who'd flown to the mansions of bliss. His speech walked the crowd through Alexander's past, from his days as a college student and a zealous

ABOVE: *ALEXANDER IS BURIED AT TRINITY CHURCH IN MANHATTAN.*

military recruit to his time in Washington's family, where he was a principal actor in the most important scenes of the Revolution. Morris reminded them of what happened in Philadelphia, where Alexander helped craft the Constitution, and followed with his years of public service.

"WOULD HAMILTON HAVE DONE THIS THING?"

"Washington sought for splendid talents, for extensive information, and, above all, he sought for sterling, incorruptible integrity—All these he found in Hamilton."

Morris talked about the dark days, too, where people criticized Alexander's work and his actions, and the way he continued to serve, even as he needed to care for his own family.

"He never lost sight of your interests," Morris told the mourners. "I declare to you, before that God in whose presence we are now so especially assembled, that in his most private and confidential conversations, the single objects of discussion and consideration were your freedom and happiness."

Yes, Alexander had been called ambitious, but he was not, except for the kind of glory that came from serving humanity. He was a veteran. A brilliant lawyer. An eloquent speaker and writer with no peer. He was a good man, a great one, too, and an inspiration for all.

"I CHARGE YOU TO PROTECT HIS FAME—It is all he has left—all that these poor orphan children will inherit from their father. But, my countrymen, that Fame may be a rich treasure to you also. Let it be the test by which to examine those who

solicit your favour. Disregarding professions, view their conduct and on a doubtful occasion, ask, *Would Hamilton have
done this thing?"*

After Morris's final words rang through the air, Alexander's
body was lowered into the earth. The circle of life, his perfect
retirement, was complete.

ALEXANDER'S DEATH HAD INDEED LEFT HIS FAM-
ily in financial straits. Oliver Wolcott wrote to a small group
of friends seeking to raise $100,000 to pay off Alexander's
debts and provide for Eliza and the children. All those rumors
that he'd stashed away money, that he'd enriched himself in
speculation, that he'd been corrupt—these were nothing more
than empty words.

"My public labours have amounted to an absolute sacrifice
of the interests of my family," Alexander had written as he
contemplated his death.

Even in his last hours, though, he had not seen everything
clearly. His public labors had left his family poor. Protecting
his honor had left them bereft of so much more.

When Nathaniel Pendleton opened the packet of papers
Alexander had left for him, he found the last two letters Alexander had written to Eliza. One asked her to be of service to
his cousin Ann Mitchell, the daughter of the Lyttons in Saint
Croix. The other was for her heart alone. He'd written it on
Independence Day, after he'd drunk wine with his fellow
soldiers and sung a song of death while Aaron Burr seethed
in the shadows.

The letter answered the mystery that was Alexander: the reason his honor was worth his life. It was something he'd only come to understand himself when the end was near.

This letter, my very dear Eliza, will not be delivered to you unless I shall first have terminated my earthly career: to begin, as I humbly hope, from redeeming grace and divine mercy, a happy immortality.

If it had been possible for me to have avoided the interview, my love for you and my precious children would have been alone a decisive motive. But it was not possible, without sacrifices which would have rendered me unworthy of your esteem. I need not tell you of the pangs I feel from the idea of quitting you, and exposing you to the anguish which I know you would feel. Nor could I dwell on the topic lest it unman me.

The consolations of Religion, my beloved, can alone support you; and these you have a right to enjoy. Fly to the bosom of your God and be comforted.

With my last idea; I shall cherish the sweet hope of meeting you in a better world.

Adieu best of wives and Best of women. Embrace all my darling Children for me.

Ever yours,

A.H.

JULY 4, 1804

HIS HONOR WAS WORTH HIS LIFE BECAUSE IT was the thing that made him worthy of love. *All for love.* That's what honor had been for, the honor he'd been born without, the honor he'd given body, heart, and mind to earn. He'd nearly thrown it away with Maria Reynolds, and when he understood what he'd almost lost, he was willing to surrender his life so that he might deserve the best thing about it, someplace better, and for all time.

ABOVE: *HIS GRAVE IS AN ELEGANT MONUMENT. ELIZA'S IS RIGHT NEXT TO HIS.*

EPILOGUE

FOUR MONTHS AFTER Alexander died, Philip Schuyler passed away as well. His estate did not leave Eliza and her family with much, and she and the children had to sell the Grange at auction. They were able to buy it back with help from Alexander's friends.

She also petitioned the government for back military pay due to Alexander, as well as a land grant he'd never applied for. It took until 1837 for her to receive $30,000.

The remainder of her years she spent serving others. She helped found the first private orphanage in New York in 1806, and she continued to take orphaned children into her own home. Her beloved sister Angelica died in 1814.

Eliza remained fiercely devoted to her Hamilton, wearing for the rest of her days both the wedding ring he had given her and a leather bag around her neck containing the poem he'd written her. She organized his papers for future biographers, and she made sure he received credit for writing George Washington's farewell address to the nation. She never forgave James Monroe for his betrayal in the Reynolds affair.

Often in Washington, D.C., to visit her daughter, Eliza joined forces with Dolley Madison, who'd married Alexander's political enemy James Madison. Together, the two women raised funds to build the Washington Monument.

Eliza died in 1854, a half century after her husband. Eliza's grave is right beside Alexander's, in the cemetery at Trinity Church in New York City.

HAMILTON'S FAMILY

JAMES
HAMILTON

ca. 1718–1799

RACHEL
FAWCETT LAVIEN

*between 1725 and 1729–
February 19, 1768*

JAMES
HAMILTON

1752 or 1753–ca. 1786

ALEXANDER
HAMILTON

*January 11, 1755–
July 12, 1804*

PHILIP

*January 22, 1782–
November 24, 1801*

JAMES ALEXANDER

*April 14, 1788–
September 24, 1878*

ANGELICA

*September 25, 1784–
February 6, 1857*

ALEXANDER JR.

*May 16, 1786–
August 2, 1875*

* All likenesses on this spread except for Philip Schuyler, Alexander Hamilton, Elizabeth Schuyler Hamilton, and Philip
Hamilton are artists' renderings. The seven younger children are depicted at their ages when their father was killed;
Philip had died almost three years before.

PHILIP SCHUYLER

*November 22, 1733–
November 18, 1804*

CATHERINE VAN RENSSELAER SCHUYLER

*November 4, 1734–
March 7, 1803*

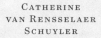

ELIZABETH SCHUYLER HAMILTON

*August 9, 1757–
November 9, 1854*

JOHN CHURCH

*August 22, 1792–
July 25, 1882*

PHILIP
(also called Little Phil)

June 1, 1802–July 9, 1884

WILLIAM STEPHEN

*August 4, 1797–
August 7, 1850*

ELIZABETH

*November 26, 1799–
October 17, 1859*

ALLIES & ENEMIES

 *ALLIES*

HUGH KNOX

Intellectual father figure to Alexander, this minister gave him access to his library, encouraged his study, and helped publish his writing, putting Alexander on a path to America.

DAVID BEEKMAN AND NICHOLAS CRUGER

New York merchants and benefactors, they supplied Alexander's mother's store and gave Alexander his first job. Nicholas Cruger set up the scholarship fund that sent Alexander to New York after the hurricane.

THOMAS STEVENS

Stevens, a respected merchant on Saint Croix, served as foster father and housed Alexander after his mother and other relatives died.

EDWARD "NED" STEVENS

Alexander's best friend from childhood, Ned also moved to America. He became a doctor and later saved Alexander's and Eliza's lives when they had yellow fever.

HERCULES MULLIGAN

An Irish immigrant turned tailor turned revolutionary spy, Mulligan was one of the first men Alexander met in New York.

ROBERT TROUP

A lifelong friend, Troup tutored Alexander in law, loaned him money, and came to hate Aaron Burr, who once called him "a great, fat fellow."

WILLIAM LIVINGSTON

A mentor of Alexander in his prep school days, Livingston was a delegate to the First and Second Continental Congresses, an active abolitionist, and a delegate alongside Alexander at the Constitutional Convention.

ELIAS BOUDINOT

A dear friend from Alexander's prep school days, Boudinot was the commissary general of prisoners during the early years of the Revolution, a member of Congress, and its president when the Treaty of Paris was signed.

MYLES COOPER

The president of Alexander's college and a loyalist, Cooper was someone Alexander defended against a violent mob.

JOHN LAURENS

Alexander's best friend during the Revolution, Laurens worked with Alexander to try to enlist enslaved men before Laurens was killed in action. He was one of the last to die in the Revolution.

LAFAYETTE

The Marquis de Lafayette and Alexander became dear friends during the war and, in the final battle, led units that stormed British redoubts side by side.

GEORGE WASHINGTON

The leader of the Continental Army and first president of the United States, Washington was a loyal and lifelong friend to Alexander.

BARON VON STEUBEN

Unable to find military work in Europe because he was accused of improper same-sex relationships, he trained Continental Army troops and wrote the first military handbook of the United States, which Alexander helped translate.

NATHANAEL GREENE

Born in Rhode Island, the self-taught soldier with a bum leg from a childhood accident became one of Washington's most trusted generals in the Continental Army, where he served so well that grateful Southerners gave him cash and land in Georgia.

JAMES McHENRY

The only one of Washington's wartime family to attend Alexander's wedding, McHenry, a surgeon, represented Maryland at the Constitutional Convention and served as secretary of war under Presidents Washington and Adams.

TENCH COXE

Coxe worked as assistant secretary of the Treasury under Alexander and helped him write some of his most famous reports.

ELIZABETH SCHUYLER HAMILTON

A devoted wife to Alexander, Eliza often acted as a sounding board and transcriptionist for his writing. After his death, she founded New York's first private orphanage, fought for Alexander's legacy, and helped raise funds for the Washington Monument.

ANGELICA SCHUYLER CHURCH

The older sister of Alexander's wife, Angelica Church was worldly, beautiful, and so desirable that Alexander's rival Thomas Jefferson once tried to seduce her.

PHILIP SCHUYLER

Father of Eliza and Angelica, Schuyler was a major general in the Continental Army and a United States senator from New York, running against Aaron Burr for the seat. He and Alexander were close; his enemies were his son-in-law's, and vice versa.

JOHN JAY

He wrote five of the *Federalist* papers arguing for the ratification of the Constitution by the states, and he negotiated the Jay Treaty between Britain and the United States, averting a war in 1795.

OLIVER WOLCOTT, JR.

Son of a signer of the Declaration of Independence, Wolcott worked for Alexander in the Treasury Department and remained a loyal friend even after the scandalous Maria Reynolds affair, which threatened the integrity of the department. He followed Alexander as Treasury secretary in 1795.

TIMOTHY PICKERING

A secretary of state under Presidents Washington and Adams, Pickering leaned on Alexander for advice.

GOUVERNEUR MORRIS

A fellow lawyer and connoisseur of women, Morris lost a leg either in a carriage accident or as he fled an irate husband. He also talked the most at the Constitutional Convention, wrote the Constitution's famous preamble, and gave Alexander's eulogy at his funeral.

E N E M I E S

HORATIO GATES

A former British soldier who became an American general, Gates replaced General Schuyler, Alexander's future father-in-law, as commander of the northern troops after a crushing loss in Ticonderoga. Gates also secretly tried to take over George Washington's job, and ultimately abandoned his own men during their retreat in the Battle of Camden in South Carolina.

CHARLES LEE

Nicknamed Boiling Water for his bad temper, Lee performed dismally at the Battle of Monmouth and was court-martialed. Afterward, he dueled John Laurens for George Washington's honor. In 1858, more than seventy-five years after his death, Lee was found to have been a traitor.

AARON BURR

A fellow orphan and soldier who fought alongside Alexander and worked with him as an attorney, Burr had no fixed political principles, which outraged Alexander and eventually led to a fatal duel between the two.

JAMES AND MARIA REYNOLDS

Maria seduced Alexander. Her husband found out, encouraged the affair, and extorted money from Alexander. Aaron Burr was their divorce attorney.

JAMES MADISON

Though he collaborated with Alexander on the final draft of the Constitution and the *Federalist* papers urging the states to ratify it, the two men diverged politically afterward, with Madison arguing for a weak federal government and Alexander arguing for an energetic one.

THOMAS JEFFERSON

The principal author of the Declaration of Independence, Jefferson was George Washington's first secretary of state. He despised Alexander but reached a critical agreement with Alexander and James Madison that put the nation's capital in Washington, D.C., in exchange for the government's assumption of state debt accrued during the Revolutionary War.

JAMES MONROE

Monroe was one of three congressmen who initially thought Alexander might have speculated in U.S. securities after a connection between James Reynolds and Alexander was discovered in a Treasury Department investigation. Monroe was in charge of letters and documents proving the affair; the documents were later leaked to a merciless political writer, nearly causing a duel between Monroe and Alexander.

TIME LINE

c. 1755

BORN ON NEVIS

1772

ARRIVES IN NEW YORK

1774

ENTERS KING'S COLLEGE

1775–1782: *Revolutionary War*

1776

BECOMES AN ARTILLERY CAPTAIN

July 4, 1776: *Congress approves the Declaration of Independence*

1777

BECOMES AN AIDE-DE-CAMP TO GEORGE WASHINGTON

1777: *Continental Congress adopts Articles of Confederation*

1778–1781: *States slowly ratify Articles*

1780

MARRIES ELIZABETH SCHUYLER

1781

LEADS CHARGE AT YORKTOWN

1783: *Treaty of Paris signed*

1783–1787

LAWYER AND CONGRESSMAN

1787

ATTENDS CONSTITUTIONAL CONVENTION

May 1787: *Constitutional Convention begins in Philadelphia*

September 17, 1787: *Constitution signed by thirty-nine delegates from twelve states*

December 1787–May 1790: *All thirteen states ratify the Constitution*

1787–1788

COWRITES *FEDERALIST* ESSAYS WITH JAMES MADISON AND JOHN JAY

1789–1795

SERVES AS FIRST SECRETARY OF THE U.S. TREASURY

1790

PERSUADES CONGRESS TO ASSUME STATES' REVOLUTIONARY DEBT, CREATING A BASIS FOR PUBLIC CREDIT

1791

PERSUADES CONGRESS TO ESTABLISH A NATIONAL BANK, HAS AFFAIR WITH MARIA REYNOLDS

1794

PUTS DOWN WHISKEY REBELLION

1796

WRITES WASHINGTON'S FAREWELL ADDRESS

1797

PUBLISHES REYNOLDS PAMPHLET ABOUT AFFAIR

1801

FOUNDS *NEW-YORK EVENING POST*; ONE WEEK LATER, HIS SON PHILIP DIES IN A DUEL

1804

KILLED BY AARON BURR

STUDENT ▸ SOLDIER ▸ SECRETARY ▸ CITIZEN

THE NATURAL WORLD: DISEASE AND HURRICANES

HOW HURRICANES WORK

THE STORM THAT SENT ALEXANDER TO NEW YORK was a hurricane—one of the most violent forms of storm on the planet. Hurricanes gather after the heat of summer has warmed the ocean. Warm, humid air rises, causing an area of low pressure below.

Air rushes in to balance the pressure. This starts a cycle where air from areas with higher air pressure zooms into areas of low pressure. In the right conditions, a spinning clot of clouds and wind forms, and this wheel of zooming air pushes the warm water ahead of it, creating a storm surge that can increase the average water level fifteen feet.

MEDICAL PRACTICES IN THE 1700s

PEOPLE IN ALEXANDER'S TIME FACED A VARIETY of diseases that could be deadly, painful, irritating, or all three: malaria, typhus, influenza, smallpox, whooping cough, tuberculosis, dysentery, scurvy, arthritis, and worms.

People then didn't understand that bacteria and viruses can cause disease, nor was it clear that an underlying disease was separate from its symptoms. Rather, they believed disease occurred when the body's four humors—blood, phlegm, yellow bile, and black

ABOVE: *ALCHEMIC APPROACH TO FOUR HUMORS IN RELATION TO THE FOUR ELEMENTS AND ZODIACAL SIGNS.*

bile—fell out of balance. As a result, medical treatments could be hit or miss and, in some cases, dangerous.

There were five main methods of treating illness: bleeding, blistering, vomiting, purging, and sweating. Doctors also used herbs, bark, and leaves, as well as toxins such as mercury, and even applied leeches (sometimes to inflamed genitalia suspected of harboring sexually transmitted illnesses).

YELLOW FEVER

THIS DEADLY VIRUS, SPREAD BY MOSQUITOES, probably killed Alexander's mother. Symptoms begin with headache, fever, nausea or vomiting, and sore muscles. After a few days, the symptoms abate. In some cases, however, the virus returns with a vengeance after the brief period of quiet, savaging the kidneys and liver.

This phase is what gives the disease its name, because the liver damage causes yellow skin and eyes. Organ damage can also make victims vomit black blood. These internal hemorrhages are fatal to 20 percent to 50 percent of the people who develop the second stage of the disease—and why bleeding was not a safe or effective treatment.

TYPHUS

BEFORE HE WAS SHOT TO DEATH, PHILIP HAMILTON contracted typhus, sometimes called ship, jail, or camp fever.

This virulent illness causes fever, chills, and delirium, and later causes a rash that covers everything but the face, palms, and soles. It can also cause brain inflammation and, without treatment, death.

Typhus is transmitted through the bites of lice, fleas, and ticks and can be cured with antibiotics.

A BRIEF HISTORY OF THE COLONIES

THE LAND THAT BECAME THE UNITED STATES WAS first inhabited by millions of indigenous people from many nations, each of which had independent and sometimes interdependent governments and economies. Starting in 1565, the territory was invaded by many European countries for a variety of reasons: to expand trade, to impose Christianity, to avoid religious persecution, to seize land and resources for the benefit of the parent nation, and to prevent colonization by European rivals. The thirteen colonies that became the original United States were under British control when Americans declared their independence.

These original colonies, established between 1606 and 1732, were Virginia, Massachusetts, New Hampshire, Maryland, Connecticut, Rhode Island, Delaware, North Carolina, South Carolina, New York, New Jersey, Pennsylvania, and Georgia.

EARLY GOVERNMENT

THE BRITISH DRAFTED WRITTEN AGREEMENTS with each of their colonies in America. Called charters, these documents specified that the king ruled the colonies and appointed local governors to represent him. Colonists elected legislatures from the ranks of men who owned property, and these legislatures set the salary of the governors, as an attempt to balance the power between the two.

One famous group of pilgrims was an exception to the charter rule. The passengers on the *Mayflower* failed to land in Virginia as planned. They landed instead on the coast of what is now Massachusetts, which was outside the boundaries of the Virginia colony. As a result, their Mayflower Compact claimed they'd rule themselves.

The longer colonists put down roots in America, the more attractive the idea of self-rule became. The colonists were also influenced by philosophers of the age, especially by the work of the seventeenth-century Englishman John Locke.

Locke argued that people have three natural rights: to life, to liberty, and to own property. The government's job is to protect these rights. Citizens give a leader the authority to rule. If the government fails to protect the natural rights of the citizens, they have the right to overthrow the ruler.

As the colonists became disenchanted with British rule, they came together to form the Continental Congress. Through that body, they coordinated their resistance to England. Congress functioned as the national government during the war, balancing states' competing interests and negotiating with foreign governments. The states' representatives in Congress drafted the nation's first constitution, the Articles of Confederation, which had certain limits that hamstrung the nation before the Constitution replaced it.

BALL GOWNS, POINTY SHOES, AND ORNATE WIGS

MANUFACTURING HAD NOT YET REACHED THE colonies—that would come after the Revolution, and thanks in no small part to Alexander's efforts. So in the years prior, much of the fabric used to make clothes was imported, which meant colonial-era clothing reflected a person's status. A wealthy planter in Virginia might wear garments made from Chinese silk or Dutch linen, and English-made shoes. Enslaved people would be dressed in inexpensive imports made specifically for them in English factories. Homespun fabrics were available on the frontier.

Gowns for women had full skirts, fitted bodices, and sleeves that ended below the elbow. Women often accessorized with kerchiefs, aprons, and ruffles. Shoes were pointed, with a bit of a heel. Men of fashion and style wore tricorn hats, buckled shoes, jackets, ruffled shirts, and pants—often bejeweled for special occasions.

And then there were wigs. In the seventeenth and eighteenth centuries, fashionable people in America wore wigs and hair powder, and sometimes both. They were a status symbol that said, "I have enough money to buy hair." Louis XIII of France started this trend to conceal his premature balding.

Head lice were a common scourge, and many people kept their hair shorn as a result. Wigs could be infested, but they were easier to pick through. Even more hair-raising, a sexually transmitted disease called syphilis could cause embarrassing, patchy hair loss. Wigs—made of human or animal hair—helped hide the problem.

Wigs and hair powder went out of style at the end of the eighteenth century, though older conservatives continued to wear them into the nineteenth century.

WHAT COMBAT WAS LIKE

THE BRITISH REGULARS WERE HIGHLY TRAINED troops who had experience with the methodical, synchronized style of warfare used on open fields. It took incredible coordination for men to march and fire in perfectly controlled formation, and Americans—who weren't professional soldiers or usually inclined to take orders—weren't good at this until Baron von Steuben drilled them. They stayed alive before then by hiding behind walls, trees, and entrenchments while taking fire.

At the outset of a battle on an open field, however, opposing forces advanced shoulder to shoulder toward each other, flags flying and music playing. Often one side would open fire with longer-range artillery, softening the enemy's lines of infantrymen. When the advancing regiments were about fifty or sixty yards apart, they would fire away. The soldiers in each line would fire in unison, and well-trained troops could crack off four or five rounds in a minute. The firing clotted the air with white smoke.

The lines advanced through the smoke until they were close enough to charge with their seventeen-inch bayonets, triangular blades attached to the ends of their muskets—these were the most accurate and devastating weapons of all.

THE ARMS WERE BARE

COLONISTS WERE AT A DISADVANTAGE WHEN IT came to weapons. Though there were individual craftsmen who made guns, there were no gun factories, thanks to the Crown, and the guns they could afford to import were obsolete or damaged. So patriots seized local arsenals when they could, and France started sending weapons in 1776, thanks in part to the diplomatic negotiations of Benjamin Franklin, Lafayette, and others. As a result, patriot troops carried a mix of muskets, rifles, and other guns.

Every soldier was issued a musket, bayonet, and cartridge box, as well as tools to keep everything working. They carried rations and gear in haversacks and slung canteens over their shoulders.

The muskets were long—five feet or more—and could fire a single ball or a cluster of pellets, called shot. Musket balls ranged from about a half inch to nine-tenths of an inch in diameter and fit loosely with the gunpowder in the gun's smooth barrel, or bore. Paper cartridges of powder and ball made the guns easy to load, but their effective range was short. Bayonets attached to the end of the muskets were used in hand-to-hand combat, causing devastating puncture wounds.

Muskets weren't as accurate as rifles, the weapon of choice of colonists along the frontier, who brought their guns with them when they joined the fight against the Crown. Long rifles had grooved barrels that spun a tight-fitting ball as it blasted out of the bore, stabilizing its flight so that it could hit a target three hundred yards away, several times the range of a musket. But rifles took longer to reload, and their grooves were easily clogged with gunpowder residue. They also couldn't be fitted with bayonets. Because they weren't as standardized as muskets, soldiers had to practice more with them.

Patriots from the frontier also armed themselves with tomahawks, the Algonquian word for the light axes American Indians used as throw weapons or in hand-to-hand combat. Originally made from stone and wood, the weapons were adopted by colonists, who crafted them from sharpened metal and wood.

ARTILLERY

ALEXANDER HAMILTON STARTED HIS CAREER AS an artillery captain. The Americans, French, and British used three types of artillery: cannons, mortars, and howitzers.

CANNONS. There were two types, field guns and siege cannons. FIELD GUNS were lighter and mounted on wheeled carriages pulled by men or horses. Used against enemy soldiers, field artillery fired solid balls and grapeshot into infantry lines. SIEGE CANNONS fired solid balls at fortifications, buildings, and ships. Against flammable targets like ships or gunpowder storehouses, artillerymen would load the cannons with red-hot iron balls that could set the enemy structures on fire. Also effective against ships were bar shot and chain shot, in which two halves or two whole cannon balls were connected by a bar or chain. In the air, the two weights would cause the chain to rotate—particularly good for taking down ship's masts or rigging.

MORTARS. With barrels that rose at an angle from a flat bed of wood, mortars were used to lob an exploding shell high over enemy fortifications (cannons shot along flatter trajectories). "Bombs bursting in air" came from mortars. When the bombs burst like this, they'd rain deadly shrapnel on the enemy below.

HOWITZERS. If a cannon and a mortar had a child, it would be a howitzer. Howitzers were mounted on wheeled carriages and could fire bombs or cannonballs at different trajectories.

HOW THE EARLY TRADE CYCLE WORKED

COLONIES WERE MEANT to generate wealth and give the colonizing nation an advantage over its rivals. This economic boon came at the expense of southeastern Indian tribes and Africans, who were enslaved and imported to perform the grueling labor.

COLONISTS ⟶ CARIBBEAN

flour, bread, corn, salted beef, wood, and American Indians captured and sent as slaves

CARIBBEAN ⟶ COLONISTS

sugar, rum, molasses, limes, cocoa, ginger

EUROPE ⟶ AFRICA

fabrics, clothes, simple manufactured goods

AFRICA ⟶ EUROPE, AMERICA, CARIBBEAN, BRAZIL

enslaved people, who were sold for sugar

NORTH AMERICA ⟶ EUROPE

rum brought by ships' captains

RELATIONS WITH TRIBAL NATIONS

EVEN THOUGH AMERICAN INDIANS ARE OFTEN referred to as a monolithic people, this is not the case. There are many sovereign Indian nations today, as there were during the time of the American Revolution, when Indian nations had treaties with England, Spain, France, and the newly formed United States. Today, tribal citizens can be citizens of their tribes, of their states, and of the United States simultaneously.

Before the Revolutionary War, land—and who owned it— created massive conflict. The Proclamation of 1763 said that lands beyond the Appalachian mountain range, considered the frontier, were out of bounds for colonial governments. The Crown, which asserted sovereignty over the lands, had "reserved" them for the indigenous tribes that lived there. This angered the colonists, especially those bent on settling and speculating that territory themselves.

Meanwhile, the colonists hoped to keep the war between themselves and England. The Second Continental Congress, in a speech to the Six Nations (a confederacy of Mohawk, Onondaga, Cayuga, Seneca, and Tuscarora tribes) said in July 1775, "This is a family quarrel between us and Old England. You Indians are not concerned in it. We don't wish you to take up the hatchet against the king's troops. We desire you to remain at home, and not join on either side, but keep the hatchet buried deep."

During the war, relationships among colonists, indigenous tribes, and England were complicated. Some Indian nations remained neutral, some took sides, and some—such as the Iroquois Confederacy—were divided.

The question before Indian nations then was how best they might protect their land and sovereignty in the face of conflict between the colonies and England. The nations that sided with the English did not do so because they were fighting for the Crown, but rather because they saw a British victory as their best chance to keep their land safe from American colonists and land speculators who viewed tribal lands as sources of potential profit.

In New England, tribes tended to support the colonists. Some volunteered to serve as minutemen, even before the war started. One of the first men killed in the conflict, Crispus Attucks, had both African and Wampanoag ancestry. Other Indians supported Washington's army at the siege of Boston, and in New York, New Jersey, and Canada.

Mohawk Indians, who were members of the Iroquois Confederacy, remained aligned with the British, along with most Cayugas, Onondagas, and Senecas. But members of the Oneida and Tuscarora nations joined the American side, making the Revolution a devastating civil war for the Iroquois.

Cherokee Indians on the Appalachian frontier were incensed at colonial land grabs. The Creeks and Catawbas sided with the British for this reason as well.

In Ohio country, the Senecas and Shawnees intended to be neutral, as did the Delawares, who signed a treaty in 1778 that promised "perpetual peace and friendship." But in 1782, after Americans massacred Indians in Gnadenhutten, Ohio, these Indians allied with the British and continued to resist American expansion long after the Revolution ended.

After the war, the 1783 Treaty of Paris made no provision to protect the land of the Indians who'd allied with England. As a result, land that England had claimed as territory—east of the Mississippi, south of the Great Lakes, and north of Florida—was ceded to the United States for future expansion. Tribes that had allied with the states, meanwhile, including the Mohicans and Oneidas, also lost land.

George Washington called on Alexander to intervene in violations of treaties by American states. These violations were a federal matter because the treaties were between the United States and sovereign Indian nations. In one case, when Alexander asked Washington for leave to care for his seriously ill toddler, Washington let him go but pleaded for advice on how to deal with Georgia citizens who were encroaching on Creek territory and trying to set up their own government there. Alexander told Washington to reassure the Creek leaders that the United States wouldn't stand for such intrusions.

Alexander advocated for peaceful relations with Indian nations, and he lent support to the Hamilton-Oneida Academy, which was meant to educate Indian children, a progressive position for the time. But he also supported policies of Washington's that eventually led to loss of land and forced migration for Indian tribes. And he served as Washington's right-hand man during the war, when Washington's devastating fighting techniques earned him the name "Town Destroyer" with members of the Six Nations.

A BRIEF HISTORY OF THE SUGAR TRADE

THE HUMAN LOVE AFFAIR WITH SUGAR GOES BACK centuries. People in India first figured out how to extract and purify sugarcane into crystals, and their technique reached Persia in the sixth century. Traveling Arabs during the medieval era brought the know-how to the Mediterranean. But it wasn't until the age of exploration that the world went mad for the stuff.

It's hard to imagine something so common today being treasured like gold, but between 1600 and 1800, the rush for sugar and its profits drove much of the world's economy, creating a trade cycle that linked Europe with Africa, Asia, and the Americas.

When it was rare, sugar was a substance for kings and was presented in elegant desserts and sculptures for their enjoyment. It could also be turned into alcohol or traded for other goods. Some considered it medicinal. Eventually, sugar became something everyone wanted—especially for their tea. By the mid-1700s, English people drank up to fifty cups of tea per day. American colonists drank even more, and they stirred several spoonfuls of sugar into each cup.

Tea in some cases was more than a comforting drink. Factories started cropping up in England to hasten production of the goods that needed to be sold to buy tea and sugar, as well as the cheap fabric used to clothe the enslaved people who produced the sugar. To keep the workers going for long hours at the factory, employers needed something inexpensive, hot, and filling.

Tea—with plenty of sugar—fit the bill.

THE LINK BETWEEN SUGAR AND SLAVERY

GREED FOR SUGAR FUELED THE AFRICAN SLAVE trade. Most enslaved people were taken to sugar plantations in the Caribbean, Brazil, and South America. Only 4 percent were sold in North America.

Alexander witnessed terrible conditions in the canebrakes. The work was arduous, and enslaved people survived an average of just seven years in the sugar islands.

First, enslaved men, women, and children had to prepare the rough soil, sometimes by hand. They worked five-foot-square patches, digging the soil five inches deep. Seeders pushed cuttings into the holes or rows and covered them with earth. Weeders—often enslaved women and small boys—removed undergrowth that choked the growing cane and attracted rats, working ten to fourteen hours a day in brutal heat. Others cut

ABOVE: *THIS LITHOGRAPH DEPICTS ENSLAVED WORKERS CUTTING SUGARCANE IN TRINIDAD, 1836.*

and transported wood to fire the boiling vats of bubbling syrup. Specialists watched the cane ripen. This was an important job: timing was everything in sugar production, and they had to bundle the cane rapidly during the harvest.

At the mill, enslaved people, often women, fed the bundled cane into dangerous machinery. They kept axes at the ready to chop off trapped limbs before people's entire bodies were ground to bits.

It took a great deal of heat to produce sugar, making the boiling houses so hot they had to be sprayed with water so they wouldn't catch fire. Huge copper cauldrons boiled sugar into a foamy syrup. Enslaved workers skimmed scum from the surface and strained the syrup repeatedly until it reached the proper purity. Inevitably, some people fell in.

Finally, the thick, clean syrup was left to crystallize. Then enslaved people sorted grains into white and brown piles. The whiter the sugar, the more valuable.

Enslaved people who were thought to have stepped out of line, attempted escape, or dared protest were whipped—sometimes hundreds of times. They were branded, castrated, chained, and locked in dungeons. An enslaved person faced losing a hand.

FEDERALISM
VS.
ANTIFEDERALISM

THE UNITED STATES DIDN'T ALWAYS HAVE AN
identity as a single nation. People thought of themselves first
as citizens of their colonies, and later, their states. When frustrations with England rose to intolerable levels, the colonies
came together for the first time as a confederation, but people
still thought of themselves primarily as citizens of their states.
It wasn't until after the Revolution that people worked to figure
out what the states' relationships would be with one another
and with the nation as a whole. The debates took years and
were deeply divisive.

The matter was partly an economic question, most urgently,
how to pay for the Revolutionary War. But part was also a political question: Were the states subject to the nation's treaties?
Could the states pass laws inconsistent with the nation's?

Eventually, and even after the Constitution was ratified, these
questions divided people into factions—groups with different
opinions about the roles of state and federal governments. In
the early years of the nation, as the abstract political principles of the Constitution were put into practice, the differences
hardened and gave rise to the nation's first political parties,
Federalists and Republicans.

Federalists believed in an "energetic" central government.
Alexander, a leader of the Federalist Party, believed a strong
government was necessary to protect and preserve liberty. He'd
seen firsthand how the war was jeopardized by the weakness of
the confederation, which could not levy taxes and pay for food,

salaries, and vital supplies. An energetic central government could raise revenue from the states and would also ensure that states adhered to international treaties and didn't fight with one another, helping minimize the risk of war when the nation was still young and vulnerable.

Thomas Jefferson and James Madison organized the Republicans to oppose the Federalists. They feared an erosion of individual liberties in the face of a strong federal government, which is why Madison drafted the Bill of Rights shortly after the Constitution was ratified. They didn't want anyone subject to the whims of a tyrannical leader or aristocracy, and these civil liberties were ratified as the first ten amendments to the Constitution on December 15, 1791.

Republicans also feared that Alexander's banking and finance system would create an aristocracy. The Southern economy was agrarian, and Jefferson in particular viewed this as an American ideal. This economy depended on slavery, though, and that was one of the "states' rights" many in the South fought to protect.

This question, more than any other, was never far below the surface of political debates. Not every state permitted the ownership of human beings. If the federal government outlawed the practice, it would throw the economy of the South into upheaval. The South became a Republican stronghold for this reason. The Northeast, meanwhile, had a more diversified economy and was better able to confront the hypocrisy of slavery and, therefore, became a Federalist base.

RULES FOR DUELS

AN INSULT COULD SOMETIMES BECOME A MATTER of life and death. If a man insulted the honor of another—say, by using words like *rascal, scoundrel*, or *impertinent puppy*—this was often seen as the first step of a formal fight, possibly to the death.

The showdown wouldn't happen immediately.

Duels followed a certain set of rules, and they weren't necessarily meant to kill or even wound. Rather, the purpose was to restore honor after an insult. This meant the conflict might be headed off with an apology negotiated by representatives of each man, who acted as seconds.

The Code Duello of 1777 outlined the steps and rules:

- No challenges were to be delivered at night unless the offending party planned to leave the area before morning.

- The challenged man could choose his own weapon, but the challenger could decline it.

- The challenged man also chose the dueling ground, while the challenger chose the firing distance.

- The seconds determined the time and terms of firing the weapons.

- The seconds loaded the pistols in each other's presence, unless they gave each other their word they've done so correctly.

- The duelers worked together to determine what signal, if any, should be given to fire.

- A misfire counted as a shot.

- Seconds had to try to reconcile the parties before their meeting for the duel, or after shots were fired.

- A wound that agitated the nerves and made a man's hands shake would end the duel.

- If the seconds disagreed and decided to duel themselves, it had to be at the same time, and at right angles to their principals.

The guns that killed both Alexander and Philip Hamilton were returned to John Church. He handed them down to his grandson. Eventually, they were purchased by JP Morgan Chase bank, which, once upon a time, was called the Manhattan Company when it was founded, through trickery, by Aaron Burr.

THE SAD LIFE OF AARON BURR

AFTER HE SHOT ALEXANDER, AARON RETURNED home and spent time in his library and ate breakfast with a cousin who'd come from Connecticut for a visit. The cousin had no idea Burr had just shot a man.

Remorseless, Burr cursed the people who sympathized with his victim. After eleven days at home, he fled on a barge during the night. He eventually made his way, by carriage, canoe, and boat, to South Carolina, where his daughter lived with her husband. The journey was a hard one.

The states of New York and New Jersey charged him with murder, but the charges were never prosecuted and were eventually dropped, thanks in part to political influence exerted on his behalf by his friends.

As vice president and leader of the Senate, Burr returned to Washington in November for the start of the legislative session. On the way, he stopped in Petersburg, Virginia, where local Republicans held a public dinner for him and took him to the theater; he received a standing ovation. His last major role in public office was presiding over the Senate's impeachment trial of Supreme Court Justice Samuel Chase, who was acquitted.

The next day Burr formally left the Senate, two days before Jefferson's new vice president would be sworn in. In his resignation speech before weeping colleagues on March 2, 1805, he called the Senate "a sanctuary; a citadel of law, of order, and of liberty; and it is here—it is here, in this exalted refuge; here, if any where, will resistance be made to the storms of political phrenzy and the silent arts of corruption; and if the Constitution be destined ever to perish by the sacrilegious hands of the demagogue or the usurper, which God avert, its expiring agonies will be witnessed on this floor."

Burr's daughter and her son—little Aaron—became the principal source of love and light in his life, but he could not see them as often as he wished.

In 1807, he was charged with treason after hatching a military expedition in the western territories, either to attack Spanish possessions and expand the United States or to stir up revolution in the West and found a nation on his own.

Thomas Jefferson believed him guilty. He wrote to the Marquis de Lafayette that Burr's conspiracy "has been one of the most flagitious of which history will ever furnish an example. He meant to separate the Western states from us, to add Mexico to them, place himself at their head, establish what he would deem an energetic government. . . . There is not a man in the US. who doubts his guilt."

Acquitted for lack of sufficient evidence of treason but condemned by the public nonetheless, Burr fled to Europe in 1808, where he thought he might be able to interest either Britain or France in his ambitions. Eventually, he ran out of money. His boots were so worn that there was not enough leather left for them to be repaired. Stuck in France with no money and no passport, he finally received one and set sail for America in 1811. However, the ship was soon boarded by the British and taken to England, where Burr was delayed another five months before he could again secure passage to the United States.

Traveling as Adolphus Arnot, he made it back in 1812. By the time he arrived in New York, he had but one wish: to see his daughter and her son. The first letter he received from his son-in-law, though, informed him that little Aaron had died and that Theodosia was inconsolable.

Grief and poor health prevented Theodosia from visiting her father until the end of the year. The schooner she boarded on

December 30, the *Patriot*, should have arrived in a week. It never did.

Burr married again, but his wife soon left him. His world grew small and dark. He had only a few words at the end of his life for his old nemesis Alexander. They sounded as though something like regret had found him at last.

"If I had read Sterne more, and Voltaire less, I should have known the world was wide enough for Hamilton and me."

ABOVE: *AARON BURR CIRCA 1834.*
HE DIED TWO YEARS LATER, AT THE AGE OF EIGHTY.

MAJOR BATTLES OF THE REVOLUTIONARY WAR

PLACES ALEXANDER SERVED

CAPTURING CANNON AT FORT GEORGE

August 23, 1775, tip of Manhattan Island

HAMILTON APPOINTED CAPTAIN OF ARTILLERY UNIT

March 14, 1776, New York City

DECLARATION OF INDEPENDENCE READ TO TROOPS

July 9, 1776, New York City

BATTLE OF HARLEM HEIGHTS

September 16, 1776, Alexander leads New York Provincial Company of Artillery between 106th Street and Broadway up to 120th Street.

BATTLE OF TRENTON

December 26, 1776, Patriots capture Hessians after crossing the Delaware on Christmas night.

SECOND BATTLE OF TRENTON

January 2, 1777

BATTLE OF PRINCETON

January 3, 1777, Alexander leads an artillery attack on Nassau Hall, the original building that housed the College of New Jersey.

WINTER CAMP IN MORRISTOWN, N.J.

January 20–May 29, 1777

HAMILTON BECOMES WASHINGTON'S AIDE-DE-CAMP

March 1, 1777

BATTLE OF BRANDYWINE

September 11, 1777, Alexander is at the front lines with George Washington; a loss for the patriots

HAMILTON ESCAPES THE BRITISH ON SCHUYLKILL RIVER

Sept. 18, 1777, Alexander almost drowns escaping British gunfire.

WINTER CAMP IN VALLEY FORGE

Winter 1777–1778, Baron von Steuben arrives to train troops.

BATTLE OF MONMOUTH

June 28, 1778, Alexander's horse is shot out from under him. He performs valiantly.

WINTER CAMP IN MORRISTOWN

Winter 1779–1780, Alexander falls in love with Elizabeth Schuyler.

TAPPAN, N.Y.

October 2, 1780, British Major John André is hanged as a spy after the discovery of Benedict Arnold's betrayal.

ALBANY, N.Y.

December 14, 1780, Alexander marries Eliza.

SIEGE OF YORKTOWN

September 28–October 19, 1781, Alexander and Lafayette storm the final two British redoubts; the British surrender ends major conflict in the war.

TIME LINE

APRIL 1775

Lexington and Concord,
Massachusetts

MAY 1775

Fort Ticonderoga, New York

JUNE 1775

Bunker Hill, Massachusetts

DECEMBER 1775

Québec

JUNE 1776

Charleston, South Carolina

DECEMBER 1776

Trenton, New Jersey

SEPTEMBER–OCTOBER 1777

Battles at Saratoga, New York

JUNE 1778

Monmouth, New Jersey

AUGUST 1778

Rhode Island

OCTOBER 1780

Kings Mountain, South Carolina

JANUARY 1781

Cowpens, South Carolina

SEPTEMBER–OCTOBER 1781

Siege of Yorktown, Virginia

The British surrender on October 19
ended major conflict.

FORT TICONDEROGA

SARATOGA

LEXINGTON & CONCORD   BUNKER HILL

RHODE ISLAND

TRENTON   MONMOUTH

YORKTOWN

KINGS MOUNTAIN
COWPENS

CHARLESTON

AUTHOR'S NOTE

THIS IS A NATION BUILT BY PEOPLE IN PURSUIT OF powerful principles.

As with everything created by humans, the nation has flaws.

But the flaws do not diminish the beauty of the ambitions that fired Alexander Hamilton. No democracy in the history of the world has lasted longer than the one he, perhaps above all, helped forge. Heart, mind, and body: he gave it all.

We, the people, owe a debt of gratitude to Alexander—an immigrant—and to the many souls who built this nation: men, women, people of color, people living in bondage, and those persecuted for their religion and sexual orientation.

It is our obligation to understand the complexity, the fragility, and the failures that have dogged us in every step of our history. We owe it to the founders, to ourselves, and to the millions of unborn souls to keep working, keep understanding, and keep doing better to make good on the promises of life, liberty, and the pursuit of happiness.

ACKNOWLEDGMENTS

To QUOTE SOMETHING GEORGE WASHINGTON NEVER said, "I cannot tell a lie."

I cannot tell a lie: I loved working on this book. I loved surrounding myself with piles of books and maps and documents from the early days of the United States. I loved inviting the legends of history into my imagination as I read their letters, essays, journal entries, and teenage love poetry.

Any errors in this book are my responsibility alone. Any successes, on the other hand, are due in no small part to the diligence of my research assistant, Nicole van derMeer. I am grateful also to Traci McClean-Sorell and Adedayo Rhuday-Perkovich for professional insights with respect to race. Olivia Liu also assisted with research, feedback, and general professional support.

Several readers provided thoughtful feedback as I wrote: Bijou Desir, Christa Desir, Elana K. Arnold, and Zach Hayward.

I am deeply grateful to Jean Feiwel and Julia Sooy at Feiwel & Friends. They are visionary, supportive, and inspirational collaborators. Likewise, I am grateful to Raphael Geroni, Patrick Collins, Jennifer Healey, Alexei Esikoff, Raymond Colon, and Sherri Schmidt for their work in making this book a beautiful and enduring work. And thank you to my literary agent, Sarah Davies, for her excellence—even if she remains one of Her Majesty's subjects.

To my Cupcake Royale crew; and to my family, for putting up with nonstop chatter about Alexander Hamilton; and especially to the McClures, who let me revise on their couch. And, finally, to Adam, Lucy, and Alice: you are my everythings.

BIBLIOGRAPHY

Aronson, Marc, and Marina Tamar Budhos. *Sugar Changed the World: A Story of Magic, Spice, Slavery, Freedom, and Science*. Boston: Clarion, 2010. Print.

Berleth, Richard J. *Bloody Mohawk: The French and Indian War & American Revolution on New York's Frontier*. Hensonville, NY: Black Dome, 2009. Print.

Brands, H. W. *The Heartbreak of Aaron Burr: A Tale of Homicide, Intrigue and a Father's Worst Fear*. New York: Anchor, 2012. Print.

Buchan, William, and Melanie King. *Can Onions Cure Ear-ache?: Medical Advice from 1769*. Oxford: Bodleian Library, 2012. Print.

Chernow, Ron. *Alexander Hamilton*. New York: Penguin, 2004. Print.

Collins, Paul. *Duel with the Devil: The True Story of How Alexander Hamilton and Aaron Burr Teamed Up to Take on America's First Sensational Murder Mystery*. New York: Crown, 2013. Print.

Ewald, Johann Von. *Diary of the American War: A Hessian Journal*. New Haven: Yale University Press, 1979. Print.

Ferling, John E. *Jefferson and Hamilton: The Rivalry That Forged a Nation*. New York: Bloomsbury, 2013. Print.

Firearms: An Illustrated History. New York: DK, 2014. Print.

Flexner, James Thomas. *The Young Hamilton: A Biography*. Boston: Little, Brown, 1978. Print.

Freeman, Joanne B. *Affairs of Honor: National Politics in the New Republic*. New Haven: Yale UP, 2001. Print.

Hamilton, Alexander. *Alexander Hamilton: Writings*. Joanne B. Freeman, ed. New York: Library of America, 2001. Print.

Johnson, Robert Amandus. *Saint Croix, 1770–1776: The First Salute to the Stars and Stripes*. Bloomington, IN: AuthorHouse, 2006. Print.

Keegan, Susanne. *History of Slavery*. New York: Chartwell, 2006. Print.

Knott, Stephen F., and Tony Williams. *Washington and Hamilton: The Alliance That Forged America*. Naperville, IL: Source, 2015. Print.

Kurin, Richard. *The Smithsonian's History of America in 101 Objects*. New York: Penguin, 2013. Print.

McCullough, David G. *1776*. New York: Simon & Schuster, 2005. Print.

Middlekauff, Robert. *Washington's Revolution: The Making of America's First Leader*. New York: Alfred A. Knopf, 2015. Print.

Nagy, John A. *George Washington's Secret Spy War: The Making of America's First Spymaster*. New York: St. Martin's Press, 2016. Print.

Neumann, George C. *Battle Weapons of the American Revolution: The Historian's Complete Reference*. Texarkana, TX: Scurlock Pub., 1998. Print.

Newton, Michael E. *Alexander Hamilton: The Formative Years*. Phoenix, AZ: Eleftheria, 2015. Print.

O'Brien, Jean M. *Firsting and Lasting: Writing Indians out of Existence in New England*. Minneapolis: U of Minnesota, 2010. Print.

Rosenfeld, Richard N., and William Duane. *American Aurora: A Democratic-Republican Returns: The Suppressed History of Our Nation's Beginnings and the Heroic Newspaper That Tried to Report It*. New York: St. Martin's Press, 1997. Print.

Sedgwick, John. *War of Two: Alexander Hamilton, Aaron Burr, and the Duel That Stunned the Nation*. New York: Berkley, 2015. Print.

Sehgal, Kabir. *Coined: The Rich Life of Money and How Its History Has Shaped Us*. New York: Grand Central, 2015. Print.

Sheinkin, Steve. *The Notorious Benedict Arnold: A True Story of Adventure, Heroism & Treachery*. New York: Roaring Brook, 2010. Print.

Stenn, Kurt S. *Hair: A Human History*. New York: Pegasus, 2016. Print.

SOURCES

1 • The storm tore homes and buildings: William F. Cissel, "Alexander Hamilton: The West Indian 'Founding Father' " (paper presented at Alexander Hamilton: The Formative Years conference, Christiansted, Saint Croix, July 2004), 16.

1 • The air itself reeked of gunpowder and sulphur: [Alexander Hamilton], Letter to the *Royal Danish American Gazette*, Sept. 6, 1772, in *A Few of Hamilton's Letters, Including His Description of the Great West Indian Hurricane of 1772*, ed. Gertrude Atherton (New York: Macmillan, 1903), 261.

3 • 1755: Historians are split on the year. Alexander Hamilton gave 1757 as the date of his birth, but there is reason to doubt this.

5 • relatives who lived a mile and a half: Cissel, 2.

5 • Rachel's mother, fooled by the glitter: Alexander Hamilton to William Jackson, Aug. 26, 1800, in Founders Online, National Archives, last modified Oct. 5, 2016, founders.archives.gov/documents/Hamilton/01-25-02-0068.

11 • One famous duel: "Trial of John Barbot, at St. Christopher's in the West-Indies, for the Murder of Matt. Mills, Esq.," *London Magazine*, August 1753, 350.

11 • he had to stand on the table next to his teacher: John C. Hamilton, *The Life of Alexander Hamilton*, vol. 1 (New York: 1840), 3.

12 • *Hark! hark! a voice from yonder sky*: Alexander Hamilton, "The Soul ascending into Bliss, In humble imitation of Popes Dying Christian to his Soul," Oct. 17, 1772, *Founders Online*, National Archives, last modified Oct. 5, 2016, founders.archives.gov/documents/Hamilton/01-01-02-0043.

13 • crammed into the bellies of overcrowded ships: A watercolor illustration of the slave ship *Marie Séraphique* painstakingly depicts the contents of the hold, steerage, and bridge, including the 307 men, women, and children lying side by side on board. The Slavery and Remembrance project describes the drawing thus: "Illustrations of captives, their positions noted with accuracy, reveal some wrapped with linen and doubtlessly suffering in the middle of the steerage. . . . Apparently, this document was created at the request of the ship owner. The general table of this slave trading voyage, begun August 25 and finished December 16, 1769, presented in the bottom, details the journey in chilling numbers." *Slavery and Remembrance: A Guide to Sites, Museums, and Memory*, "Plan, profile and layout of the ship *Marie Séraphique*," ca. 1770, Nantes History Museum, Castle of the Dukes of Brittany, slaveryandremembrance.org/collections.

15 • Lavien sent a court summons: Cissel, 4.

15 • "She has shown herself to be shameless . . .": Holger Utke Ramsing, "Alexander Hamilton og hans mødrene stoegt Tidsbilleder fra Dansk Vestindiens barndom," *Personalhistorisk tidsskrift*, 24 cm., 10 Raekke, 6bd. (Copenhagen, 1939), 244.

18 • Family members helped: Probate court transactions for Rachel Lewine, February 19, 1768–December 11, 1769, in the Alexander Hamiltons Papers Publication Project Records (Columbia University, Rare Book & Manuscript Library).

19 • Alexander, always great at math . . . chairs from Uncle James: Ramsing, 244.

20 • the financial vultures arrived an hour later: "Probate Court Transaction on Estate of Rachel Lavien," Feb. 19, 1768, *Founders Online*, National Archives, last modified June 29, 2016, founders.archives.gov/documents/Hamilton/01-01-02-0001.

21 • She was buried the next day in the family cemetery: Gertrude Atherton, "The Hunt for Hamilton's Mother," *The North American Review* 175 (August 1902), 229–242, jstor.org/stable/25119289.

21 • their cousin grew distraught about his finances: Cissel, 13.

24 • "I sent all that were able to walk": Alexander Hamilton to Nicholas Cruger, Feb. 24, 1772, *Founders Online*, National Archives, last modified Oct. 5, 2016, founders.archives.gov/documents/Hamilton/01-01-02-0026.

25 • "I wish there was a War": Alexander Hamilton to Edward Stevens, Nov. 11, 1769, *Founders Online*, National Archives, last modified Oct. 5, 2016, founders.archives.gov/documents/Hamilton/01-01-02-0002.

30 • Ships moored there: Archaeologists excavating the remains of the wharf in modern times found a ton of stuff from the era: bottles, pottery, rigging from ships, shoes, and the like. From this, they learned a lot of the imports came from Bristol, and activity at the wharf was bustling enough that people frequently lost their belongings and portions of shipments. Paul R. Huey, "Old Slip and Cruger's Wharf at New York: An Archaeological Perspective of the Colonial American Waterfront," *Historical Archaeology* 18, no. 1 (1984): 15–37.

31 • "a deep azure, eminently beautiful": New York *Mirror*, n.c. Co[y in LC-AHP, reel 31, as cited in Chernow, 51.

33 • The company Alexander kept: During the Revolution, Hessian mercenaries targeted Livingston's grand house, Liberty Hall, which was finished with elegant details and wood paneling that held small cupboards. The mercenaries hacked away at the staircase with their swords, but Liberty Hall survived, as did a tree one of his daughters planted in 1770. Alexander's school didn't. It and the church burned during the Revolutionary War. Liberty Hall still stands today, greatly expanded from the original fourteen-room Georgian-style house.

34 • He once wrote a letter: Martha J. Lamb, *History of the City of New York: Its Origin, Rise and Progress*, vol. 2 (New York, 1880), 82.

35 • *For the sweet babe, my doating heart*: Alexander Hamilton, "Poem on the Death of Elias Boudinot's Child," Sept. 4, 1774, *Founders Online*, National Archives, last modified Oct. 5, 2016, founders.archives.gov/documents/Hamilton/01-01-02-0052.

36 • the plan was contrary to the usage of the college: Hercules Mulligan, "Narrative," in Nathan Schachner, "Alexander Hamilton Viewed by His Friends: The Narratives of Robert Troup and Hercules Mulligan," *William and Mary Quarterly* 4 (April 1947) 209, jstor.org/stable/1915991.

37 • "None of the Pupils . . .": "Laws and Orders of the College of New York, Adopted June 3, 1755," in *A History of Columbia University, 1754–1904* (New York: Columbia University Press, 1904), 447.

42 • "nest of locusts": As quoted by Professor Joanne Freeman, "The American Revolution: Lecture 7," retrieved Dec. 9, 2016, openmedia.yale.edu/projects/iphone/departments/hist/hist116/transcript07.html.

46 • "The only distinction between freedom and slavery . . .": [Alexander Hamiton], *A Full Vindication of the Measures of the Congress. . . .* (New York, 1774) on *Founders Online*, National Archives, last modified

Oct. 5, 2016, founders.archives.gov/documents/
Hamilton/01-01-02-0054.

47 • "scorpions" who would "sting us to death":
[Samuel Seabury], *The Congress Canvassed or an
Examination into the Conduct of the Delegates at
Their Grand Convention. . . .* (New York, 1774) on
Project Canterbury, anglicanhistory.org/usa/seabury/
farmer/02.html.

47 • he preferred the man's disapproval . . . :
[Alexander Hamilton], *The Farmer Refuted. . . .* (New
York, 1775) on *Founders Online,* National Archives,
last modified Oct. 5, 2016, founders.archives.gov/
documents/Hamilton/01-01-02-0057.

52 • The *Asia* could burn down the city: James
Thomas Flexner, *The Young Hamilton: A Biography*
(New York: Fordham University Press, 1997), 81.

55 • The men lashed ropes to the cannons: Flexner,
The Young Hamilton, 82.

56 • "I was born to die . . .": "Extract of a Letter from
a Gentleman in New York, Dated February 18th,"
Royal Danish American Gazette, March 20, 1776, as
cited in Chernow, 72.

56 • New York Provincial Company of Artillery:
This unit is still active today as the U.S. Army's First
Battalion, Fifth Field Artillery Regiment.

58 • Washington, a strict disciplinarian,
approved: founders.archives.gov/documents/
Washington/03-04-02-0248.

61 • Patriots tore down the statue: connecticutsar.
org/king-georges-head/.

61 • New York was difficult territory to defend:
Middlekauff, (New York: Random House, 2015), 116.

63 • "Unsoldierly Conduct must grieve . . .":
George Washington, general orders, July 13 1776,
Founders Online, National Archives, last modified
Oct. 5, 2016, founders.archives.gov/documents/
Washington/03-05-02-0207.

63 • "The Movements of the enemy . . .": George
Washington, general orders, Aug. 8, 1776, *Founders
Online,* National Archives, last modified Oct.
5, 2016, founders.archives.gov/documents/
Washington/03-05-02-0464.

64 • "Good God, what brave fellows . . .": Quoted
in David McCullough, *1776* (New York: Simon and
Schuster, 2006), 145.

65 • "Are these the men . . .": Rufus Rockwell Wilson,
ed., *Heath's Memoirs of the American War.* (1798;
repr. New York, 1904), 70.

66 • Burr raced toward gunfire: Newton, 163.

66 • "These are the times . . .": Thomas Paine,
"The American Crisis: Number 1," Dec. 19, 1776, in
Collected Writings (New York: Library of America,
1955).

67 • "I noticed a youth, a mere stripling . . .": John
C. Hamilton, *Life of Alexander Hamilton: A History
of the Republic of the United States,* vol. 1 (Boston:
1879), 137.

70 • "a valorous knight . . .": Alexander Hamilton
to Susanna Livingston, March 18 , 1779, *Founders
Online,* National Archives, last modified Oct.
5, 2016, founders.archives.gov/documents/
Hamilton/01-02-02-0061.

75 • "I have won the bet . . .": Max Ferrand, ed. *The
Records of the Federal Convention of 1787, Volume 3.*
(New Haven: Yale University Press, 1911), 85.

76 • "I am compelled to desire you": George
Washington to Alexander Hamilton, Sept. 21, 1777,
Founders Online, National Archives, last modified
Oct. 5, 2016, founders.archives.gov/documents/
Hamilton/01-01-02-0288.

78 • On the night of October 3: George Washington,
general orders for attacking Germantown, Oct.
3, 1777, *Founders Online,* National Archives, last
modified July 12, 2016, founders.archives.gov/
documents/Washington/03-11-02-0404.

79 • the patriots "were flying": Extracts from the
Journal of Mrs. Henry Drinker, of Philadelphia,
from September 25, 1777, to July 4, 1778 . Mrs.
Henry Drinker, *The Pennsylvania Magazine of
History and Biography,* Vol. 13, No. 3 (Oct., 1889),
298–308. Published by the Historical Society of
Pennsylvania. jstor.org/stable/20083329.

79 • "He does himself the pleasure . . .": George
Washington to William Howe, Oct. 6 , 1777,
Founders Online, National Archives, last modified
July 12, 2016, founders.archives.gov/documents/
Washington/03-11-02-0432.

81 • "impudence . . . folly . . . rascality": Alexander
Hamilton to John Laurens, April 1779, *Founders
Online,* National Archives, last modified Oct.
5, 2016, founders.archives.gov/documents/
Hamilton/01-02-02-0100.

81 • "I am astonished . . .": Horatio Gates to George
Washington, Nov. 7, 1777, *Founders Online,* National
Archives, last modified July 12, 2016, founders.
archives.gov/documents/Washington/03-12-02-0140.

83 • "Sir, I cannot forbear Confessing": Alexander
Hamilton to Israel Putnam, Nov. 9, 1777, *Founders
Online,* National Archives, last modified Oct.
5, 2016, founders.archives.gov/documents/
Hamilton/01-01-02-0338.

85 • The lack of shoes was so dire: "The Commander-
in-Chief offers a reward of *Ten dollars,* to any person,
who shall by nine o'clock on Monday morning,
produce the best substitute for shoes, made of
raw hides." George Washington, general orders,
Nov. 22, 1777, *Founders Online,* National Archives,
last modified Oct. 5, 2016, founders.archives.gov/
documents/Washington/03-12-02-0342.

85 • a group of rivals had been plotting: The plot was
called the Conway Cabal after one of its instigators.
General Thomas Conway, an Irishman who was a
veteran of the French military, thought Washington
was a weak general and told Horatio Gates as much.
Gates, who should have squelched such talk, didn't—
most likely because he thought he'd be a better leader
of the army. In November 1777, Congress created the
War Board to oversee Washington and named Gates
president of it. Conway was made inspector general
a month later. Some members of Congress had begun
to question Washington's leadership ability, but as
president of the Congress, Henry Laurens, John's
father, made sure no more shenanigans could take
place. Conway ended up resigning in April 1778, but
he couldn't stop criticizing Washington. Neither could
Gates. Both were challenged to duels. Gates wept and
apologized, and his duel was called off. Conway did
not. General John Cadwalader shot him in the mouth.
The musket ball sailed through his mouth and out
the back of his head. He lived, but he was finished in
the army.

86 • "vermin bred in the entrails . . .": Alexander
Hamilton to George Clinton, Feb. 13, 1778,
Founders Online, National Archives, last modified
Oct, 5, 2016, founders.archives.gov/documents/
Hamilton/01-01-02-0365.

87 • "It is easy to see that if their privations": Louis
Duportail to Comte de St. Germain, Nov. 17, 1777,
in Arthur P. Watts, "A Newly Discovered Letter of
Brigadier-General Duportail," *Pennsylvania History* 1
(April 1934), 105.

87 • soldiers who got ill had to discard their clothing:
The doctors insisted on it. A December 26 entry in
Weedon's Valley Forge Orderly Book read, "It appears
also that many men who go into the Hospitals well
clad are in a manner naked when they get well and
cannot return to their regiment till new cloathed, to
prevent a continuance of this evil."

89 • "A part of the army has been": George
Washington to George Clinton, Feb. 16, 1778,
Founders Online, National Archives, last modified
Oct. 5, 2016, founders.archives.gov/documents/
Washington/03-13-02-0466. Did Alexander Hamilton
write this letter of his own accord and present it to
George Washington for a signature? It seems possible,
even likely. Hamilton was a New Yorker, so writing to
his own governor for aid in desperate times would be

a logical move for him, less so for Washington. The length of the letter and vividness of the descriptions are pure Hamilton. And Hamilton wrote a great deal of Washington's correspondence. The men established a rhythm where Hamilton understood Washington's intentions, and Washington trusted him to convey them with force and style.

91 • "ancient fabled god of war": *The Life of Ashbel Green, V.D.M.*, ed. Joseph H. Jones (New York, 1849), 109.

92 • "You say to your soldier . . .": Steuben to Baron de Gaudy, 1787–88, in Friedrich Kapp, *The Life of Frederick William von Steuben* (New York, 1859), 699.

92 • "The American soldier, never having . . .": Kapp, *The Life of Frederick William von Steuben*, 117.

93 • "My good republicans wanted . . .": Steuben to Baron Von de Goltz, 1785, in Kapp, 698.

93 • "'Tis unquestionably to his efforts . . .": Alexander Hamilton to John Jay, Dec. 7, 1784, *Founders Online*, National Archives, last modified Oct. 5, 2016, founders.archives.gov/documents/Hamilton/01-03-02-0393.

94 • "I think I see the reason . . .": From Alexander Hamilton to Baron von Steuben, March–April 1778, *Founders Online*, National Archives, last modified October 5, 2016, founders.archives.gov/documents/Hamilton/01-01-02-0412. Translated by Eric Yves Garcia, April 17, 2017.

95 • Alexander wrote up Washington's orders: George Washington, orders for march from Valley Forge, June 17, 1778, *Founders Online*, National Archives, last modified July 12, 2016, founders.archives.gov/documents/Washington/03-15-02-0443.

96 • In further orders delivered by horseback: "Proceedings of a General Court-Martial for the Trial of Major General Charles Lee," July 4, 1778, *Founders Online*, National Archives, last modified July 12, 2016, founders.archives.gov/documents/Hamilton/01-01-02-0498. Alexander Hamilton was a witness in Charles Lee's court-martial. Lee cross-examined Hamilton, who provided clear, specific, and unemotional testimony.

97 • "I will stay here with you . . .": John C. Hamilton, *The Life of Alexander Hamilton*, vol. 1 (New York, 1840), 201.

97 • "You damned poltroon, you never tried them!": Washington, George Parke Custis. *Recollections and Private Memoirs of Washington by His Adopted Son* (New York: Derby & Jackson, 1860), p 218. *Poltroon* and *poultry* share the same etymological roots. Washington essentially called him a damn chicken.

98 • At one point, a British cannonball: Private Joseph Plumb Martin described the moment in his narrative: "Looking at it with apparent unconcern, she observed that it was lucky it did not pass a little higher, for in that case it might have carried away something else, and continued her occupation." Joseph Plumb Martin, *Narrative of the Some of the Adventures, Dangers and Sufferings of a Revolutionary Soldier* (1830), 96–97. This woman was one of many to fight in the Revolution. Some dressed as men. Margaret Corbin, the first woman given a pension by the Continental Congress, was buried at the Military Academy at West Point, New York. Patriotic literature commonly refers to Margaret Corbin as "Captain Molly." Historian Linda Grant DePauw describes Margaret Corbin as a soldier who wore a uniform but made no attempt to conceal her sex. Emily J. Teipe, "Will the Real Molly Pitcher Please Stand Up?" *Prologue Magazine*, Summer 1999, on archives.gov/publications/prologue/1999/summer/pitcher.html.

98 • "mouth of a heated oven": Martin, *Narrative*, 92.

98 • "America owes a great deal . . .": From Alexander Hamilton to Elias Boudinot, July 5, 1778, *Founders Online*, National Archives, last modified October 5, 2016, founders.archives.gov/documents/Hamilton/01-01-02-0499.

99 • "A certain preconceived and preposterous . . .": Alexander Hamilton to Elias Boudinot, July 5, 1778, *Founders Online*, National Archives, last modified Oct. 5, 2016, founders.archives.gov/documents/Hamilton/01-01-02-0499.

101 • "I must conclude that nothing . . .": Charles Lee to George Washington, June 30, 1778, *Founders Online*, National Archives, last modified Oct. 5, 2016, founders.archives.gov/documents/Washington/03-15-02-0651.

101 • "unnecessary, disorderly, and shameful": George Washington to Charles Lee, June 30 , 1778, *Founders Online*, National Archives, last modified Oct. 5, 2016, founders.archives.gov/documents/Washington/03-15-02-0652.

101 • He dashed off another letter: Charles Lee to George Washington, June 30, 1778, *Founders Online*, National Archives, last modified Oct. 5, 2016, founders.archives.gov/documents/Washington/03-15-02-0653.

102 • Lee had defenders: Lee to Burr, October 1778, *Memoirs of Burr*, vol. 1, 135. Only Lee's response survives. No one knows what Burr said.

102 • All things considered, it was a light sentence: In 1858, evidence turned up that indicates Charles Lee wasn't incompetent and that he was worse than disobedient. He was a traitor. While Lee was held a prisoner of war in 1777, he'd created a plan the British could use to capture Alexandria and Annapolis. "I will venture to assert with the penalty of my life, if the plan is fully adopted and no accidents (such as a rupture betwixt the Powers of Europe) intervenes, that in less than two months . . . not a spark of this desolating war remains unextinguish'd in any part of the Continent." In other words, he swore on his life that his plan would end the war in British victory, barring intervention from other European nations. "General Charles Lee's Treason in 1777," *Bulletin of the New York Public Library* 1 (April 1897), 92. The British general Henry Clinton's papers contained a note from Lee dated June 4, 1778—weeks before the Battle of Monmouth. Lee wished Clinton health and happiness and assured him he was a "most respectful and obliged humble servant." Charles Lee to Henry Clinton, June 4, 1778, Henry Clinton Collection, Clements Library, University of Michigan.

103 • at three thirty in the afternoon: Alexander Hamilton and Evan Edwards, "Narrative of an Affair of Honor Between General Lee and Col Laurens," Dec. 24, 1778, *Founders Online*, National Archives, last modified July 12, 2016, founders.archives.gov/documents/Hamilton/01-01-02-0687.

104 • he had killed the Italian: Edward Langworthy, "Memoirs of Major General Lee," March 10, 1787, in *The Life and Memoirs of the Late Major General Lee* (New York, 1813), 10.

105 • "Mr. Chouin the French Gentleman": Alexander Hamilton to ———, Sept. 12, 1778, *Founders Online*, National Archives, last modified July 12, 2016, founders.archives.gov/documents/Hamilton/01-01-02-0556.

106 • "I think that we Americans . . .": David Duncan Wallace, *Life of Henry Laurens* (New York: G.F. Putnam's Sons, 1915), 474.

106 • "We have sunk the Africans . . .": David Duncan Wallace, *Life of Henry Laurens* (New York: G.F. Putnam's Sons, 1915), 474.

108 • "I have not the least doubt . . .": Alexander Hamilton to John Jay, March 14, 1779, *Founders Online*, National Archives, last modified Oct. 5, 2016, founders.archives.gov/documents/Hamilton/01-02-02-0051.

109 • "I foresee that this project . . .": Hamilton to Jay, March 14, 1779.

110 • "We are much disgusted here . . .": Gregory Massey, *John Laurens and the American Revolution*, (Columbia: University of South Carolina Press, 2000), 140.

110 • "Prejudice and private interest . . .": Alexander Hamilton to John Laurens, Sept. 11, 1779, *Founders Online*, National Archives, last modified July 12, 2016, founders.archives.gov/documents/Hamilton/01-02-02-0446.

111 • "I wish, my Dear Laurens . . .": Alexander Hamilton to John Laurens, April 1779, *Founders Online*, National Archives, last modified Oct. 5, 2016, founders.archives.gov/documents/Hamilton/01-02-02-0100.

112 • "She must be young . . .": Hamilton to Laurens, April 1779.

113 • "If I did, I am sure I have missed my aim": His family thought so. Someone reviewing the letter later cut out words from the sentence, "Mind you do justice to the length of my nose and don't forget that I—" What was Laurens to remember? We'll never know.

113 • "ALL FOR LOVE is my motto": Alexander Hamilton to Catharine Livingston, May 1777, *Founders Online*, National Archives, last modified Oct. 5, 2016, founders.archives.gov/documents/Hamilton/01-01-02-0170.

113 • "I am chagrined and unhappy . . .": Alexander Hamilton to John Laurens, Jan. 8, 1780, *Founders Online*, National Archives, last modified July 12, 2016, founders.archives.gov/documents/Hamilton/01-02-02-0568.

116 • "Hamilton is a gone man": Tench Tilghman to William Tilghman, May 12, 1780, in *Memoir of Lieut. Col. Tench Tilghman* (Albany, 1876), 173.

117 • "the soldier-lover was embarrassed": Benson John Lossing, *Hours with the Living Men and Women of the Revolution* (New York: Funk & Wagnalls, 1889), 140.

118 • "She is most unmercifully handsome . . .": Alexander Hamilton to Margarita Schuyler, February 1780, *Founders Online*, National Archives, last modified Oct. 5, 2016, founders.archives.gov/documents/Hamilton/01-02-02-0613.

118 • He wrote a poem in response: Alexander Hamilton, "Answer to the Inquiry Why I Sighed," in Allan McLane Hamilton, *The Intimate Life of Alexander Hamilton* (New York: Scribner's, 1910), 126.

119 • "She wore a plain, brown gown . . .": Schuyler's description is from Hugh Howard, *Houses of the Founding Fathers* (New York: Artisan, 2007), 147, in *Following the Drum: Women at the Valley Forge Encampment* (Dulles, Va.: Potomac, 2009), 190n8.

120 • "Though I have not the happiness . . .": Alexander Hamilton to Catherine Schuyler, April 14, 1780, *Founders Online*, National Archives, last modified Oct. 5, 2016, founders.archives.gov/documents/Hamilton/01-02-02-0648.

120 • "I give up my liberty to Miss Schuyler": Alexander Hamilton to John Laurens, June 30, 1780, *Founders Online*, National Archives, last modified Oct. 5, 2016, founders.archives.gov/documents/Hamilton/01-02-02-0742.

121 • "I love you more and more every hour": Alexander Hamilton to Elizabeth Schuyler, July 2-4, 1780, in *The Papers of Alexander Hamilton* vol. 2, 1779-1781, ed. Harold Syrett, (New York: Columbia University Press, 1961), 350-352.

121 • "My heart overflows with every thing . . .": Alexander Hamilton to Elizabeth Schuyler, August 1780, *Founders Online*, National Archives, last modified Oct. 5, 2016, founders.archives.gov/documents/Hamilton/01-02-02-0834.

121 • "Tell me my pretty damsel . . .": Alexander Hamilton to Elizabeth Schuyler, August 1780, *Founders Online*, National Archives, last modified July 12, 2016, founders.archives.gov/documents/Hamilton/01-02-02-0834.

122 • "I shall again present him . . .": Alexander Hamilton to Elizabeth Schuyler, June–October 1780, *Founders Online*, National Archives, last modified Oct. 5, 2016, founders.archives.gov/documents/Hamilton/01-02-02-0746.

122 • "Mrs. Washington most cordially . . .": George Washington to Alexander Hamilton, Dec. 27, 1780, *Founders Online*, National Archives, last modified Oct. 5, 2016, founders.archives.gov/documents/Washington/99-01-02-04348.

126 • "Gates has had a total defeat . . .": Alexander Hamilton to Elizabeth Schuyler, Sept. 6, 1780, in *The Papers of Alexander Hamilton*, vol. 2, 422.

128 • "Arnold has betrayed us!": Washington is quoted in Flexner, *Young Hamilton*, 308.

128 • "It was the most affecting scene . . .": Alexander Hamilton to Elizabeth Schuyler, Sept. 25, 1780, *Founders Online*, National Archives, last modified Oct. 5, 2016, founders.archives.gov/documents/Hamilton/01-02-02-0869.

130 • Above all, Washington was furious: George Washington to John Jameson, Sept. 25, 1780, in *The Writings of George Washington*, vol. 20, ed. John C. Fitzpatrick (Washington, D.C.: Government Printing Office, 1937), 86-87.

130 • "He came within our lines in the night . . .": George Washington to Nathanael Greene, Sept. 29, 1780, *Founders Online*, National Archives, last modified Oct. 5, 2016, founders.archives.gov/documents/Washington/99-01-02-03430.

131 • "Let me hope, Sir": John André to George Washington, Oct. 1, 1780, *Founders Online*, National Archives, last modified Oct. 5, 2016, founders.archives.gov/documents/Washington/99-01-02-03449.

132 • "It has so happened . . .": Alexander Hamilton to Henry Clinton, Sept. 30, 1780, *Founders Online*, National Archives, last modified July 12, 2016, founders.archives.gov/documents/Hamilton/01-02-02-0879.

132 • A B: Because the letter is written in disguised handwriting with false initials, we can't be certain Alexander Hamilton is the writer. But he did have the motive to write it and the opportunity to pass along the letter, leading many historians to believe he's the author. He'd also used these initials elsewhere, and later in his life disguised his handwriting when he felt it necessary.

132 • "One of their principal excellencies . . .": Alexander Hamilton to Elizabeth Schuyler, March 17, 1780," *Founders Online*, National Archives, last modified July 12, 2016, founders.archives.gov/documents/Hamilton/01-02-02-0622.

132 • It would have meant death for Arnold: Hamilton to Clinton, Sept. 30, 1780.

134 • "*Must* I then die in this manner?": Alexander recounted André's last words in Alexander Hamilton to John Laurens, Oct. 11, 1780, *Founders Online*, National Archives, last modified Oct. 5, 2016, founders.archives.gov/documents/Hamilton/01-02-02-0896.

134 • "I say this to you . . .": Alexander Hamilton to John Laurens, Sept. 12, 1780, *Founders Online*, National Archives, last modified Oct. 5, 2016, founders.archives.gov/documents/Hamilton/01-02-02-0851.

137 • In that time, he rarely: Michael E. Newton, *Alexander Hamilton: The Formative Years* (Phoenix: Eleftheria, 2015), 435.

138 • "I am sorry that you are not better known . . .": John Laurens to Alexander Hamilton, Dec. 18, 1779, *Founders Online*, National Archives, last modified July 12, 2016, founders.archives.gov/documents/Hamilton/01-02-02-0546.

139 • "There was a batalion without a field officer . . .": Alexander Hamilton to George Washington, Nov. 22, 1780, *Founders Online*, National Archives, last modified July 12, 2016, founders.archives.gov/documents/Washington/99-01-02-04021.

139 • "I am unable to ansr . . .": George Washington to John Sullivan, Feb. 4, 1781, *Founders Online*, National Archives, last modified Oct.

5, 2016, founders.archives.gov/documents/
Washington/99-01-02-04754.

141 • Washington found little better: Newton, *The Formative Years*, 431.

141 • One witness said his face: "Did George Washington Swear During the Battle of Monmouth?" *Reader's Almanac*. N.p., n.d. Web. Dec. 1, 2016.

141 • "Colonel Hamilton," he said: Alexander recounted the incident in a letter to his father-in-law. Alexander Hamilton to Philip Schuyler, Feb. 18, 1781, *Founders Online*, National Archives, last modified Oct. 5, 2016, founders.archives.gov/documents/Hamilton/01-02-02-1089.

143 • "Your Excellency knows I have been . . .": Alexander Hamilton to George Washington, April 27, 1781, *Founders Online*, National Archives, last modified July 12, 2016, founders.archives.gov/documents/Hamilton/01-02-02-1163.

143 • "I beg you to be assured . . .": George Washington to Alexander Hamilton, April 27, 1781, *Founders Online*, National Archives, last modified Oct. 5, 2016, founders.archives.gov/documents/Hamilton/01-02-02-1164.

144 • "Indeed Betsey, I am intirely changed . . .": Alexander Hamilton to Elizabeth Hamilton, July 13, 1781, *Founders Online*, National Archives, last modified Oct. 5, 2016, founders.archives.gov/documents/Hamilton/01-02-02-1180.

146 • Then he made sure his men: Alexander Hamilton to Timothy Pickering, Aug. 7, 1781, *Founders Online*, National Archives, last modified July 12, 2016, founders.archives.gov/documents/Hamilton/01-02-02-1184.

146 • During an oppressively hot afternoon . . . the family's silver: Benson John Lossing, *Reflections of Rebellion: Hours with the Living Men and Women of the Revolution* (Charleston, S.C.: History Press, 2005), 123–124.

147 • "It has felt all the horror . . .": Alexander Hamilton to Elizabeth Hamilton, Aug. 16, 1781, *Founders Online*, National Archives, last modified July 12, 2016, founders.archives.gov/documents/Hamilton/01-02-02-1188.

148 • He wanted only to be happy: Alexander Hamilton to Elizabeth Hamilton, Sept. 6, 1781, *Founders Online*, National Archives, last modified July 12, 2016, founders.archives.gov/documents/Hamilton/01-02-02-1195.

149 • "would be our misfortune . . .": *Reminiscences of James A. Hamilton* (New York: Charles Scribner & Co, 1869), 11.

150 • "a modern Hannibal": Newton, 466 [Footnoted as Nathanael Greene to Anthony Wayne, probably July 1781, in Charles J. Stillé, *Major-General Anthony Wayne*, (London: Forgotten Books, 2012), 271].

151 • Everything depended on speed: George Washington to Benjamin Lincoln, Aug. 24, 1781, in *The Writings of George Washington*, vol. 23, ed. John C. Fitzpatrick (Washington, D.C.: Government Printing Office, 1937), 43.

151 • "I cannot announce the fatal necessity . . .": Alexander Hamilton to Elizabeth Hamilton, Aug. 22, 1781," *Founders Online*, National Archives, last modified Oct, 5, 2016, founders.archives.gov/documents/Hamilton/01-02-02-1189.

151 • Over the next fifteen days . . . of their houses: James Thacher, *A Military Journal During the American Revolutionary War, from 1775 to 1783* (Boston: Richardson and Lord, 1823), 325–326.

154 • "Circumstances that have just come . . .": Alexander Hamilton to Elizabeth Hamilton, Sept. 6, 1781, *Founders Online*, National Archives, last modified July 12, 2016, founders.archives.gov/documents/Hamilton/01-02-02-1195.

154 • Cash in hand . . . : Ludwig Closen and Evelyn Martha Acomb. *The Revolutionary Journal of Baron Ludwig Von Closen, 1780–1783* (Chapel Hill: Published

for the Institute of Early American History and Culture at Williamsburg, Va., by the University of North Carolina, 1958), 124.

155 • "How chequered is human life!": Alexander Hamilton to Elizabeth Hamilton, Sept. 15–18, 1781, *Founders Online*, National Archives, last modified July 12, 2016, founders.archives.gov/documents/Hamilton/01-02-02-1196.

155 • "The present moment offers . . .": George Washington, general orders, Sept. 30, 1781, *Founders Online*, National Archives, last modified July 12, 2016, founders.archives.gov/documents/Washington/99-01-02-07054.

158 • "Five days more the enemy . . .": Alexander Hamilton to Elizabeth Hamilton, Oct. 12, 1781, *Founders Online*, National Archives, last modified July 12, 2016, founders.archives.gov/documents/Hamilton/01-02-02-1199.

158 • Clinton had never imagined: *Narrative of Lieutenant General Sir Henry Clinton* (London, 1783), 26–27.

159 • "We have it! . . .": John C. Hamilton, *The Life of Alexander Hamilton* (New York, Halsted & Voorhies, 1834), 382.

161 • "Your father will tell you the news . . .": Alexander Hamilton to Elizabeth Hamilton, Oct. 18, 1781, *Founders Online*, National Archives, last modified July 12, 2016, founders.archives.gov/documents/Hamilton/01-02-02-1202.

161 • "You cannot imagine . . .": Alexander Hamilton to Richard Kidder Meade, March 1782, *Founders Online*, National Archives, last modified July 12, 2016, founders.archives.gov/documents/Hamilton/01-03-02-0011.

163 • Philip was perfect: Alexander Hamilton to Richard Kidder Meade, Aug. 27, 1782, *Founders Online*, National Archives, last modified July 12, 2016, founders.archives.gov/documents/Hamilton/01-03-02-0064.

163 • "You know the circumstances . . .": Alexander Hamilton to Elizabeth Hamilton, 1782, *Founders Online*, National Archives, last modified Oct. 5, 2016, founders.archives.gov/documents/Hamilton/01-03-02-0137.

165 • "I was out-voted . . .": John Laurens to Alexander Hamilton, July 1782, *Founders Online*, National Archives, last modified Oct. 5, 2016, founders.archives.gov/documents/Hamilton/01-03-02-0044.

165 • "Quit your sword my friend . . .": Alexander Hamilton to John Laurens, Aug. 15, 1782, *Founders Online*, National Archives, last modified Oct. 5, 2016, founders.archives.gov/documents/Hamilton/01-03-02-0058.

166 • "Intrepidity bordering on rashness": David Duncan Wallace, *The Life of Henry Laurens, with a Sketch of the Life of Lieutenant-Colonel John Laurens* (New York: Russell & Russell, 1967), 489.

166 • "You know how truly . . .": Alexander Hamilton to Marquis de Lafayette, Nov. 3, 1782, *Founders Online*, National Archives, last modified July 12, 2016, founders.archives.gov/documents/Hamilton/01-03-02-0102.

166 • "How strangely are human affairs . . .": Alexander Hamilton to Nathanael Greene, Oct. 12, 1782, *Founders Online*, National Archives, last modified July 12, 2016, founders.archives.gov/documents/Hamilton/01-03-02-0090.

166 • "The more I see . . .": Alexander Hamilton to Robert Morris, Sept. 28, 1782, *Founders Online*, National Archives, last modified July 12, 2016, founders.archives.gov/documents/Hamilton/01-03-02-0082.

167 • he wanted Washington to secretly: Alexander Hamilton to George Washington, Feb. 13, 1783, *Founders Online*, National Archives, last modified Oct. 5, 2016, founders.archives.gov/documents/Washington/99-01-02-10638.

167 • Washington, grateful, wrote back: George Washington to Alexander Hamilton, March 4, 1783, *Founders Online*, National Archives, last modified Oct. 5, 2016, founders.archives.gov/documents/Washington/99-01-02-10767.

168 • "You will give one more . . .": George Washington to Officers of the Army, March 15, 1783, *Founders Online*, National Archives, last modified Oct. 5, 2016, founders.archives.gov/documents/Washington/99-01-02-10840.

169 • "I have not only grown gray but . . .": Joseph J. Ellis, *Founding Brothers: The Revolutionary Generation* (New York: Vintages Books, 2000), 130.

169 • He saw now that: Alexander Hamilton to George Washington, March 17, 1783, *Founders Online*, National Archives, last modified July 12, 2016, founders.archives.gov/documents/Washington/99-01-02-10850.

170 • Congress refused to negotiate: Edmund C. Burnett, ed., *Letters of Members of the Continental Congress*, vol. 7, (Washington, D.C., 1935), 193–94.

171 • "and the peace of this City . . .": Continental Congress, "Resolutions on Measures to be Taken in Consequence of the Pennsylvania Mutiny," June 21, 1783, *Founders Online*, National Archives, last modified July 12, 2016, founders.archives.gov/documents/Hamilton/01-03-02-0256.

172 • Fed up, Alexander wrote a resolution: Alexander Hamilton, "Unsubmitted Resolution Calling for a Convention to Amend the Articles of Confederation," July 1783, *Founders Online*, National Archives, last modified July 12, 2016, founders.archives.gov/documents/Hamilton/01-03-02-0272.

174 • "I am strongly urged to stay . . .": Alexander Hamilton to Elizabeth Hamilton, July 22 , 1783, *Founders Online*, National Archives, last modified Oct. 5, 2016, founders.archives.gov/documents/Hamilton/01-03-02-0267.

174 • But New York felt pride in these men: James Grant Wilson, ed., *The Memorial History of the City of New-York*, vol. 2 (New York, 1892), 556.

176 • "Nothing is more common . . .": [Alexander Hamilton], "A Letter from Phocion to the Considerate Citizens of New York," Jan. 1–27, 1784, *Founders Online*, National Archives, last modified July 12, 2016, founders.archives.gov/documents/Hamilton/01-03-02-0314.

177 • Though he joked to Lafayette: Alexander Hamilton to Marquis de Lafayette, Nov. 3, 1782, *Founders Online*, National Archives, last modified July 12, 2016, founders.archives.gov/documents/Hamilton/01-03-02-0102.

177 • Alexander's passion was for principles: James Parton, *The Life and Times of Aaron Burr*, vol. 1 (Boston, 1888), 154.

178 • "He is a grave, silent . . .": Roger G. Kennedy, *Burr, Hamilton, and Jefferson: A Study in Character* (London: Oxford University Press, 1999).

179 • Burr helped Alexander: Alexander Hamilton to Elizabeth Hamilton, March 17, 1785, *Founders Online*, National Archives, last modified July 12, 2016, founders.archives.gov/documents/Hamilton/01-03-02-0416. The house number later changed from 57 to 58.

180 • A newspaper advertisement invited: [Alexander Hamilton], Constitution of the Bank of New York, Feb. 23–March 15, 1784, *Founders Online*, National Archives, last modified July 12, 2016, founders.archives.gov/documents/Hamilton/01-03-02-0332.

182 • "The abandonment of [enslaved black people] . . .": Alexander Hamilton, "The Defence No. III," July 29, 1795, *Founders Online*, National Archives, last modified Oct. 5, 2016, founders.archives.gov/documents/Hamilton/01-18-02-0317.

183 • A few months later, he helped lobby: *The Works of Samuel Hopkins, D.D.* vol. 1 (Boston, 1852), 117.

184 • He listened to little Angelica: Alexander Hamilton to Elizabeth Hamilton, 1783–1789, *Founders Online*, National Archives, last modified July 12, 2016, founders.archives.gov/documents/Hamilton/01-03-02-0312.

184 • "I confess for my own part . . .": Alexander Hamilton to Angelica Church, Aug. 3, 1785, *Founders Online*, National Archives, last modified July 12, 2016, founders.archives.gov/documents/Hamilton/01-03-02-0448.

184 • "The situation you describe . . .": Alexander Hamilton to James Hamilton, June 22, 1785, *Founders Online*, National Archives, last modified Oct. 5, 2016, founders.archives.gov/documents/Hamilton/01-03-02-0444.

185 • "Let me know how . . .": Alexander Hamilton to James Hamilton, June 22, 1785.

185 • "I feel that nothing can ever . . .": Alexander Hamilton to Elizabeth Hamilton, Sept. 8, 1786, *Founders Online*, National Archives, last modified Oct. 5, 2016, founders.archives.gov/documents/Hamilton/01-03-02-0554.

187 • "Pardon me my love . . .": Alexander Hamilton to Elizabeth Schuyler, Sept. 6, 1780, *Founders Online*, National Archives, last modified Oct. 5, 2016, founders.archives.gov/documents/Hamilton/01-02-02-0843.

190 • With Madison's influence: Alexander Hamilton, address, Annapolis Convention, Sept. 14, 1786, *Founders Online*, National Archives, last modified July 12, 2016, founders.archives.gov/documents/Hamilton/01-03-02-0556.

190 • "The heat of the day . . .": Benjamin Brown, "Hot, Hot, Hot: The Summer of 1787," July 31, 2012, Constitution Daily, National Constitution Center, blog.constitutioncenter.org/2012/07/hot-hot-hot-the-summer-of-1787/.

191 • "assembly of demigods": Thomas Jefferson to John Adams, Aug. 30, 1787, *Founders Online*, National Archives, last modified Oct. 5, 2016, founders.archives.gov/documents/Adams/99-02-02-0188.

196 • "with a little change of sauce": James Madison, Notes on the Debates of the Federal Convention, June 18, 1787, n11, Avalon Project, Yale Law School, avalon.law.yale.edu/18th_century/debates_618.asp.

197 • "Colo. Hamilton is deservedly . . .": Notes of Major William Pierce (Georgia) in the Federal Convention of 1787, Avalon Project, Yale Law School, avalon.law.yale.edu/18th_century/pierce.asp.

197 • "I own to you Sir . . .": Alexander Hamilton to George Washington, July 3, 1787, *Founders Online*, National Archives, last modified July 12, 2016, founders.archives.gov/documents/Hamilton/01-04-02-0110.

197 • "The Men who oppose . . .": George Washington to Alexander Hamilton, July 10, 1787, *Founders Online*, National Archives, last modified Oct. 5, 2016, founders.archives.gov/documents/Washington/04-05-02-0236.

198 • Acting on orders during the war: Alexander Hamilton to Elias Dayton, July 7, 1777, *Founders Online*, National Archives, last modified July 12, 2016, founders.archives.gov/documents/Hamilton/01-01-02-0211.

199 • Alexander determined how: Attendance, Society for Promoting the Manumission of Slaves meeting, Feb. 4, 1785, *Founders Online*, National Archives, last modified July 12, 2016, founders.archives.gov/documents/Hamilton/01-03-02-0409.

199 • And then there were the enslaved people: Allan McLane Hamilton, *The Intimate Life of Alexander Hamilton* (London: Dalton House, 2015), 268.

199 • "It will however by no means . . .": Alexander Hamilton, remarks, New York Ratifying Convention, June 20, 1788, recorded by Francis Childs, *Founders Online*, National Archives, last modified Oct. 5, 2016, founders.archives.gov/documents/Hamilton/01-05-02-0012-0005.

202 • "I have the happiness to know . . .": James Madison, Notes on the Debates, Sept. 17, 1787, avalon.law.yale.edu/18th_century/debates_917.asp.

202 • "Nine states will fail . . .": Madison, Notes on the Debates, Sept. 17, 1787.

204 • "This I confess hurts my feelings": Alexander Hamilton to George Washington, Oct. 11, 1787, *Founders Online*, National Archives, last modified Oct. 5, 2016, founders.archives.gov/documents/Washington/04-05-02-0335.

205 • "I do therefore, explicitly declare . . .": George Washington to Alexander Hamilton, Oct. 18, 1787, *Founders Online*, National Archives, last modified July 12, 2016, founders.archives.gov/documents/Hamilton/01-04-02-0148.

206 • Parts of Virginia were enthusiastic: Washington to Hamilton, Oct. 18, 1787.

206 • "The constitution proposed has . . .": Alexander Hamilton to George Washington, Oct. 30, 1787, *Founders Online*, National Archives, last modified July 12, 2016, founders.archives.gov/documents/Hamilton/01-04-02-0153.

206 • It was based on an outline: Katharine Schuyler Baxter, *A Godchild of Washington: A Picture of the Past* (New York, 1897), 219.

208 • "If men were angels . . .": [James Madison and Alexander Hamilton], "The Federalist No. 51," February 6, 1788, *Founders Online*, National Archives, last modified Oct. 5, 2016, founders.archives.gov/documents/Hamilton/01-04-02-0199.

210 • "We think here that . . .": Alexander Hamilton to James Madison, May 19, 1788, *Founders Online*, National Archives, last modified Oct. 5, 2016, founders.archives.gov/documents/Hamilton/01-04-02-0236.

211 • "Our adversaries greatly outnumber us": Alexander Hamilton to James Madison, June 19, 1788, *Founders Online*, National Archives, last modified July 12, 2016, founders.archives.gov/documents/Hamilton/01-05-02-0011.

211 • "I am very sorry to find . . .": Alexander Hamilton to James Madison, June 25, 1788, *Founders Online*, National Archives, last modified July 12, 2016, founders.archives.gov/documents/Madison/01-11-02-0115.

211 • The next week, on June 28 . . . adjourned for the day: "Convention Debates and Proceedings," New York, June 28 , 1788, in *The Documentary History of the Ratification of the Constitution* Digital Edition, ed. John P. Kaminski, Gaspare J. Saladino, Richard Leffler, Charles H. Schoenleber and Margaret A. Hogan, (Charlottesville: University of Virginia Press, 2009), upress.virginia.edu/rotunda.

212 • A group of antifederalists attacked: Alexander Hamilton to James Madison, July 8, 1788, *Founders Online*, National Archives, last modified July 12, 2016, founders.archives.gov/documents/Hamilton/01-05-02-0012-0057.

212 • The best of all, though: "Description of the New York City Federal Procession, New York Daily Advertiser," Aug. 2, 1788, in *The Documentary History of the Ratification of the Constitution* Digital Edition.

215 • "I take it for granted, Sir": Alexander Hamilton to George Washington, Aug. 13, 1788, *Founders Online*, National Archives, last modified July 12, 2016, founders.archives.gov/documents/Hamilton/01-05-02-0016.

215 • Washington wrote back: George Washington to Alexander Hamilton, Aug. 28, 1788, *Founders Online*, National Archives, last modified July 12, 2016, founders.archives.gov/documents/Hamilton/01-05-02-0025.

216 • "I am particularly glad . . .": George Washington to Alexander Hamilton, Oct. 3, 1788, *Founders Online*, National Archives, last modified Oct. 5, 2016, founders.archives.gov/documents/Hamilton/01-05-02-0038.

216 • If any other man should get the votes: In another letter to George Washington in November 1788, the thrust of which was to return a watch that had been plucked from the body of a British officer, Alexander included a postscript: "It is no compliment to say that no other man can sufficiently unite the public opinion or can give the requisite weight to the office in the commencement of the Government. These considerations appear to me of themselves decisive. I am not sure that your refusal would not throw every thing into confusion. I am sure that it would have the worst effect imaginable. Indeed as I hinted in a former letter I think circumstances leave no option." Alexander Hamilton to George Washington, Nov. 18 1788, *Founders Online*, National Archives, last modified July 12, 2016, founders.archives.gov/documents/Hamilton/01-05-02-0051.

217 • "Your advices from the South . . .": Alexander Hamilton to James Wilson, Jan. 25, 1789, *Founders Online*, National Archives, last modified Oct. 5, 2016, founders.archives.gov/documents/Hamilton/01-05-02-0075.

219 • He wore a brown suit: The brown suit was woven at the Hartford Woolen Manufactory in Connecticut. It sent a symbol that the future of America included manufacturing—something that would be a controversial idea in the years to come. *George Washington Digital Encyclopedia*, s.v. "Material Culture of the Presidency," mountvernon.org/digital-encyclopedia/.

220 • nearby Masonic lodge: After the September 11, 2001, terrorist attack on New York City, the George Washington Inaugural Bible was rescued from the Fraunces Tavern by the director of the Masonic Museum. New York Police Department officers escorted him and the Bible to safety.

224 • "Tomorrow I open the budget . . .": Alexander Hamilton to Angelica Church, Jan. 7, 1790, *Founders Online*, National Archives, last modified Oct. 5, 2016, founders.archives.gov/documents/Hamilton/01-06-02-0072.

226 • "a general without an army . . .": Andrew Hamilton, eulogy on Nathanael Greene, July 4 1789, *Founders Online*, National Archives, last modified July 12, 2016, founders.archives.gov/documents/Hamilton/01-05-02-0141.

226 • He called Alexander a liar: Joanne B. Freeman, *Affairs of Honor: National Politics in the New Republic* (New Haven: Yale University Press, 2001), 30.

226 • "The attack which I conceived . . .": Aedanus Burke to Alexander Hamilton, April 1, 1790, *Founders Online*, National Archives, last modified July 12, 2016, founders.archives.gov/documents/Hamilton/01-06-02-0216.

229 • "sombre, haggard, and dejected . . .": Ellis, 48.

231 • The nation's finances were so haphazard: Alexander Martin to Alexander Hamilton, June 1, 1790, *Founders Online*, National Archives, last modified July 12, 2016, founders.archives.gov/documents/Hamilton/01-26-02-0002-0196.

231 • Jefferson even sniped to Madison: From Thomas Jefferson to James Madison, October 1, 1792, *Founders Online*, National Archives, last modified October 5, 2016, founders.archives.gov/documents/Jefferson/01-24-02-0392.

235 • That night, he stashed money: He lived at 79 South Third Street.

235 • Alexander played up his concern: Alexander Hamilton to Elizabeth Hamilton, Aug. 2, 1791, *Founders Online*, National Archives, last modified Oc. 5, 2016, founders.archives.gov/documents/Hamilton/01-09-02-0004.

236 • "A promise must never be broken . . .": Alexander Hamilton to Philip A. Hamilton, Dec. 5, 1791, *Founders Online*, National Archives, last modified Oct. 5, 2016, founders.archives.gov/documents/Hamilton/01-09-02-0419.

238 • "Burst with Greef": Maria Reynolds to Alexander Hamilton, Jan. 23–March 18, 1792,

Founders Online, National Archives, last modified July 12, 2016, founders.archives.gov/documents/Hamilton/01-10-02-0125.

239 • "Oh my God I feel more . . .": Maria Reynolds to Alexander Hamilton, Dec. 15, 1791, *Founders Online*, National Archives, last modified Oct. 5, 2016, founders.archives.gov/documents/Hamilton/01-10-02-0031.

239 • "I find the wife always weeping . . .": James Reynolds to Alexander Hamilton, Dec. 17, 1791, *Founders Online*, National Archives, last modified Oct. 5, 2016, founders.archives.gov/documents/Hamilton/01-10-02-0037.

239 • Alexander, fearing he was: Alexander Hamilton to ———, Dec. 18, 1791, *Founders Online*, National Archives, last modified July 12, 2016, founders.archives.gov/documents/Hamilton/01-10-02-0040.

240 • He'd feel much better: James Reynolds to Alexander Hamilton, Dec. 19, 1791, *Founders Online*, National Archives, last modified July 12, 2016, founders.archives.gov/documents/Hamilton/01-10-02-0045.

240 • the first, of $600: James Reynolds to Alexander Hamilton, Dec. 22 , 1791, *Founders Online*, National Archives, last modified July 12, 2016, founders.archives.gov/documents/Hamilton/01-10-02-0053.

240 • the second on January 3, 1792: James Reynolds to Alexander Hamilton, Jan. 3, 1792, *Founders Online*, National Archives, last modified July 12, 2016, founders.archives.gov/documents/Hamilton/01-10-02-0080.

240 • "I have kept my Bed those tow . . .": Maria Reynolds to Alexander Hamilton, Jan. 23–March 18, 1792, *Founders Online*, National Archives, last modified July 12, 2016, founders.archives.gov/documents/Hamilton/01-10-02-0125.

240 • "If my dear freend . . .": Maria Reynolds to Alexander Hamilton, Jan. 23–March 18, 1792, *Founders Online*, National Archives, last modified Oct. 5, 2016, founders.archives.gov/documents/Hamilton/01-10-02-0126.

241 • Its author? James Reynolds: Broadus Mitchell, *Alexander Hamilton: Youth to Maturity 1755-1788* (New York: Macmillan, 1957), 407.

242 • "It has been maintained . . .": Alexander Hamilton, *Report on the Subject of Manufactures*, Dec. 5, 1791, *Founders Online*, National Archives, last modified Oct. 5, 2016, founders.archives.gov/documents/Hamilton/01-10-02-0001-0007.

244 • Alexander considered it a "religious duty": Alexander Hamilton to ———, Sept. 21, 1792, *Founders Online*, National Archives, last modified July 12, 2016, founders.archives.gov/documents/Hamilton/01-12-02-0309.

244 • "As a public man he . . .": Alexander Hamilton to ———, Sept. 26, 1792, *Founders Online*, National Archives, last modified July 12, 2016, founders.archives.gov/documents/Hamilton/01-12-02-0334.

245 • Reynolds should be held: Oliver Wolcott, *Reynolds Pamphlet*, Appendix No. XXIV, July 12, 1792, *Founders Online*, National Archives, last modified July 12, 2016, founders.archives.gov/documents/Hamilton/01-21-02-0138-0009.

245 • In a meeting on December 13, 1792: Frederick A. C. Muhlenberg, *Reynolds Pamphlet*, Appendix No. I (a), Dec. 13, 1792, *Founders Online*, National Archives, last modified July 12, 2016, founders.archives.gov/documents/Hamilton/01-21-02-0138-0003.

246 • Alexander hoped the thorough confession: The next year, Maria and James Reynolds divorced, and Aaron Burr, his life becoming increasingly intertwined with Alexander's, represented Maria in court. He also became the guardian of Maria's child and placed the girl in the home of a congressman so she could escape the stain of her mother's reputation. Nancy Isenberg, *Fallen Founder: The Life of Aaron Burr* (New York: Viking, 2007), 121. Maria later

married Jacob Clingman, her husband's accomplice. Marriage Records of Gloria Dei Church 'Old Swedes',' Philadelphia: Compiled from the Original Records 1750–1863 (Philadelphia, 1879). 179.

247 • "Was I with you . . .": Henry Lee to Alexander Hamilton, May 6, 1793, *Founders Online*, National Archives, last modified July 12, 2016, founders.archives.gov/documents/Hamilton/01-14-02-0278.

250 • "You can not immagin . . .": Isaac Heston to his brother, Sept. 19, 1793, in Edwin B. Bronner, "Letter from a Yellow Fever Victim," *Pennsylvania Magazine of History and Biography*, April 1962, 204.

251 • As many as a hundred: Henry Knox to George Washington, Sept. 18, 1793, *Founders Online*, National Archives, last modified July 12, 2016, founders.archives.gov/documents/Washington/05-14-02-0073.

251 • In all, at least five thousand: "Contagion: Historical Views of Diseases and Epidemics," *Contagion* digital collection, Open Collections Program, Harvard University Library.

251 • All day and night, the bereaved: Joshua Cresson, *Meditations Written During the Prevalence of the Yellow Fever. . . .* (London, 1803), Houghton Library, Harvard University, Cambridge, Mass.

251 • They recovered in five days: John Sedgwick, *War of Two: Alexander Hamilton, Aaron Burr, and the Duel that Stunned the Nation* (New York: Penguin, 2015).

251 • "Hamilton is ill of the fever . . .": Thomas Jefferson to James Madison, Sept. 8, 1793, *Founders Online*, National Archives, last modified Oct. 5, 2016, founders.archives.gov/documents/Jefferson/01-27-02-0058.

253 • The townspeople wanted to be certain: Alexander Hamilton to Abraham Yates Jr., Sept. 26, 1793, n1, *Founders Online*, National Archives, last modified July 12, 2016, founders.archives.gov/documents/Hamilton/01-15-02-0268.

254 • Some people had even spread: Tobias Lear to Alexander Hamilton, Oct. 10, 1793, *Founders Online*, National Archives, last modified July 12, 2016, founders.archives.gov/documents/Hamilton/01-15-02-0281.

254 • he wanted to be cleared again: Alexander Hamilton to Frederick A. C. Muhlenberg, Dec. 16, 1793, *Founders Online*, National Archives, last modified July 12, 2016, founders.archives.gov/documents/Hamilton/01-15-02-0387-0002.

254 • "I am just where I do not wish to be . . .": Alexander Hamilton to Angelica Church, Dec. 27, 1793, *Founders Online*, National Archives, last modified Oct. 5, 2016, founders.archives.gov/documents/Hamilton/01-15-02-0421.

255 • "the Secretary of the Treasury . . .": *Report of the Committee Appointed to Examine into the State of the Treasury*, U.S. House of Representatives, May 22, 1794, (Philadelphia, 1794), 82.

255 • "War may come upon us . . .": Alexander Hamilton to George Washington, March 8, 1794, *Founders Online*, National Archives, last modified July 12, 2016, founders.archives.gov/documents/Hamilton/01-16-02-0107-0002.

256 • War was such a threat: Alexander Hamilton to George Washington, April 14, 1794, *Founders Online*, National Archives, last modified July 12, 2016, founders.archives.gov/documents/Hamilton/01-16-02-0208-0002.

257 • A mentally ill man: Alexander Hamilton to George Washington, Aug. 5, 1794, *Founders Online*, National Archives, last modified Oct. 5, 2016, founders.archives.gov/documents/Washington/05-16-02-0357.

257 • Around this time, Henry Knox: Knox to Washington, Aug. 8, 1794, *Founders Online*, National Archives, last modified Oct. 5, 2016, founders.archives.gov/documents/Washington/05-16-02-0367.

257 • "They are all I can now offer . . .": Alexander Hamilton to Elizabeth Hamilton, Aug. 12, 1794, *Founders Online*, National Archives, last modified July 12, 2016, founders.archives.gov/documents/Hamilton/01-17-02-0042.

258 • He asked Washington's permission: Alexander Hamilton to George Washington, Sept. 19, 1794, *Founders Online*, National Archives, last modified July 12, 2016, founders.archives.gov/documents/Hamilton/01-17-02-0217.

258 • "to attack and subdue the wicked . . .": Alexander Hamilton to Angelica Church, Oct. 23, 1794, *Founders Online*, National Archives, last modified July 12, 2016, founders.archives.gov/documents/Hamilton/01-17-02-0324.

259 • He quit his job that day: Alexander Hamilton to George Washington, Dec. 1, 1794, *Founders Online*, National Archives, last modified July 12, 2016, founders.archives.gov/documents/Hamilton/01-17-02-0392.

259 • "Don't let Mr. Church be alarmed . . .": Alexander Hamilton to Angelica Church, Dec. 8, 1794, *Founders Online*, National Archives, last modified Oct. 5, 2016, founders.archives.gov/documents/Hamilton/01-17-02-0407.

261 • "After so long an experience . . .": George Washington to Alexander Hamilton, Feb. 2, 1795, *Founders Online*, National Archives, last modified July 12, 2016, founders.archives.gov/documents/Hamilton/01-18-02-0148.

261 • He had $500: Ron Chernow, *Alexander Hamilton* (New York: Penguin, 2004), 483.

262 • Not long after Alexander left office: Robert Troup to Alexander Hamilton, March 31, 1795, *Founders Online*, National Archives, last modified July 12, 2016, founders.archives.gov/documents/Hamilton/01-18-02-0207.

262 • "I dont want to be rich . . .": Alexander Hamilton to Robert Troup, April 13, 1795, *Founders Online*, National Archives, last modified Oct. 5, 2016, founders.archives.gov/documents/Hamilton/01-18-02-0218.

266 • "Philip inherits his father's talents . . .": A. M. Hamilton, *Intimate Life*, 212.

266 • Alexander's role was secret: Chernow, 508.

267 • Someone had written the newspaper: Noah Webster Jr., *Reynolds Pamphlet*, Appendix No. XLIII, July 3, 1797, *Founders Online*, National Archives, last modified July 12, 2016, founders.archives.gov/documents/Hamilton/01-21-02-0138-0013.

268 • "I shall take no notice . . .": John Adams to Abigail Adams, Jan. 9, 1797, *Founders Online*, National Archives, last modified July 12, 2016, founders.archives.gov/documents/Adams/04-11-02-0251.

268 • Writing as Phocion: Chernow, 511–512.

268 • Although Angelica had a husband: Thomas Jefferson to Angelica Schuyler Church, Aug. 17, 1788, *Founders Online*, National Archives, last modified July 12, 2016, founders.archives.gov/documents/Jefferson/01-13-02-0400.

269 • Philip was also distinguishing: A. M. Hamilton, *Intimate Life*, 217.

270 • "He has such skill . . .": Callender, James Thompson. *The history of the United States for 1796; including a variety of interesting particulars relative to the federal government previous to that period*, 108.

272 • Alexander stormed into . . . reluctantly agreed: "David Gelston's Account of an Interview between Alexander Hamilton and James Monrow, 11 July 1797," *Founders Online*, National Archives, last midified March 30, 2017, http://founders.archives.gov/documents/Hamilton/01-21-02-0093. [Original source. *The Papers of Alexander Hamilton*, vol. 21, April 1797–July 1798, ed. Harold C. Syrett. New York: Columbia University Press, 1974, pp. 159-162.]

273 • "I pray you to present my best wishes . . .": George Washington to Alexander Hamilton, Aug. 21, 1797, *Founders Online*, National Archives, last modified July 12, 2016, founders.archives.gov/documents/Washington/06-01-02-0276.

275 • Philip was delirious: Chernow, 544–545.

275 • Angelica once dropped: Emery, Moemie. *Alexander Hamilton: An Intimate Portrait*. New York: Putnam, 1982, p. 126.

276 • "I seldom write to a lady . . .": Alexander Hamilton to Angelica Church, Dec. 6, 1787, *Founders Online*, National Archives, last modified July 12, 2016, founders.archives.gov/documents/Hamilton/01-04-02-0172.

276 • "Tranquillize your kind and good heart . . .": Sedgwick, *War of Two*, 260.

278 • "superabundance of secretions . . .": John Adams to Benjamin Rush, Nov. 11, 1806, *Founders Online*, National Archives, last modified July 12, 2016, founders.archives.gov/documents/Adams/99-02-02-5152.

278 • "You will be compelled . . .": Alexander Hamilton to George Washington, May 19, 1798, *Founders Online*, National Archives, last modified July 12, 2016, founders.archives.gov/documents/Washington/06-02-02-0211.

278 • "If you command . . .": Alexander Hamilton to George Washington, June 2, 1798, *Founders Online*, National Archives, last modified Oct. 5, 2016, founders.archives.gov/documents/Hamilton/01-21-02-0264.

279 • "the bastard brat of a Scotch Pedler": John Adams to Benjamin Rush, Jan. 25, 1806, *Founders Online*, National Archives, last modified October 5, 2016, founders.archives.gov/documents/Adams/99-02-02-5119.

279 • "That he is ambitious . . .": George Washington to John Adams, Sept. 25, 1798, *Founders Online*, National Archives, last modified Oct. 5, 2016, founders.archives.gov/documents/Adams/99-02-02-3028.

280 • In response, Jefferson and Madison: Chernow, 573–574.

281 • The Saturday, December 14, edition: Richard N. Rosenfeld, *American Aurora* (New York: St. Martin's Press, 1997), 725.

282 • Two days earlier, Washington: *George Washington Digital Encyclopedia*, s.v. "The Death of George Washington," mountvernon.org/digital-encyclopedia.

282 • The day Washington took ill: George Washington to Alexander Hamilton, Dec. 12, 1799, *Founders Online*, National Archives, last modified Oct. 5, 2016, founders.archives.gov/documents/Washington/06-04-02-0402.

284 • "I have been acquainted . . .": Report of the Trial of Levi Weeks on an indictment for the murder of Gulielma Sands, on Monday the thirty-first of March, and Tuesday the first day of April, 1800. New York, John Fuhrman, 1800, p. 82.

284 • "He must not Depart . . .": Alexander Hamilton, "Rules for Philip Hamilton," 1800, *Founders Online*, National Archives, last modified July 12, 2016, founders.archives.gov/documents/Hamilton/01-25-02-0152.

285 • "The poor old Man . . .": Oliver Wolcott Jr. to Alexander Hamilton, Sept. 3, 1800, *Founders Online*, National Archives, last modified Oct. 5, 2016, founders.archives.gov/documents/Hamilton/01-25-02-0080.

285 • Madison snickered to Jefferson: James Madison to Thomas Jefferson, Nov. 1, 1800, *Founders Online*, National Archives, last modified July 12, 2016, founders.archives.gov/documents/Jefferson/01-32-02-0145.

286 • "Of all the Libellers of me . . .": John Adams to Benjamin Rush, June 23, 1807, *Founders Online*, National Archives, last modified July 12, 2016, founders.archives.gov/documents/Adams/99-02-02-5190.

286 • "hideous hermaphroditical character": James Callender, *The Prospect Before Us*, vol. 2 (Richmond, Va., 1800–01), 57.

286 • "murder, robbery, rape, adultery and incest . . .": The Lehrman Institute, "The Election of 1800—American History—Thomas Jefferson, John Adams." N.p., n.d. Web, retrieved Dec. 3, 2016. lehrmaninstitute.org/history/1800.html. [They cite: Gordon S. Wood, *Empire of Liberty: A History of the Early Republic, 1719–1815* (Oxford: Oxford UP, 2009), 586.]

286 • Burr's election would be a disgrace: Alexander Hamilton to Theodore Sedgwick, Dec. 22, 1800, *Founders Online*, National Archives, last modified July 12, 2016, founders.archives.gov/documents/Hamilton/01-25-02-0139.

286 • He was bankrupt beyond redemption: Alexander Hamilton to Gouverneur Morris, Dec.24, 1800, *Founders Online*, National Archives, last modified July 12, 2016, founders.archives.gov/documents/Hamilton/01-25-02-0141.

286 • Worse, his financial distress: Alexander Hamilton to James A. Bayard, Dec. 27, 1800, *Founders Online*, National Archives, last modified July 12, 2016, founders.archives.gov/documents/Hamilton/01-25-02-0146. .

287 • "We are all Republicans . . .": Thomas Jefferson, First Inaugural Address, March 4, 1801, *Avalon Project*, Yale Law School, avalon.law.yale.edu/19th_century/jefinaul.asp.

287 • "Viewing all that she had endured . . .": Alexander Hamilton to Elizabeth Hamilton, March 16, 1801, *Founders Online*, National Archives, last modified July 12, 2016, founders.archives.gov/documents/Hamilton/01-25-02-0195.

288 • "to diffuse among the people . . .": Allan Nevins, *The Evening Post: A Century of Journalism* (New York: Boni and Liveright, 1922), 19.

288 • "the most elegant piece of workmanship . . .": Nevins, 20.

288 • "a set of rascals": An account of the duel between Philip Hamilton and George Eacker and the newspaper coverage of it can be found in "The Duels Between—Price and Philip Hamilton, and George I. Eacker," *The Historical Magazine*, vol. 2, ser. 2, Oct. 1867, 193–204.

290 • "The highest as well as the eldest hope . . .": Alexander Hamilton to Benjamin Rush, March 29, 1802, *Founders Online*, National Archives, last modified Oct. 5, 2016, founders.archives.gov/documents/Hamilton/01-25-02-0312.

293 • "My Dear Sir . . .": Alexander Hamilton to Charles Cotesworth Pinckney, Dec. 29, 1802, *Founders Online*, National Archives, last modified July 12, 2016, founders.archives.gov/documents/Hamilton/01-26-02-0001-0056.

295 • "To men who have been so much harassed . . .": Alexander Hamilton, "Explanation of His Financial Situation," July 1, 1804, *Founders Online*, National Archives, last modified Oct. 5, 2016, founders.archives.gov/documents/Hamilton/01-26-02-0001-0244.

296 • For indeed my Eliza you are very essential . . .": Alexander Hamilton to Elizabeth Hamilton, Oct. 25, 1801, *Founders Online*, National Archives, last modified July 12, 2016, founders.archives.gov/documents/Hamilton/01-25-02-0252.

296 • "there was a furious and dreadful storm . . .": James Kent to his wife, April 26, 1804, in *Memoirs and Letters of James Kent*, L.L.D., ed. William Kent (Boston, 1898), 143.

299 • But he was financially corrupt: A. M. Hamilton, *Intimate Life*, 379.

299 • "1. He is in every sense a profligate . . .": Alexander Hamilton, "Enclosure: Opinions on Aaron Burr," Jan. 4, 1801, *Founders Online*, National Archives, last modified Oct. 5, 2016, founders.archives.gov/documents/Hamilton/01-25-02-0156-0002.

299 • "I consider Burr as a man to be shunned": James Monroe to James Madison, Aug. 5, 1795, *Founders Online*, National Archives, last modified Oct. 5, 2016, founders.archives.gov/documents/Madison/01-16-02-0038.

299 • "His conduct very soon inspired . . .": Thomas Jefferson, "Notes on a Conversation with Aaron Burr," *The Papers of Thomas Jefferson*, Volume 42: 16 November 1803 to 10 March 1804, (Princeton University Press, 2016), 346-9.

300 • "*Discretion* is the mentor . . .": Alexander Hamilton, "Enclosure: Thesis on Discretion," June 1804, *Founders Online*, National Archives, last modified July 12, 2016, founders.archives.gov/documents/Hamilton/01-26-02-0001-0242-0002.

300 • "I can only regret the circumstance . . .": Alexander Hamilton to Aaron Burr, June 20, 1804, *Founders Online*, National Archives, last modified Oct. 5, 2016, founders.archives.gov/documents/Hamilton/01-26-02-0001-0205.

301 • "Why, Soldiers, Why": "What Was Hamilton's 'Favorite Song'?" *The William and Mary Quarterly*, Vol 12, no. 2 (1955): 298-307. doi:10.2307/1920510.

302 • "These were his last moments . . .": Judah Hammond to John C. Hamilton, Dec. 13, 1843, Columbia University Libraries, in "From Alexander Hamilton to Theodore Sedgwick, 10 July 1804," n4, *Founders Online*, National Archives, last modified Oct. 5, 2016, founders.archives.gov/documents/Hamilton/01-26-02-0001-0264.

302 • Should he be killed: John C. Hamilton, *Life of Alexander Hamilton: A History of the Republic of the United States of America*, vol. 7 (Boston, 1879), 823.

302 • he enumerated his reasons: Alexander Hamilton, "Statement on Impending Duel with Aaron Burr," June 28–10 July 1804, *Founders Online*, National Archives, last modified July 12, 2016, founders.archives.gov/documents/Hamilton/01-26-02-0001-0241.

303 • The night before the duel: A. M. Hamilton, *Intimate Life*, 407.

304 • The account of the duel and Alexander's death come from reports Alexander's and Burr's seconds made to the editor of *The New-York Evening Post*. Their accounts and additional details from letters, visitor accounts, and additional family documents are collected in *The Intimate Life of Alexander Hamilton* by Allan McLane Hamilton, his grandson.

308 • "My dear Brother . . .": Angelica Church to Philip J. Schuyler, July 11, 1804, Gilder Lehrman Collection, New York Historical Society, gilderlehrman.org.

309 • "My Dear Dearly Beloved . . .": Philip Schuyler to Elizabeth Hamilton, July 13, 1804, in A. M. Hamilton, *Intimate Life*, 410.

310 • "Thus has perished . . .": Oliver Wolcott to Mrs. Wolcott, July 11, 1804, in A. M. Hamilton, *Intimate Life*, 407.

310 • "Yesterday General Hamilton expired . . .": Oliver Wolcott to Mrs. Wolcott, July 13, 1804, in A. M. Hamilton, *Intimate Life*, 407.

312 • "Washington sought for splendid talents . . .": Gouverneur Morris, Funeral Oration, July 14, 1804, in "The Funeral," *Founders Online*, National Archives, last modified Oct. 5, 2016, founders.archives.gov/documents/Hamilton/01-26-02-0001-0271.

313 • "My public labours have amounted . . .": Alexander Hamilton, "Explanation of His Financial Situation," July 1, 1804.

INDEX

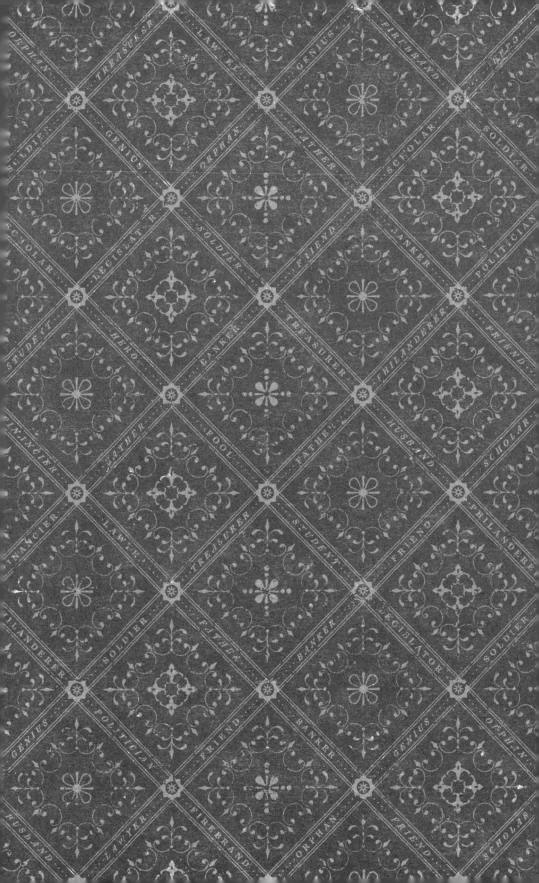

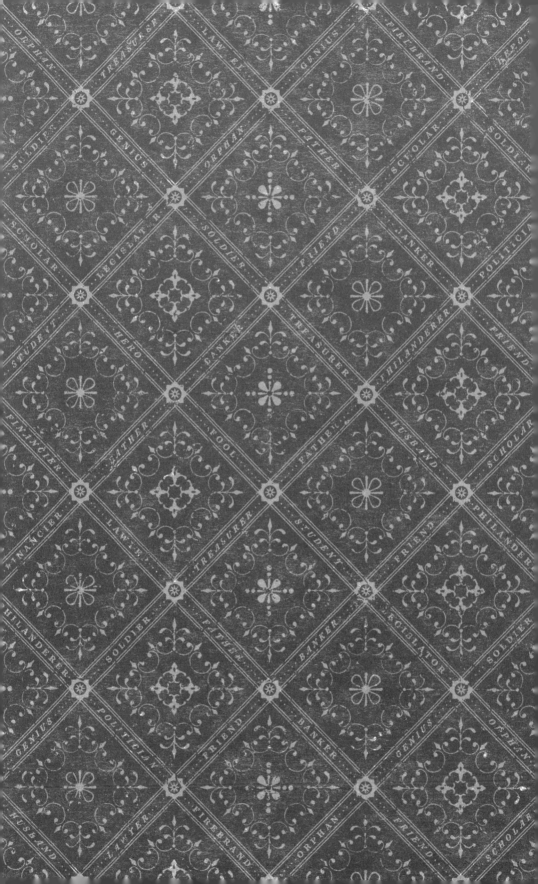